# death by chocolate

## WHAT YOU MUST KNOW BEFORE TAKING A CRUISE

# Ross A. Klein

# BREAKWATER

# death by chocolate

**WHAT YOU MUST KNOW BEFORE TAKING A CRUISE**

## Ross A. Klein

Breakwater
100 Water Street
P.O. Box 2188
St. John's, NF
A1C 6E6

**Canadian Cataloguing in Publication Data**
    Klein, Ross A.-
Death by chocolate: what you must know before taking a cruise
    **ISBN 1-55081-172-X**

1. Ocean travel.
2. Crusie ships.
I. Title.

    **G550.K58 2001**        **910'.2'02**        **C2001-900742-6**

The Canada Council | Le Conseil des Arts
for the Arts | du Canada

We acknowledge the financial support of The Canada Council for the Arts
for our publishing activities.

We acknowledge the financial support of the Government of Canada
through the Book Publishing Industry Development Program
(BPIDP) for our publishing activities.

Printed in Canada.

Cover design and illustrations by Darren Whalen

# ACKNOWLEDGEMENTS

A book such as this cannot be done without the help of others. Unfortunately, those to whom I am most indebted—the crew and staff on cruise ships— cannot be thanked by name. Many spoke openly about things that they shouldn't have, and many offered information that while invaluable to me could lead to loss of their livelihood. Fortunately, many of these people know who they are and know that they contributed to this work. As a small statement of my appreciation for their contribution, 10% of my royalties from this work will be donated to the International Transport Worker's Federation's—an international organization that stands up for the fundamental rights of crew members on all ships. The funds will be specifically directed to the Seafarers' Trust. Mine is a small gesture, but it will hopefully give back something to those who have given me so much of themselves.

I also acknowledge the assistance provided by librarians who were helpful and infinitely patient with my odd and curious needs and requests. I particularly thank the Government Documents section at E. S. Bird Library at Syracuse University, and the staff at Dr. C. R. Barrett Library at the Marine Institute of Memorial University of Newfoundland. A special thank you to Ruth Wilson who simplified navigating and utilizing the library at the Marine Institute.

I also thank those who have helped and provided support along the way. Invaluable comments on the manuscript were made by Helene Davis, Boyd Laing, Mike Ungar, Allan Duddle, Larry Hoffman, and Kathleen Halley. I am indebted to the support for this project from family and friends, and to Memorial University of Newfoundland for its financial support for library research and for providing time to undertake the research and to complete this book. Also, thanks to Ulrich Wiechmann for insights and comments he provided and to Llotd's List for access to their online archive.

Special thanks to the support and administrative staff of the School of Social Work (Collette Cluett, Donna O'Driscoll, Judy Doyle, Arlene Ivany, and Barbara Noel) for showing genuine interest and unconditional support for this work. Also, thanks to my colleagues in the Department of Sociology at Syracuse University for allowing me to present a colloquium based on my work and for providing useful feedback. And thanks to my travel agent, Shana Lalani, for her work and follow through—little did she know what was in store for her when I came through the door and booked the first of many cruises with her.

Finally, thanks to my partner in life who has been with me every step of the way. While she was on a cruise to enjoy her vacation, I was busily doing my research—constantly intruding on her peace and quiet with another insight, another observation, or another story. Her tolerance and patience with me, and with some of the less-than-pleasant cruise experiences we shared, can never be thanked enough.

online:  www.cruisejunkie.com

# CONTENTS

# 1 Introduction

If you have picked up this book and are looking for a guide to cruise ships, **then put this down now!!!** This book will be a disappointment. However, if you are looking for information that makes you better able to understand what is being said in a guidebook, then you should read on. If you are interested in the kind of information that will not be found in any guidebook—the kind of information most cruise lines would prefer you not to have—then you should definitely read on.

## Why Not a Guidebook?

I am often asked, "What is the best cruise line?" This is often more a question asking "What is the best cruise line for me?" This is also the underlying question as most people approach a guidebook on cruise ships and cruising. A guidebook is used to find the "best" cruise for that particular person.

There is nothing wrong with doing this. When I first began to cruise I relied on a guidebook to familiarize myself with the choices, and the costs associated with those choices. However, what I learned as I began cruising was never discussed in any of the guidebooks.

I am particularly cautious about a guidebook's assessment of the food on any ship, given the personal preferences implicit in those assessments. I also never assume that the food on one ship belonging to a cruise line will be comparable to the food on another ship with the very same line.

The executive chef, alone, can account for significant differences in the food served on a particular ship. I have seen two different executive chefs on Norwegian Cruise Line prepare the exact same dish of "Jerk Pork", but they produced a totally different product. One chef was first-rate in both presentation and taste. The other chef sliced the pork more thickly—he placed three thick slices of pork over a bed of rice rather than six or seven very thin slices. The thick slices gave a less delicate presentation, and the pork (because it is thicker) was tough and less flavourful. Though one chef used 25% more meat than the other chef, thereby spending more money, he

9

served a less pleasing dish. Such variations are quite common. They are also interesting given the budget restrictions, discussed in chapter two, under which most executive chefs on cruise ships must operate.

## A Guidebook Can't Account for Personal Preferences

When we take a cruise, each of us has a different set of expectations. We also have a different base, or point of comparison, for making judgments about what is good or bad. Our final assessment is based on the specific set of expectations we bring to a particular cruise, and the similarity between these expectations and the personal experience we have. As well, our assessment is based on one individual ship at one particular point in time.

Given the individual nature of personal preferences, it is difficult to assess a guidebook's review of a cruise ship without knowing the reviewer's preferences, and his or her likes and dislikes. Also, given the tendency for overgeneralization, it is difficult to base a decision about a cruise line or a cruise ship on the guidebook alone. Brand name provides a general guide, but it is never a guarantee in the cruise industry.

Stated simply, that a reviewer has received good service on a ship is not an indication that you too will receive good service. You may. But it is as likely that you may not. Likewise, that a reviewer received bad service does not mean that your experience or assessment would be the same. Service on cruise ships, quite realistically, varies widely. It varies somewhat predictably between cruise lines, but it can vary unpredictably between ships within the very same cruise line.

An answer I give when asked, "What is the best cruise line?" is, "It is the luck of the draw." I then go on to explain that I have had one of the best cruise experiences in my life with Norwegian Cruise Line, but I've also had one of the absolute worst. As well, I have had several fantastic experiences with Holland America Line, but I've also had one poor and one good experience with the company.

Thus, my bottom line answer is that "the best cruise line is the one on which you are traveling at the time, and you have to make the best of what you have been given." If you read on, this book will provide an understanding of the cruise industry that makes it easier to realize the control you give up when you board a cruise ship. It also identifies the control you still retain, and it provides insights into how to use that control.

## Choosing a Cruise

Choosing a cruise is often a difficult decision. Not only does the choice of a particular cruise ship indicate that we trust a company with our valuable (and limited) vacation time, but it also reflects a considerable investment of our resources. We have chosen a cruise over another vacation option, and now we want to have the vacation we believe we have been promised.

One way to avoid disappointment is to learn to read cruise brochures. As discussed in chapter one, all cruise lines claim to have the best food, the best shows, the best accommodations...the best of everything there is to offer. Cruises are described in superlatives.

As a first time passenger, one often goes on a cruise and expects to find everything the advertising has promised. A passenger may be quickly disappointed, but that doesn't mean they will leave the ship dissatisfied. Instead, their expectations for what is a cruise are being shaped by reality rather than by advertising. Most people like what they find, and many return with a better a sense of what to expect.

Another way to avoid disappointment is to know yourself well enough to know why you are choosing a cruise and what you want to get out of a cruise vacation. While my style of cruising is certainly not the norm, it will give you a sense of how my own personal preferences are a major factor in my choice of a particular cruise itinerary, a particular cruise line, and a particular ship.

When I choose a cruise I have three main priorities. I like to have days at sea —the more the better. I want a ship that has sufficient outdoor public areas so that it is not difficult to find a place to sit or lay in the sun—at least one of these areas must provide an unobstructed view of the ocean. If this is not available, then the ship must have reasonably priced cabins with a private verandah. The third priority is that the food must be palatable. It doesn't need to be "gourmet" or "international": just good tasting with good ingredients. I do not want meals that are (as is common with some cruise lines) prepared onshore and then reheated in the galley, or desserts that come frozen out of a box and served when thawed. With these three criteria, I can eliminate many of the options available.

I also avoid ships that have a single pool in the centre of the ship because the bulk of outdoor public space is around the pool (an arrangement that many people prefer). This alone eliminates 60 or 70% of the ships available. When I add my preferences for food, the list is further shortened so that my choices are limited to a handful of cruise lines.

Two items that are not on my list, but which rank very high for most people on a cruise is the quality of the shows and the variety of onboard activities being offered. These priorities provide direction to their own set of cruise lines.

Cruises provide a wide range of options and activities. Individual cruise lines and ships tailor their options and activities to fit the clientele they want to attract and to provide a particular type of cruise experience. Though clearly different, if taken for what they are, the product provided by one cruise line is qualitatively as good in their own right as that provided by any other cruise line. The product is advertised as different, and its delivery will reflect these different personalities—"cruise ship style."

With our personal preferences and individual wants, each of us is attracted to a ship that we believe will satisfy our needs. We consciously (or unconsciously) choose a ship based on its size (e.g., 300 passengers versus 1000 passengers versus 2000 passengers versus 3000 or more passengers), on its dining options (e.g., availability of alternative dining rooms, open seating versus two seatings, dining with a time limit versus dining with no time limit), and on the activities and entertainment it provides (e.g., do they offer art auctions, do they offer gold by the inch, do they have a large show lounge, what's the casino like...is there enough to do that I can be sure I won't get bored). This book helps identify some of the choices we may not know we are making.

## A Guidebook Can Overgeneralize About a Cruise Line

Guidebooks tend to overgeneralize about cruise lines and cruise ships. Readers are given an overall assessment of a company and its ships, but variations between ships belonging to the same cruise line aren't always discussed. There is only limited comparison of ships belonging to different cruise lines.

The overall assessments offered can be misleading. For example, all guidebooks have very high ratings for the *Seabourn Goddess I—Stern's 2001 Guide to the Cruise Vacation* awards the Seabourn ships Six Plus Black Ribbons, the highest award for excellence in the luxury category, noting the *Seabourn Goddesses'* "impeccable service, the finest cuisine, and unparalleled personal attention." However, one week after Seabourn Cruise Line issued a press release quoting Stern's Guide and touting their product, claiming "we offer the best of the best on board", I sailed on the *Seabourn Goddess I*. The first time I used the washroom I was shocked by the toilet paper being used on this "ultra-luxury" ship. It was the worst toilet paper I had ever seen on a cruise ship, and was even worse than the toilet paper provided in the public washrooms at Charles de Gaulle Airport in Paris, where I had a stopover on the way to the ship. I brought home with me some of the toilet paper from the ship in order to show it to my travel agent. If I hadn't, she would have never believed that the toilet paper was as bad as it was. The comparison was a source of humour for the entire office.

While guidebooks have consistently given very high ratings to Seabourn Cruise Line generally, and to the *Seabourn Goddess I* and *II* specifically, what I experienced starkly contrasts with the image they present. Is it the fault of the guidebook? No!!

Is it my fault? Not really. It is just a reminder, when taking a cruise, to always be prepared for the unexpected. Do not be lulled into trusting an overgeneralization in a book, or the tone of a cruise line's brochure. I left the cruise not knowing whether the toilet paper on the *Seabourn Goddess* was the same as on the other Seabourn ships, or whether I had experienced an anomaly. When I wrote to the chief executive officer of Seabourn Cruise Line to clarify this, the initial response did not indicate that the toilet paper quality was different than what is normally used. Even if it had been an anomaly, the fact remained that the toilet paper was inferior to that provided by other ships claiming to be "ultra-luxury", and inferior to that provided by most (if not all) ships in the range from budget to premium.

Just as toilet paper on Seabourn's ships can vary considerably from ship to ship, time to time, the product on all cruise lines can vary widely from one ship to another. Mentioned above is the Jerk Pork prepared by two different executive chefs; the differences can be more fundamental and far reaching.

On any one line, the executive chefs may be drawn from a number of different countries. Some may be from Austria or Germany, others from France or Italy, and still others from North America, Belgium, or Switzerland. Though the cruise line has centrally planned menus and recipes, the final product still varies depending on the executive chef; normally it will reflect his tastes, his preferences, and how he believes the final product should appear. Even the vegetables may be different.

On one particular cruise line, entrees provided under the direction of an executive chef from Germany are heavier and utilize more cabbage and root vegetables. The same entrees prepared by one of the line's chefs from France are more delicate and there is greater use of baby vegetables. The same entrees take on still another character when prepared by one of the other chefs with the cruise line.

The meals reflect the orientation of the chef, perhaps more than they reflect the orientation of the cruise line, and they will appeal differently to passengers based on the passenger's personal taste. What one passenger finds pleasing, another may find unsatisfactory. That is a challenge continually being faced by guidebooks and by cruise ships.

## So, Who's in Charge?

In addition to the executive chef, another pivotal person on a cruise ship—one who has direct impact on the cruise experience—is the hotel manager. It is ultimately his or her standards that define quality control with regard to the dining room (service and food quality) and housekeeping (cabin and public room cleanliness). This isn't meant to diminish the importance of the maitre d' or chief housekeeper. Most do an excellent job and maintain their own high standards. However, at the same time, I have seen the same maitre d' perform significantly better under the direction of one hotel manager than under another. The hotel manager was the main difference in the two different situations.

The hotel manager sets standards for all onboard departments. Aside from ensuring quality control, the hotel manager can play an important role in maintaining staff morale. Hotel managers who show sincere concern for the individuals on their staff can maintain high staff morale and at the same time demand high standards for the staff. As I have been told by a number of waiters and room stewards, "happy staff means good service; unhappy staff means poor service."

What this gets at is that it isn't just the standards that are set and enforced by a hotel manager. Equally important, if not more important, is the way staff members are treated and how they feel about their home aboard ship. This is not a trivial point given that many will be away from their home and families for as long as nine or twelve months.

Let me try to illustrate. I was on Holland America Line's *Maasdam* in April 1999. Staff morale was high, as were standards for service—as good as I have seen on any ship of any cruise line. What I learned from watching is that the hotel manager had standards that were not only high, but were unwavering. And staff knew it. They did their jobs well because they knew that there were consequences if they didn't. At the same time, the hotel manager was very approachable to his staff. I watched one day when a bar waitress waited outside his office in order to proudly show him the leather jacket she had just bought (at a good price) on shore. He shared her excitement and treated her like he would a family member—with sincere interest and genuine warmth. She was beaming a smile when she left his office, undoubtedly feeling good about herself and about the workplace in which she spent her time. She returned to her assigned duties in a good mood.

I have also observed hotel managers who were afraid to take a hard line with their staff and who allowed standards for cleanliness and service to fall below acceptable levels. More than once I have seen a hotel manager who had being liked by his staff as a high priority. Quality control was allowed to suffer. The product provided by the cruise line under his direction is significantly different than that provided by a hotel manager whose first priority is customer service and customer satisfaction. But there isn't much you can do about it at the time. It is just part of the cruise experience. The unexpected should always be expected.

## How About the Cruise Director?

For many passengers, the most important person on board a cruise ship is the cruise director. It is under his/her direction and supervision that all activities are planned and carried through. While the nature and mix of activities are largely defined by the particular cruise line, the personality of the cruise is often defined by the personality and tone set by the cruise director. Passengers pick up on the energy and style of those directing activities and those hosting the evening shows, and it directly affects their cruise experience.

The importance of the cruise director to a passenger will vary with how much the passenger is involved in activities and entertainment. For me, the cruise director has very little impact because I don't go to the shows and I generally do not get involved in activities. I don't know who the cruise director is on many cruises. For others—those who go to the shows and who take part in activities (which is more common than my approach to cruising) —the cruise director and cruise staff are important elements in their overall enjoyment of the cruise. A good, entertaining cruise director produces a better experience for all passengers—in part a result of the general good mood onboard the ship—than one who "simply does his or her job."

No guidebook reviews cruise directors. There is no way they could. So what is one to do? Just being aware of the variations (every cruise director I have ever met was doing the best job they possibly could), allows one to minimize the degree to which these variations influence their enjoyment of their vacation. It is possible to overlook something that could otherwise be upsetting. After all, there is no point to complain directly to someone who is doing the best they can. Comments only further frustrate the person, and you as a passenger on a vacation become focused on something other than enjoying the cruise.

## So What Do I Do If Something Happens?

As illustrated in chapter four, cruises are not trouble-free. There is a wide number of possible problems encountered on a cruise: an accident at sea, mechanical breakdowns or fires, sexual assaults, food borne illness or airborne illness, etc. Though only a small fraction of passengers are affected by these events each year, they are viewed quite differently when it is you to whom it is happening. One sexual assault a year is one too many to the victim of that assault.

Experiencing a serious event is remote. More likely, you will experience little wrinkles in your cruise, and perhaps some minor disappointments. This is normal.

One common pastime on cruises is to complain. People will complain about almost anything. I have heard people blame the cruise line for the weather as well as for the condition of the port of call—things over which the cruise line has no control. Carnival Cruise Line was unsuccessfully sued in 1992 by a group of 250 passengers who were caught in a Pacific storm on board the company's vessel, *Tropicale*, in January 1988. The suit alleged that the ship sailed into the storm without due regard for their safety. Several years later, in 1995, hundreds of passengers on Carnival Cruise Line's *Jubilee* refused to leave the ship, demanding refunds because the captain refused to sail into a hurricane off Baja California. They finally left, after more than six hours, after the captain called the police and threatened to have their luggage impounded. Many passengers spent the entire one week cruise protesting and trying to negotiate refunds.

Sometimes, the cruise line just can't win. During the 2000 hurricane season, Carnival Cruise Line was criticized one week for sailing in rough seas and criticized another week for cancelling a cruise because of rough seas. In January 2001, I watched as groups of passengers on Holland America Line's *Maasdam* complained loudly about the fact that the ship left Fort Lauderdale eight hours late in order to accommodate close to 200 passengers who were delayed in arrival by a winter storm in the Northeast. The delay had no effect on arrival at the first port, but people still complained and they demanded compensation.

Most people go on a cruise expecting things to go smoothly—both smooth seas and a relaxing life onboard. Thus, when something goes wrong, they are taken by surprise. At first they may wonder whether it is them that is wrong—maybe they are expecting too much. They are likely to tell others they meet on the cruise. As others get drawn in, a minor occurrence (like a delayed departure from port) can become transformed into a major event. One part of enjoying a cruise is to avoid getting drawn into this way of thinking. No doubt, there will be minor lapses in service or minor problems. But it is how one handles these that is the key.

In the past year or two there has been a growing segment of the cruising population that believes upgrades and "freebies" are to be expected. Messages appear on Internet chat boards that ask how many categories one should expect to be upgraded on "x" ship, and others actually respond with a number. Some travel agents tell their customers to expect an upgrade when they board the ship. As a result, many passengers begin their cruise disappointed that the upgrade "promised" didn't materialize. Realistically, the cabin you book and pay for is the cabin you should plan to occupy.

There is also a growing trend on cruise ships for people to complain, in hopes of getting a "freebie". I have been told by more than one Maitre d' of different ways that passengers use to scam a free bottle of wine. There are similar scams played out on many other levels on a cruise ship. Unfortunately, the result is that it is increasingly difficult for management on a cruise ship to distinguish between a legitimate concern or complaint and one that is part of an ulterior motive that seeks something for nothing. The result is that complaints are often not taken seriously, particularly initially. Even repeated complaints may fall on deaf ears, depending on the cruise line.

To their credit, most cruise ships will do as much as possible to "fix" anything wrong. However, concerns need to be raised to the right people: the best bet is first the reception desk, and failing that to try the hotel manager. Cruise lines would prefer to fix a problem so you leave happy rather than have you leave dissatisfied.

They do their best, but there are still times when things either can't be fixed or they just aren't fixed. In that situation, you have just fallen into a special group— one of the 5 % of passengers considered by some cruise lines as malcontents. A chief executive officer of a major cruise line once stated that he expected 5% of passengers to leave dissatisfied. As far as he was concerned, it was OK as long as dissatisfaction was kept below 10 %. The result is that many passenger complaints are attributed to a problem with the passenger rather than to a problem with the product. Sometimes your concerns will be addressed after you return home, and sometimes they won't be addressed at all.

The bottom line is that when on a cruise, expect the unexpected. It is the way you handle the unexpected that determines whether it ruins your vacation. I have endured high seas, fearing that the ship may break apart; I have been on a ship that was at anchor waiting three days to get into port, two of those days without running water; and I have been on a cruise of the western Caribbean with temperatures of one hundred and four degrees in Belize City and no air conditioning on the ship. In none of those cases would it have done any good to complain. That was the reality. Some people grumbled and complained and had a horrible time. Others simply looked beyond the problem and had as enjoyable a vacation as the conditions allowed. The cruise provides the setting; the passenger has to bring the attitude.

## Getting the Right Attitude

The information in this book provides the kind of knowledge and insight that makes it easier to take and enjoy a cruise. It discusses how cruise lines advertise and market their product; the nature of food and dining on cruise ships; the nature of the cruise ship's society; the types and frequency of accidents at sea, including health related problems; and, the industry's record with regard to the environment. It also discusses at length, in the chapter entitled "You Can Squeeze Blood from a Turnip", how the industry makes its money. This is a must-read for anyone who considers him/herself an informed consumer.

The right attitude depends on being realistic in expectations, appropriate in expressing concerns and complaints, and realizing that some things cannot be resolved while on board. Getting drawn into complaining interferes with your enjoyment of your vacation. If the problem is service, repetitive complaints can actually result in worse service rather than better service.

Basically, the right attitude is keeping straight why you are on a cruise—for a vacation. Expect the unexpected, be willing to "go with the flow", and have a good time.

## For Those Who Are Curious

Many will wonder how this book came about. It grew out of my own cruise experiences. I took my first cruise in 1963, and several more in the ten years that followed. I then returned to cruises in 1992. In sum, I have taken thirty cruises, comprising roughly three hundred days. In recent years, cruises taken include budget cruise lines, mass market cruise lines, premium cruise lines, and ultra luxury cruise lines. As would be expected, it has been an interesting and fun couple of years.

The idea for the book initially grew out of some odd and unusual experiences in cruising. I quickly became aware of the potential for the unexpected. In 1993, I experienced terribly dangerous weather conditions while in South America and went three full days with no running water. I had a number of curious experiences in 1994: there was no air conditioning on one cruise; on another, when we stopped in Cozumel, I was told by an officer about seven bodies that had been taken off "that cruise ship over there" three weeks before; on the first day of another cruise it was discovered that a casino employee had hanged himself in his cabin after receiving a letter from his girlfriend; and one other cruise ended six hours late because one of the engines had failed and it was sailing on reduced power. These events each provided their own set of interesting experiences and their own fresh set of insights.

My awareness widened in 1995, when I became aware of the use of concessionaires (and what their use means for the cruise line both financially and in terms of liability). I suffered an injury from a shard of porcelain pottery in a dessert and found it was the concessionaire with whom I had to deal; not the cruise line. This, followed by two different cruises of twenty-four days each, on two different ships with the same cruise line, formed the basis for saying, "yes, there is something here to write about." The idea for this book was formally born.

It was never intended to make this book a review of cruise lines or cruise ships. However, the reader will find specific comments about some ships and some cruise lines. These are used for illustration. They obviously reflect my experience, and they should not be taken as an indication of what your experience of the same ship or cruise line has been or will be. The illustrations are not intended to dissuade you from taking a cruise on a particular ship or a particular cruise line. They do, however, provide a concrete base on which to base expectations for the unexpected.

Since 1996, I have been on seventeen cruises (comprising 175 days). Eighty of these days (46 %) were spent on mass market cruise ships, sixty-five days (37 %) were spent on premium cruise ships, and thirty days (17%) were spent on ultra luxury cruise ships. These form part of the information on which this book is based.

However, the time spent on cruise ships is only a small part of the information drawn together in this book. Historical and background information is drawn from a range of sources, including the news media; congressional hearings; government documents from the U.S., Canada, and the U.K.; trade publications; maritime and shipping newspapers; and, international maritime and shipping organizations. However, the most valuable source of information has been from talking and listening. Listening to passengers, to staff, and to crew. Listening to concessionaires, to onboard management and to onshore management. And, listening to senior management in cruise lines. While my own cruise experiences can be used to amusingly bring points to life, they are just a small part of what this book is about. Read on and you will find out.

[1] "Seabourn Head in Attack on Discounts," Lloyd's List, April 13, 1993, page 10
[2] "Seabourn Head in Attack on Discounts," Lloyd's List, April 13, 1993, page 10
[3] Wong, Betty. "Companies Are Entering New Waters With Theme Cruises," Los Angeles Times, July 3, 1990, page D-7
[4] "Cruising Into Bank for a Vacation Loan," Los Angeles Times, March 9, 1997, page L-3

# 2 The Art of Advertising and Marketing

It is likely you are among the 67 % of North Americans who indicate a strong desire to take a cruise vacation. You may even be among the 12 % of North Americans who have taken a cruise in past. In either case, you have been attracted by an industry that is the fastest growing segment of the leisure market. The number of North Americans taking a cruise roughly doubled from 1980 to 1986 (from 1.4 million to 2.6 million passengers) and almost doubled again between 1986 and 1998 (from 2.6 million to 5.05 million passengers). In 2000, almost 7 million North Americans took a cruise.

In 1986, the cruise industry believed that 20 % of Americans fit their target population: age twenty-five or older with an income of over $20,000. By 1998, this target population had grown to over 50 % of the population (or 133 million Americans).

With these figures in mind, an obvious question is how the cruise industry has attained the growth that it has, and how it intends to attract increasing numbers of passengers. This need for new passengers is great given the gap between capacity and occupancy. While occupancy on new ships such as the *Carnival Destiny, Carnival Triumph,* and *Grand Princess* can exceed 110 %—because 100 % occupancy is based on two persons per cabin, when there are more than two persons per cabin the occupancy rate exceed 100 %. They can run as high as 113 % or 114 % on some ships, but for the industry as a whole they are not as high. In 1998, industry-wide occupancy rates for cruises to the Far East ran 60 %; for the Caribbean they were approximately 90 %.

With new ships, the industry has increased considerably the number of passengers needed in order to maintain both occupancy rates and profits. Based on past experience (a 600 % growth in passengers from 1970 to 1991) the industry has projected a growth of 47 % in the first five years of the new millennium. It has undertaken a vigorous construction of new ships to keep pace with the projected growth in demand. Now they must create the demand to fill this space.

Consider the scope of this expansion. From 1995 through 1997, the worldwide cruise industry added 51,000 new berths. A similar number were again added in the three years that followed. In the North American fleet of cruise ships, there were roughly 100,000 berths in 1995. At the end of 1998 this figure was 122,635; and, by the year 2000 this number increased to over 160,000 berths—a 60 % increase in just five years. A similar pattern of growth is scheduled for the next five years.

In this chapter we look at how the cruise industry seeks to attract new business to fill these berths. To put the discussion into context, consider that the cruise industry spent $50 million on media advertising in 1980; fifteen years later, in 1995 this figure had increased seven-fold to $350 million. Informed sources suggest that media spending by the cruise industry exceeded $500 million in the year 2000.

## Appealing To Emotions

For many years, the cruise industry advertised its product by showing its ships and the activities commonly found on those ships. The basic assumption was that if consumers were shown the product, passengers would be attracted and would book a cruise. However, in the mid-1990's, the tact taken in advertising began to change. With much controversy, Norwegian Cruise Line's President, Adam Aron, undertook a $30 million advertising campaign that departed from the norm.

Norwegian Cruise Line's advertising campaign used the slogan "it's different out here". It shifted focus from the ship to the benefits of cruising, or more accurately to what the cruise experience entailed —to its lifestyle. It made its appeal to emotions rather than attempting to sell the virtues of cruising.

For those unfamiliar with NCL's campaign, the printed copy in one advertisement reads:

> There is no law that says you can't make love at 4:00 in the afternoon on a Tuesday
> Shall not study a sunset or train butterflies
> Must pay tax on itemized moments of pleasure
> May not have extra mushrooms with your steak
> Can't disembark in Tortola and stay there
> Must pack worry along with your luggage
> Can't learn about love from a turtle
> Must contribute to the GNP every single solitary day of your life
> Absolutely must act your chronological age not your shoe size
> Shall maintain strict economies of emotion
> Can't make love again at 5:00 in the afternoon on the Tuesday we spoke of earlier
> Because the laws of the land do not apply
> The laws are different out here

This advertising is further reflected in the following text from a brochure:

> Out here,
> the laws of the land do not apply.
> Time not only slows down,
> but runs backwards.
> Fantasy and reality cooperate in a joint venture.
> Relationships are renewed,
> washed in salt water and blown dry by trade winds.
> It's calm. It's warm. It's tempting.
> It's different out here.

The campaign was successful insofar as advertising is concerned. According to *Roper Starch Worldwide*, the magazine ads scored higher than average on readers' memory of seeing the ad in a particular issue of a publication and on noting whom the advertiser was. The Magazine Publishers Association awarded the advertising campaign the Kelly Award. It also received a prize from the One Club of New York, and the television advertisements received a CLIO award. Though the advertisements captured the viewer's imagination, they did not result in higher sales for Norwegian Cruise Line. Consequently, Adam Aron was replaced as NCL's president several years later.

Though initially criticized by others in the industry, the tact taken by Norwegian Cruise Line is now reflected in the advertising campaigns of other major companies. It was suggested by an advertising executive in June 1997 issue of *Advertising Age* that the new ads need to focus on emotional appeal. That was viewed as the best way to sell cruises.

> *We want to strike out in a new direction that gets people who historically might have been put off by yet more classic cruise imagery, to say that the kind of vacation we offer is connected with some of their most fundamental vacation and personal needs.*

He goes on to explain that these ads are designed to compete with land-based resorts, which have traditionally shown the fun to be had at the resort rather than just showing the resort.

Carnival Cruise Line's use of "the Fun Ship" as a descriptor for its fleet is a good example of just such an emotional appeal. Originally based on Commodore Cruise Line's self-identification in advertising as "the Happy Ship", Carnival's projection of the Fun Ship showed images of passengers engaged in "fun" activities onboard their ships. Recall Kathie Lee Gifford singing, "If my friends could see me now..." while enjoying herself at dinner or in a show bar. Fun was portrayed as synonymous with a Carnival Cruise Line cruise.

In 1997, Carnival Cruise Line introduced their dancing fish and dancing palm trees campaign. No longer was Kathie Lee Gifford seen in the ads—she had been replaced by computer-generated graphics—but she was heard at the end saying, "I guess some vacations are just more fun than others." In describing the new campaign, Carnival Cruise Line's President, Bob Dickinson, stated:

> We were looking for a fresh approach to convey the fun aboard Carnival ships. Fun, being something that is subjective to each individual, the commercials are meant to encourage individuals to draw their own conclusions of what type of fun they will find on a Carnival ship by minimizing the copy and onboard visuals

This advertising theme was expanded almost two years later when Carnival Cruise Line introduced a $20 million television advertising campaign with dancing starfish and dancing beach chairs and umbrellas. These advertisements, targeting the viewers of such shows as *Good Morning America, Dharma and Greg, Chicago Hope, Late Night with David Letterman,* and *Wonderful World of Disney*, continued to use Kathie Lee Gifford for the voice-overs. In these ads, the tag line was: "Looks like one vacation is just more fun. We guarantee it. Carnival. The most popular cruise line in the world." Carnival Cruise Line's newest advertisements feature candid conversations with actual first-time cruisers who were sent on a "Fun Ship" vacation and whose accolades were then videotaped.

At the same time that Carnival Cruise Line introduced its dancing fish, Princess Cruises unveiled four new television ads which conjured up the image of a storybook princess who creates an enchanted world that embodies the essence of cruising. Each ad carried the theme: "Princess. Let her take you away." In describing the ads, Rick James, the line's Senior Vice President of Sales, stated:

> Our new Grand Class fleet of ships is defining the future of cruising for Princess and our new television advertising extends our reach to everyone who has ever dreamed of cruising. The campaign builds upon the brand equity in the Princess name, which we've established over the years with our linkage to the ever-popular "Love Boat". Princess cruisers have a deep love of discoveries and new experiences, and also have an appreciation of the finer things in life. The commercials personify our brand as an enchanting princess whose special world promises that kind of experience. They create a strong emotional attraction to the Princess brand that sets us apart from other cruise products.

In line with the strategy used by its competition, Royal Caribbean International in 1999, replaced its "We're not just a cruise, we're a vacation" campaign with advertising that used as its tag line: "Like no vacation on earth". The visual images used with the television commercial include a ship shown from offshore, but there are no images that reflect the ship or shipboard activities. Taken at face value, the tagline is meaningless—is there such a thing as a nonearthly vacation experience. However, if the tag line isn't given a second thought, it produces an emotionally appealing image of cruising generally and of the Royal Caribbean product in particular.

## Distinguishing Oneself From the Competition

A common theme in a cruise line's efforts to attract passengers is to distinguish itself from the competition. There are a number of ways that this is done. One is to identify the product with a national or international image. For example, Costa Cruises, which coined "Euro-Luxe" as a trademark in the early 1990s (with the entry to the North American market of its newest ship, the *Costa Classica*), several years later identified itself as "Italian Style Cruising."

In the Fall of 1997, Norwegian Cruise Lines introduced "cruising the Norwegian Way." Initially the company's identification with Norway was reflected in new names for its ships (e.g., the *Windward* became the *Norwegian Wind*, the *Seaward* became the *Norwegian Sea*, etc). Its advertising, in addition to touting its "Norwegianess"—capitalizing on what they say is the most obvious thing about the line, but also the most ignored—attempts to distinguish Norwegian Cruise Line from the mega-ships being built by the competition. In an advertising campaign that was initially focused on trade papers, and which later appeared in newspapers and magazines, the company attacked the move to mega-liners with statements such as: "We believe a ship should be a ship, not a floating mall." and: "As other cruise lines launch ever-larger ships, they become less of a cruise and more of a line." Consumer versions of these advertisements began to appear in January 1998.

A year later, the company launched an advertising campaign that more strongly projected its Norwegian brand image. Through five different print ads and a thirty second television commercial, the company depicted experiences and activities found on an NCL ship. The tag line used in the television advertisement stated: "As far from the everyday as a ship can take you. That's the Norwegian Way." The copy in the print advertisements included:

*Today I met three legends of jazz. Today I discovered a buffet made entirely of chocolate. Today I swam with dolphins. This is not a normal day. This is a Norwegian day.*

While the Norwegian identity refers to the company's name, it also subliminally connects with Norway as a country. The value as an advertising strategy is similar to the coining of "Haagen Dasz" as a brand name in the 1970's. The product, produced in the U.S. by a U.S. company, was given a name that tapped into the appeal of European brands to the American consumer.

These ads from Norwegian Cruise Line were specifically targeted toward those between age thirty-five and sixty-five. The television advertisements were placed on programs such as *ER* and *NYPD Blue*, and appeared on cable channels such as the Travel Channel, the Food Network, the Discovery Channel, and TBS. The print advertisements were focused on magazines such as *Travel and Leisure, Conde Nast Traveler, Gourmet, Smithsonian,* and *Architectural Digest*. This is a different niche than the target market for the Carnival Cruise Line ads discussed above.

An effort to distinguish itself from the competition was a major element in advertising offered by Princess Cruises for its Alaska cruises in 1997. However, rather than maintain past practices which were to extol the virtues of cruising with "us" while publicly ignoring the competition, Princess Cruises took direct aim at Holland America Line, which was its major competitor in the Alaskan market. The campaign, directed to travel agents, involved sales kits which provided a detailed comparison between the two lines, and pointedly tells the reader that Princess Cruises is a better choice than Holland America Line. These kits included a videotape entitled "Princess versus Holland America: Discover the Princess Difference." The text of the accompanying sales guide pointed out such things as: Holland America's fleet is twice as old as Princess'; Princess offers a wider choice in cruise itineraries; Princess charges less in port charges than Holland America Line; Princess has more balcony cabins on its ships than Holland America Line; and, Princess has more entry permits for Glacier Bay National Park than Holland America Line.

Holland America Line responded to the Princess Cruises campaign by making an effort to define their "premium" product, but it did not name Princess Cruises in its advertising. Through advertisements placed in trade publications, Holland America Line spotlighted such things as larger staterooms, a policy of "tipping not required," and a quality youth program. According to an article in *Tour and Travel News* in September 1996, Jack Anderson, Holland America Line's Vice President of Marketing, said the campaign "...is an integral part of our objective to clearly define the uniqueness of our service and make it easy for travel agents to describe us to their clients." This approach is reflected in the headline of one ad, which states: "Defining the premium cruise line is no longer a matter of opinion. It is now a matter of fact."

The advertising campaign for the 1998 season saw further efforts by Princess Cruises to directly show its superiority to Holland America Line. In the Fall of 1997, they distributed another sales kit to travel agents that in addition to a video, included a day-by-day comparison of Princess' Gulf of Alaska and Holland America's Inside Passage tours. In one comparison, referring to day #5 of Holland America Line's Inside Passage cruise/tour, the materials state:

> *A taste of things to come: five hours on a bus traveling to Whitehorse. The scenery is pleasant, but this is a long trip, and once you arrive you have to look for "something" to do in Whitehorse— which, by the way, is not in Alaska. Were you really ready to leave the ship behind?*

It then goes on to tell the reader how much better a Princess Cruises' Gulf of Alaska itinerary would be. Holland America again responded to the Princess Cruises advertising, but continued to take an approach which focused on its positive attributes and which did not directly name or attack Princess.

An obvious question is why Princess Cruises would depart from a long-standing norm of lines not directly attacking one another. An explanation offered by many industry observers is that the attacks are directly the result of overcapacity in the Alaska market. Alaska cruises depend much less on repeat passengers than those in the Caribbean, so as additional ships and larger ships are deployed, companies need to make stronger efforts to fill the space.

In late 1999, Premier Cruises introduced a novel way to distinguish itself from the competition. Under the direction of Bruce Nierenberg, President and Chief Executive Officer of the company (who previously introduced the idea of private islands while with NCL, who later introduced a family-focused cruise line as co-founder of Premier Cruises and founder of American Family Cruises, and who subsequently was back with NCL as executive vice president when it introduced "the Norwegian Way" campaign), the company announced "Seven Star Service" and projected a profile that included "the official cruise line of the individual". Premier Cruises, a mass market cruise line that utilizes a fleet largely comprised of ocean liners built in the 1950's and 1960's, is working to carve a niche for itself with a number of amenities that it associates with "Seven Star Service." While labelling itself as "Seven Stars" certainly distinguishes it from other cruise lines—typically ultra luxury cruise line such as Silversea and Seabourn are classified as six stars —the long term effect of this strategy will never be seen. The company went bankrupt less than one year later.

We might have anticipated that Premier's "Seven Star Service" moniker would have gone the way of Costa's aborted "Euro-Luxe" campaign. The "Euro-Luxe" campaign was launched when Bob Mahmarian was Costa's Executive Vice President. Mahmarian, who previously worked for Revlon cosmetics, said that selling a cruise was like selling lipstick. With its introduction to the North American market of the Costa Classica, the company felt the need for more glamour; so Euro-Luxe was born. To quote the ship's brochure definition: "...a standard of elegance, entertainment and personal service so unprecedented, there was not even a name for it until now. Euro-Luxe."

Advertising by cruise lines shapes both conscious and unconscious expectations that consumers have when they go on a cruise. There is continuing debate as to whether the expectations created can be realized.

## Shaping Expectations

Anyone who has looked at an advertisement for a cruise has had his or her expectations shaped for the cruise experience. These expectations take clearer form when one looks at the brochures produced by the cruise lines. Not only do these brochures create expectations, some even promise that they will exceed our expectations, regardless of what constitutes those expectations.

This idea of "exceeding expectations" was first introduced by Celebrity Cruises. It is a concept that has more recently been used by other cruise lines and by the Cruise Line International Association (CLIA). At first blush, it is an appealing way to attract passengers. But it is also quite dangerous. How can the very same company promise to exceed every person's expectations?

Celebrity Cruises has since introduced a new, but similar, approach to shaping expectations. In advertisements appearing in 1999, they say: "We'll take you to the edge of your imagination...and beyond." This, again, is quite appealing, but without knowing the viewer's imagination, the expectations being created can be so many and varied that they can't be realized.

The shaping of expectations is not always as abstract as this. A review of any cruise line's brochure tends to project clear images and expectations about such things as the food, the accommodations, the entertainment, and the activities. Some provide photos that are clearly misleading. The 2000 and 2001 brochure for Seabourn Cruise Line shows pictures that project an impression that suites on deck five of the *Seabourn Goddess I* and *II* have a private balcony and that the suites are open to the outside deck. One picture shows a room service tray being delivered to an exterior door, as though it is a suite. In fact, the picture appears to be of dirty dishes being returned to the galley via a "staff only" entrance. Ironically, every cruise line makes almost the same claims. This was recognized by Larry Pimentel, when as President of

Seabourn Cruise line, he pointed out that "...the cruise industry is shooting itself in the foot...in the positioning of its products. Every cruise ship is said to be luxurious. All cabins are said to be deluxe. All cruise line food is said to be excellent."[1]

## Food, Glorious Food

Many of us remember the performance of "Food, Glorious Food" in Lionel Bart's fabulous musical *Oliver*. Though his lyrics were as far from cruising as one can imagine, refrains such as the following could easily be used to reflect the expectations many passengers bring to a cruise:

> *Food, glorious food!*
> *We're anxious to try it*
> *Three banquets a day*
> *Our favourite diet!*
> *Just picture a great big steak*
> *Fried, roasted or stewed*
> *Oh, food,*
> *Wonderful food,*
> *Marvellous food,*
> *Glorious food*

Brochures for most cruise lines give the impression that one will be dining in a fine restaurant while on board the ship. Some even suggest their dining room is equivalent to a Michelin starred restaurant. Pictures show food presentation that is exquisite, and the ambiance of the dining rooms is refined. Aside from the visual representations, superlatives abound: "delicious adventures," "always in excellent taste," "exquisite," "inspired," "ingenious," "superb," and "beyond compare" are common ways to describe the dining on board a ship. One brochure promises "culinary creations that are as outstanding as the settings in which they are served," and another suggests that "the food was so good, passengers ran out of superlatives." Regardless of the type of dining to which we are accustomed, these brochures set up high expectations. Whether these expectations will be met, much less exceeded, is a challenge the cruise lines create for themselves. Most fall short.

In addition to grand statements about their food, cruise lines have increasingly added to their advertising the names of "world renowned" chefs who are said to be responsible for the food on board. The best example is Celebrity Cruises. It prominently advertises "Michel Roux Cuisine", referring to the fact that Michel Roux has created the menus and the recipes. Michel Roux is the Chef at the Waterside Inn in Berkshire, England, but he is often confused with his nephew Michel Roux, the Chef at Le Gavroche in London.

More recently, Norwegian Cruise Line announced its "President's Menu" which is created by former White House Executive Chef, Henry Haller. The menu, which debuted in November 1999, is presented one evening on cruises of seven days or more and features a commemorative cover with a photograph of Chef Haller posing in front of the White House. In a slightly different vein, Seabourn Cruise Line offers a series of "Presidential Menus" which are identical to meals served at the White House to Heads of State. These are selectively offered on most cruises.

The use of celebrity chefs is not new to the cruise industry. For example, Paul Bocuse (who owns a Michelin three star restaurant near Lyon, France) developed the menus for The Royal Grill, an extra tariff upscale restaurant on the *Royal Viking Sun* that charged $45 per person when it first appeared in 1990. Wolfgang Puck, of California fame, developed the original menu for Orient Lines. Several years later, Orient Lines began an association with The Cafe Royal, a Michelin-starred London restaurant whose Executive Chef, Herbert Berger, prepared a special menu for "An Evening at The Cafe Royal" which is offered once every cruise.

Wolfgang Puck, like many other chefs, now serves as a guest chef on special sailings of select cruise ships. However, there is a clear difference between these celebrities working in the kitchens on select cruises, and the practice of lending their name to a cuisine. This will be discussed in greater depth in the chapter on food and dining.

Another way that cruise lines draw attention to the quality of their food is through their association with the Chaîne des Rôtisseurs, an international gastronomic society devoted to promoting fine dining. Initially established as a French guild of roasters in 1248, the Chaîne des Rôtisseurs was suppressed in 1789. In 1950, it was re-established and today has more than 90,000 members in one hundred and twenty countries. Ten cruise lines are affiliated with the Chaîne des Rôtisseurs: America Hawaii Cruises, Crystal Cruise Line, Cunard Line (and by association, Seabourn Cruise Line), Costa Cruises, Holland America Line, Norwegian Cruise Line, Princess Cruises, Radisson Seven Seas Cruises, Royal Caribbean Cruises and Silversea.

Companies use their membership in the Chaîne des Rôtisseurs to project an image for their product, and in so doing attempt to distinguish themselves from their competition. I recall in 1996 being told that Norwegian Cruise Line was unique because they were allowed to display the Chaîne's plaque on all their ships—a right generally reserved only for kitchens where one of the chefs is a member of the Chaîne. I learned later that Norwegian Cruise Line was not alone in this distinction. On May 27, 1998, Holland America Line issued a press release, marking their induction in the

Chaîne des Rôtisseurs, indicating that "this was the first time a culinary operation of a cruise ship became a member of the Chaîne as a unit." Also, referring to its induction as a fleet to the Chaîne, in their case on February 14, 1999, Princess Cruises indicated in a press release dated November 9, 1999 that "earlier this year, Princess was...recognized with its fleet wide induction into the prestigious Chaîne des Rôtisseurs....Princess is the first and only cruise line to have been awarded this honour." In June 2000, Royal Caribbean International announced its fleet wide induction, touting that their induction represented the largest number of chefs—twenty-five—ever inducted from any cruise line.

These comments are not intended to detract from induction of cruise lines into the Chaîne. Instead, it places into context what the distinction really means. There are ten cruise lines displaying the Chaîne's plaque—eleven if we count Seabourn Cruise Line which displays the plaque as an affiliated brand with Cunard Line—and each of these cruise lines claims to have the best food at sea. It is interesting to note that one becomes a member of the Chaîne by being nominated by a current member. Membership is open to anyone who has an interest and who shares an enjoyment and appreciation of fine food, especially food that is grilled or roasted, and who pays the membership fees. The designation is not an award of merit, nor is it an impartial statement about food quality.

## I Want a Cabin Like That

On a Mediterranean cruise aboard Royal Caribbean Cruise Line's *Song Of Norway*, I overheard a fellow passenger's conversation with the staff at the Purser's Desk. Holding a picture from the ship's brochure, and in an agitated tone, the passenger implored that he had booked "that" room and wanted to be assigned the room he had booked.

What had escaped his notice, which is a mistake made by most first-time cruisers, is that while the brochures describe the cabins as spacious, gracious, luxurious, deluxe, and so forth, the pictures shown are taken with a wide angle lens. This presents an appearance that is different than reality. A cabin measuring 130 or 140 square feet is made to appear two or three times larger than it actually is. The pictures also reflect the cabin's appearance when the ship was brand new. After years of use there is wear and tear that may be surprising when one first enters their accommodations. After one's first cruise, they become accustomed to the difference between pictures and reality.

The tendency to overstate the size of cabins is most clearly reflected in two examples where cruise lines re-categorized a cabin after receiving passenger complaints. Several months after it first appeared, cabins on Celebrity Cruises' *Galaxy* had their description changed from "mini-suite" to "premium stateroom." More recently, Norwegian Cruise Lines changed their initial advertising of the *Norwegian Sky's* S1: Superior Deluxe Suite" to a category "AA: Superior Deluxe Oceanview Stateroom." While the category's labels were changed to more accurately reflect the cabin's size, the pricing differential was not affected.

The recategorization of cabins can also be done for other reasons. In order to bring their prices down to a level to better compete with Silversea Cruises, Seabourn Cruise Line, beginning in 1998, revised their category-A cabins. What were previously sold as same-category cabins, were now divided between A, A1, A2, and A3. All cabins were still the same, but pricing was changed to reflect different locations on the ship: passengers now paid a premium for a midship location as compared to a location toward the bow or stern of the ship. Significant increments were also introduced for each of the two higher decks with cabins.

Windstar Cruises introduced a similar change in categories in 2000. Previously, all cabins on a Windstar ship, except for the Owner's Suite, were sold for the same price. Now, the line charges a differential of $200 per week, per person, for a cabin on deck one versus a cabin on deck two. The cabins are identical; the difference is simply which floor the cabin occupies. Ironically, the cabins on the lower deck are more stable in rough seas, yet they are lower in cost.

Perhaps the most interesting surprise in cabins is found on the original *Love Boats*. Reflecting the norm for ship construction when they were built, neither the *Pacific Princess* nor the *Island Princess* had/has a double bed. Contrary to the images reflected on the television show (which showed spacious cabins of perhaps 400 or 500 square feet), the majority of cabins on the ships measured 128 to 150 square feet. In addition, all cabins had twin beds that were fixed in place and could not be combined to make a double bed. This is not the image conveyed in my memory of the television series. Except for ships of their vintage (i.e., built before 1980), it is uncommon to find ships that do not have beds that convert to double or queen-sized configurations.

## Entertainment and "All that Jazz"

Given the importance to many passengers of the entertainment on board ships, cruise brochures do not spare superlatives in describing their Las Vegas-style or Broadway-style shows. The shows are described by mainstream cruise lines as dazzling, spectacular, splashy, exhilarating, and award winning. The costumes are described as stunning, lavish, individually designed, and hand-stitched. These descriptors are used to somehow distinguish "our" shows from "theirs"; however, whether one cruise line's shows are actually better than another's is not the focus of brochures. Each brochure projects a simple view that our's is the best.

Cruise lines consistently produce expectations that the quality of the live shows will be comparable to the performances found in Las Vegas or Broadway. However, for all of their efforts, the response to shows appears to be similar across cruise lines. Most passengers are pleased with the live entertainment on ships, regardless of the cruise line. Whether it is one troupe or company or another appears to have little influence on choice of a particular cruise or cruise line.

## So Much to Do, So Little Time

There are two common views expressed by those who have not cruised. One view is a fear that there will not be enough to do on the ship—that the cruise will be boring. The other view, in direct contrast, is that with all the activities, cruises are overly regimented. Cruise line brochures may create the latter view.

Cruise lines consistently advertise the range of activities offered. They suggest that one can pick and choose those of interest, but that no matter what one won't find their self with nothing to do. This is the essence of Princess Cruises' "Personal Choice Cruising" advertising campaign that appeared in January 2001. Traditionally, cruise lines have advertised organized activities (such as Bingo, horse racing, dance instruction), demonstrations (such as ice carving, napkin folding, bridge and/or galley tours), the casino, and their spa and exercise programs. They continue to introduce new activities and new facilities.

Beginning in the early 1990s, there has been increasing competition between cruise lines for the biggest, the best, and the most modern spa facilities. New treatments are continually being offered, and new settings are being designed. One of the most interesting is Crystal Cruises' introduction in July 2000 of Feng Shui to the Crystal Harmony's spa. According to Crystal Cruise's press release:

> *The goal of Feng Shui, known as the Asian Art of Placement, is to create a harmonious space evoking health, prosperity and happiness. With origins dating back four thousand years, the practice is designed to allow the Qi (pronounced Chi) or "life force" to flow freely within a given environment.*
>
> *To reach ultimate harmony, Crystal Cruises enlisted the expertise of noted Feng Shui practitioner Carol Cannon. Working from a floor plan, she made key changes to all areas of the luxurious 3,000 square-foot Crystal Spa. Simplifying the spa's appearance, strategically placing furnishings and adding vital Feng Shui elements were part of the redesign process.*

*Decorative features such as Chinese tiles symbolizing the seasons now cover the walls outside of beauty rooms. Zen rock gardens grace waiting rooms. Incense and fountains enhance therapy and common areas while wind chimes, crystals and specially placed mirrors throughout combine to suggest feelings of peace and harmony. This ancient art of placement and spiritual balance is being embraced with increasing frequency and adopted within homes and businesses in the U.S. and abroad.*

It remains to be seen whether others copy Crystal Cruises' innovation.

In addition to spas, most cruise lines have their own version of an exercise program. These programs often provide incentives or awards that may be earned for participation: a t-shirt, a cap, or a windbreaker. The programs have creative names like Passport to Fitness, Cruisercise, ShipShape, and Sports Afloat.

This offering of activities has reached new heights in recent years. In 1995, with release of the *Legend of the Seas*, Royal Caribbean Cruise Line introduced an eighteen-hole miniature golf course; in the same year, Carnival Cruise Line introduced a twenty-four-hour pizzeria on the *Imagination*. In 1996, with its introduction of *Destiny*, Carnival Cruise Line advertised not just its pizzeria, but also the largest water slide afloat and a virtual reality game room. In 1998, the *Grand Princess* appeared and offered computerized golf play at some of the world's greatest courses, a virtual reality centre with motion-based undersea theme rides, and a nine-hole putting green. In 1999, with its release of *Vision of the Seas*, Royal Caribbean International offered cruisers a rock-climbing wall, regulation ice skating rink (with seating for 800 spectators), and a Johnny Rockets franchised food outlet. (Not surprisingly, the very first franchised food outlet on a passenger ship was a MacDonald's; it appeared on a Baltic ferry.)

As each cruise line innovates new attractions, cruise ships become increasingly competitive with one another and with land-based resort vacations. They raise the standards for future ships, and they effectively shape passengers' perceptions of what constitutes a cruise. The simplicity of being at sea, which was the main attraction of cruising in the 1960s, has given way to a view of cruising that is based on multiple options from an endless list of activities, anytime night or day.

## Innovative strategies for attracting passengers

Cruise lines have created many innovative strategies for attracting passengers. Some of these have become industry norms, while others have been copied by some competitors but are not generalized to the industry.

## Air/Sea Programs

The introduction of air/sea packages was an innovation initially introduced by Costa Cruises in 1968. The company moved the *Franca C.* from Miami to San Juan, in an effort to market cruises to the Southern Caribbean. In order to remove the cost and time required to arrange air connections to the cruise, Costa Cruises introduced packages that included the cruise and the airline ticket.

Royal Caribbean Cruise Line (RCCL) took a similar tact in 1971. In order to contain the cost of air fare RCCL chartered aircraft and focused its marketing efforts on two markets: Los Angeles and San Francisco, which together accounted for 35 % to 40 % of their total passenger load. The company was able to fill the chartered back-to-back flights of wide-body aircraft from each city. The flights would deliver embarking passengers and return home those passengers who had just disembarked. With this efficient use of the aircraft, RCCL was able to provide the transcontinental airfare, and a quick sightseeing tour of Miami, for less than $60. A one week cruise on the *Song of Norway*, including airfare, port charges, and transfers could be had for as little as $368 per person.

The offer of air/sea programs has become an industry norm today. It is likely that the majority of passengers traveling any distance to a port depend upon a cruise line's air/sea offers for their flight arrangements before and after a cruise. Cruise lines have taken further advantage of this fact by offering pre-and post-cruise packages that are conveniently accommodated by their air/sea arrangements. However, unlike the airline tickets, which are usually reasonably priced, pre-and post cruise packages are often priced to provide a substantial profit margin. The advantage of using a cruise line's air/sea program is that if a plane is delayed in getting you to the ship, or if the ship is late returning you to port, the cruise line will take responsibility for making whatever arrangements are necessary for you to make the necessary connections. Passengers who book their own air arrangements are often left to deal with the situation on their own, including expenses associated with any changes.

## Discounts

There has been considerable debate in the industry about discounting cruise fares. A philosophy expressed by some is that it is better to bundle something with a cruise fare (i.e., give something away or offer onboard spending credits) than to accustom passengers to the idea that they will pay less than the rates listed in brochure. Larry Primentel, President of Seabourn Cruise Line, succinctly pointed out in 1993 that the "...cruise industry has conditioned the consumer to expect a discount with a cruise purchase." He went on to say that:

> ...it is far more sensible for Seabourn to offer [discounts]...to the guest than to allow our competitors to steal market share. If our competitors are destroying the market, it is incumbent upon us not to sit by and do nothing but instead to participate in the battle. The cruise market is a war zone, and the weapons are rampant and uncontrolled price-cutting. [2]

His comments reflect that discounting had become a common practice in the late 1980s and early 1990s; periods during which there was an overcapacity of space and a need to fill those empty cabins. As revenues dropped because of lower fares, the product being offered increasingly reflected lower budget operations. Cruise lines of all types and qualities have cut back considerably over the past decade in order to make their product affordable to a larger market. The quality of the product has suffered in the process.

Take for example the Seabourn Goddesses. Discounted fares in 2000 were so low that one could pay less for one week than the amount that would have been previously charged for a single day when the ships were part of Cunard Line. The ship is the same, but the cruise product has to suffer when per passenger revenues are cut so drastically.

## Early Booking or Last Minute

It was common practice in the early 1990s to provide last-minute discounts in order to fill the unused space. However, this produced problems in that passengers were given a disincentive to book their cruises too far in advance since the price may fall considerably as the departure date nears.

Confronted by an increasing gap between supply and demand, and the need for discounts to attract passengers, cruise lines introduced in 1992 (in most cases for implementation in 1993) early booking discounts. For the first time, the early bird got a bigger discount than the last-minute booker on sailings of a number of lines. Many of the programs established then, continue today. It was then that Royal Caribbean Cruise Line introduced its "Breakthrough Program"; Carnival Cruise Line began its "Super Savers Plan"; Holland America Line's introduced its "Keep it simple" program (which is now called "Early Booking Discounts"); NCL advertised "Dream Fares" (which are now "Leadership Fares"); and Princess Cruises started its "Love Boat Saver" program which guaranteed early booking passengers the best fares, even if a lower fare is introduced later on for any reason. These innovations, created out of necessity, are industry standards today.

With continuing overcapacity, cruise lines still offer discounts to fill ships. Some will offer the best discounts as the departure date nears in order to fill the last remaining empty cabins. While already-booked passengers are technically entitled to a refund of the difference between this discounted fare and what they paid, few are ever told it is available. These offers are made, changing day to day, and it is the passenger's responsibility to watch for them. If you are lucky enough to find one on a cruise you have booked, you can request and will receive a refund of the difference between what you paid and the new fare. However, if one is not requested, a refund is not automatically given.

## Theme Cruises

Another innovation from the mid-1980s and early 1990s, which has become a common marketing tool today, is theme cruises. As early as February 3, 1985, an article in the *Miami Herald* proclaimed "Themes Are In On Ships". The article goes on to discuss the things that can be explored on a cruise ship, including fitness and fashion, cosmetics, and computers. Later articles talk about children's programs. These were popularized by Premier Cruises (and its Big Red Boat), which was initially focused on the family market.

The motivation for theme cruises is simple: to attract passengers. James Godsman, President of the Cruise Line International Association, stated in 1990: "As the cruise industry consistently strives to enhance the on-board cruise product...individual lines are offering more themes." Natalie Kaye, Vice President of Marketing Communications for Cunard Line, goes on to say, "It's a way to put an edge of distinction, set yourself apart and expand your market to people who might not have considered a cruise."[2]

What are some of the popular theme cruises of the day? In 1989, Princess Cruises introduced a very successful ten day chocoholic theme cruise. Days were filled with classes in chocolate cooking and candy making and tastings. A different chocolate treat was presented each night at bedtime. Also in 1989, Princess offered cruises that featured magic, country music, big bands, and even a cruise built around the Academy Awards and hosted by actor Karl Malden.

Cunard Line offered an interesting array of theme cruises in 1989 and 1990. These included classical music—on a special anniversary cruise they had an onboard performance by the London Philharmonic—theatre, sports, and food. A sports-themed cruise included players from the New York Mets and their wives, who participated in autograph sessions and mingled with passengers. A series of "Epicurean Voyages" were offered which included an award-winning chef who prepared food and a renowned vintner who selected wines.

For today's cruiser, these may sound pedestrian and common. A review of current offerings includes the following:

> Holland America Line (among others) has their annual "Big Band" and "Swing" cruises, featuring the orchestras of Guy Lombardo, Glenn Miller, and Tommy Dorsey;
>
> Silversea Cruises has an impressive program of theme cruises based on enrichment lecturers and on guest chefs, the latter based on an association with Relais & Chateaux—the Relais Gourmands;
>
> Radisson Seven Seas Cruises has a guest chef program based on a program in association with the world-renowned Le Cordon Bleu Culinary Academy;
>
> Crystal Cruises offers Olympic Games cruises, opera cruises, classical music cruises, and art and architecture cruises;
>
> Disney Cruise Lines has its very existence based on a theme;
>
> Norwegian Cruise Lines has become known for its music theme cruises, most notably country and western and jazz, and for their Sports Afloat program that is in association with Sports Illustrated and which includes a Sports Bar and sport celebrities on all their ships.
>
> Interestingly, Norwegian Cruise Line's association with sports began in the early 1990s. It was reflected in 1996, when Norwegian Cruise Line was the official cruise line of the National Basketball Association's Miami Heat. Ironically, the Miami Heat is owned by Micky Arison, President and CEO of Carnival Corporation, the parent company of Carnival Cruise Line, Holland America Line, Windstar Cruises, Costa Cruises, Cunard Line, and Seabourn Cruise Line.

## Mini Cruises

Cruises of short duration became popular in the late 1980s and early 1990s. A number of articles appeared in 1990 proclaiming that the mini vacation would be the trend for the 1990s. Over 90 % of those taking three-or-four day cruises with Carnival Cruise Line in 1990 were first time cruisers. It was reasonably expected that 85 % of these would return in the future for another cruise, and this likely would be of longer duration. The mini cruise was seen as something of a sampler that would introduce to cruising those who were otherwise hesitant to devote a week to a cruise, or who did not have a full week for a vacation.

Short cruises, of two to five days, are the fastest growing segment of the cruise industry. In 1991, more than 37 % of the four million cruise passengers took a cruise that was three or four days in length. By 1997, 12 % of the sixty-eight itineraries offered by Royal Caribbean Cruise Line were three or four days in length. Between 1982 and 1997, there had been a 325 % increase in mini cruises. This growth continues.

The growth in mini cruises has contributed to the boom in growth of cruising. It was facilitated by cruise lines directly marketing these mini vacations, and by designing ships for this niche market. Royal Caribbean Cruise Line, which had pioneered through its subsidiary Admiral Cruises the three and four day market to the California market, introduced the *Nordic Empress* in 1990. A year later the *Viking Serenade* was deployed in the California market following a $75 million refit that included 260 new cabins (for a total passenger load of 1500). The *Nordic Empress* was unique in that it was the first ship that had been built specifically for the three and four day market. Because passengers would spend less time on the ship, it had no library, no card room, and no cinema. This space was instead used for additional cabins.

Royal Caribbean Cruise Line was not alone in the mini cruise market. Carnival Cruise Line introduced the *Fantasy* to the Miami/Bahamas market in 1990. The *Fantasy* was Carnival's newest ship, replacing the Mardi Gras, which was moved to Port Canaveral for mini cruises. It was deployed four months before RCCL's *Nordic Empress* was delivered. Today, more than half of the Carnival Cruise Line fleet is devoted to cruises of five days or less.

In the California market, RCCL had competition from Norwegian Cruise Line's *Southward*, an older, smaller, more intimate vessel with the additional attraction of costumed Universal Studios characters often on board; characters ranging from Groucho Marx and Frankenstein to Woody Woodpecker and Marilyn Monroe would show up on deck and pose for photographs.

There were other ships as well in the mini cruise market. One of particular interest is the *Royal Majesty*, a ship built by Dolphin Cruise Line for Majesty Cruise

Line, its upscale offshoot and introduced in 1992. The *Royal Majesty*, which operated from Miami, brought to the industry the first smoke-free policy. For the first time, a cruise ship prohibited smoking in the dining room and it designated 132 (26 %) of its 505 cabins as strictly nonsmoking.

## Nonsmoking

Carnival Cruise Line introduced the *Paradise* in November 1998. With a huge "no smoking" sign on its side, the ship has been given considerable attention because of its comprehensive prohibition of smoking by anyone on board the ship. Since the *Paradise* entered service, an average of four to six people per month are fined and sent home for violating the line's no-smoking policy.

Not only does Carnival Cruise Line require passengers to sign a contract prior to boarding the ship that promises they will abide by the no-smoking requirement, but any tobacco found when passenger baggage is x-rayed before being place on the ship is confiscated. Once on board, security personnel and ship staff monitor passenger activity to ensure that no one lights up anywhere on board the ship. If a passenger is discovered smoking, they are fined $250 and escorted ashore by security personnel at the next port of call. From there, it is the passenger's responsibility to find his or her own way home. According to Carnival President Bob Dickinson, the strict policies and penalties are necessary:

> *"...to effectively insure that the integrity of the smoke-free environment is maintained."*

This policy earned Carnival Cruise Line the Guest Choice Network's "Nicotine Nanny Award" in 2000. Regardless, the *Paradise* has been a marketing success, with occupancy rates exceeding 100 %. There is speculation that additional nonsmoking ships will be introduced.

Carnival Cruise Line, however, was not the first to introduce nonsmoking as a marketing tool. The Royal Majesty (mentioned above) is an example of a very progressive effort, particularly when considered in light of the fact that it predated the Paradise by more than six years. Carnival followed the Royal Majesty's example in 1994 by making all its dining rooms nonsmoking.

Norwegian Cruise Line also used nonsmoking as a marketing tool in the mid-1990s. They made the dining room nonsmoking, except for a very small area in the corner. They also designated all cabins on the starboard side of the ship as nonsmoking; smoking was permitted only in cabins on the port side. However this policy of nonsmoking cabins was eliminated in 2001. Interestingly, just one year earlier, in January 2000, Crystal Cruises made their dining rooms nonsmoking.

## Newer is Bigger—Bigger is Better

The cruise industry has used "newest" and "biggest" as advertising tools at least since 1985. There appears to be friendly competition for bragging rights of whose is bigger, including inclusion in the Guinness Book of World Records. The media have cooperated in this competition by providing coverage of each newer and bigger ship.

The competition appears to have begun in 1985, when Carnival Cruise Line unveiled the 46,000-ton *Holiday*, and touted it as the largest ship ever built for vacation cruises. Three years later, in January 1988, Royal Caribbean Cruise Line welcomed the *Sovereign of the Seas*, "the world's largest cruise ship." Built at a cost of $185 million, and at a weight of 73,192 tons, the ship could carry as many as 2852 passengers. As these new ships began to appear, the celebratory hoopla became more colourful and grand.

Though not the largest cruise ship, Carnival Cruise Line's 2600 passenger *Fantasy*, which began service in February 1990, was advertised as having the largest atrium in the cruise world. Built at a cost of $225 million, the 70,000-ton vessel was also the largest ship making three and four day cruises. Other notable descriptions that appeared at the time included the fact that the *Fantasy* has fifteen miles of neon tubing—described by one journalist as like walking into a giant jukebox. Another journalist referred to the *Fantasy* as the only ship in the world whose decor is best described in wattage.

Four months after the *Fantasy* began service, Royal Caribbean Cruise Line claimed the newest cruise ship with its *Nordic Empress*. Several months later, following a two-month, $40 million expansion, Norwegian Cruise Line claimed the *S.S. Norway* as the largest cruise ship afloat. The ship was physically the largest, but it did not accommodate the largest number of passengers.

There was a building frenzy during the 1990s that produced a continual flow of newer and bigger ships. The *Monarch of the Seas*, at 73,941 tons and with a passenger capacity of 2744, became the newest cruise ship in November 1991. Though it was 2000 tons lighter than the NCL's *Norway*, it had a passenger capacity of 350 more than the *Norway*, thereby claiming to be the largest in passenger capacity, even if not the largest in size. In 1995, Princess Cruises came out with the *Sun Princess*—the largest cruise ship ever built at 77,000 tons, but with a passenger capacity of only 1950.

Competition for the most passengers carried first appeared in July 1992, when the *Monarch of the Seas* set a record for the most passengers to embark on a single voyage on a modern cruise ship: 2655. Royal Caribbean Cruise Line announced that it had submitted the necessary documentation to the Guinness Book of World Records.

Competition for the biggest was renewed in November 1996 with the entry to the cruise market of mega ships. Carnival Cruise Line began with the $400 million, 101,000 ton *Destiny*, which had a maximum passenger capacity of 3400. It entered the Guinness Book of World Records for carrying 3269 passengers on a single voyage on December 22, 1996; this was surpassed to 3315 on March 29, 1997, and its sister ship, the *Triumph* took the honour August 22, 1999 with 3413 passengers.

Princess Cruises re-entered the competition in May 1998 for the biggest with its *Grand Princess*. The ship's capacity was only 2600 passengers, but built at a cost of $400 million it weighed in at 109,000 tons. A year and a half later, Royal Caribbean International reclaimed the title of having the biggest when it christened the *Voyager of the Seas*. This latest ship, built at a cost of $500 million, was the largest in both weight—143,000 tons—and in passenger capacity—3840 passengers. The *Voyager of the Seas* claimed the title for most passengers on a single voyage on several successive voyages. On its millennium cruise, December 26, 1999, the *Voyager of the Seas* attracted 3537 passengers. In June 2000, it exceeded 3600 passengers on a single cruise.

# Special Promotions

## Loan Programs

Cruise lines have used a variety of promotions to increase awareness of their product and to increase the attractiveness and accessibility of cruising. Princess Cruises helped remove the usual financial barrier to taking a cruise when it unveiled in February 1997 its Love Boat Loan cruise financing. Administered through an arrangement with MBNA America Bank, passengers can spread the cost of their cruise over a period of two to four years, with an annual interest charge as low as 14.99 %; the rate can be as high as 26.99 %.[4]

Royal Caribbean Cruise Line announced in October 1997, a Cruise Loan program administered through Citibank at interest rates of 14.5 % for new passengers and 12 % for past passengers, however it is unclear whether this program continued beyond its first year or two. Similarly, Carnival Cruise Line announced a loan program in May 1997, but it appears to have been short-lived.

Windjammer Cruises took an opposite tact in marketing their product. Using a scheme similar to a layaway plan found in many retail stores, they offer potential passengers a payment schedule over a set period of time. At the end of the period, they have paid enough for the desired cruise.

## Vacation Guarantee

Carnival Cruise Line introduced a "Vacation Guarantee" program as a marketing tool in May 1996. The Vacation Guarantee provides that guests may disembark in the first non-U.S. port of call for any reason and receive a prorated refund for the unused portion of their cruise fare, along with reimbursement for coach air transportation back to the ship's home port, by notifying the purser's office prior to arrival at the first port of call.

Initially tested over a four month period, from August 8 through November 22, the program has become a part of Carnival Cruise Line's marketing strategy. During the first seventy-eight sailings of the time period where the guarantee offer was in place, Carnival carried 160,000 passengers. Only 24 passengers (with only three sailings involved) had invoked the guarantee and disembarked. That is less than 0.02 %, or less than one in every 6500 passengers.

Carnival Cruise Line was not dissuaded from renewing its vacation guarantee by the fact that three days before it expired, 213 passengers (less than 10 % of the total passenger load) aboard the *Sensation* exercised their option after the ship broke down on its way to San Juan. In that case, a faulty battery led to a power outage, that was quickly restored, but which curtailed the ship's cruising speed and caused it to arrive in San Juan a day late.

Though the vacation guarantee has been credited by Carnival Cruise Line executives for contributing to a 16 % increase in sales in the four month trial period, it has not been copied by the competition. According to Bob Dickinson, Carnival Cruise Line's President, in a poll of guests as they left the ship during the initial four month trial period, 28 % of their passengers indicated they were aware of the program, and more than half of those said the guarantee played a major role in their decision to cruise with Carnival. By the end of its first year, Carnival Cruise Line logged a 42 % increase in bookings and 50 % of their guests indicated that the vacation guarantee was a positive influence to their purchasing decision. The number of passengers who have exercised the guarantee remained very small.

## Marketing Alliances

Another tool that Carnival Corporation has used effectively has been marketing alliances. In the Fall of 1998, it launched a joint marketing effort for its six cruise brands which were presented as the "World's Leading Cruise Lines." The first activity, and a test to see how it works, was an eight-page newspaper insert produced jointly with VISA, presenting Carnival Cruise Line, Costa Cruises, Cunard Line, Holland America Line, Seabourn Cruise Line, and Windstar Cruises. The tag line on the cover read: "The World's Leading Cruise Lines make it easy to find the cruise vacation that's right for you."

The insert, which cost about $1.5 million, was expected to reach 16 million households in fourteen of the nation's major markets. It was placed in the Sunday, October 18, 1998 issue of papers in New York, Los Angeles, Philadelphia, Boston, San Francisco, Washington, Dallas/Ft. Worth, Detroit, Atlanta, Miami/Ft. Lauderdale, New Orleans, Tampa, and Seattle. The cost was trivial if considered in light of the combined media spending for the six brands, which exceeded $100 million per year. The link with VISA provided cardholders with exclusive discounts and onboard credits ranging from $50 to $1000 per cabin, depending on the length of cruise and the cruise line, when booked with a VISA card.

This was not the first time that Carnival Cruise Line had linked with VISA. Following Royal Caribbean Cruise Line's link with VISA in December 1990, Carnival Cruise Line joined in a broad marketing partnership with the credit card in June 1991 (though it had stopped taking American Express two years earlier). The two lines became part of the well-known advertisements that featured companies that did not take American Express. One year later, VISA and Carnival Cruise Line went a step further with an advertisement filmed on Carnival's *Fantasy* as it sailed to Nassau. In November 1993, Carnival announced that it would offer its own VISA card, allowing card holders to earn points toward the purchase of cruise vacations. One year later, in December 1994, Carnival Cruise Line returned to accepting the American Express credit card and was named a preferred supplier for American Express' travel agencies. Royal Caribbean Cruise Lines also shifted back to American Express shortly thereafter.

The Carnival Corporation began marketing their "World's Leading Cruise Lines" in combined brochures in the United Kingdom in 1998. In the United States, Carnival Corporation has introduced "Vacation Stores" that specialize in their products. The concept was test marketed in June and July 1997, with the introduction of Carnival Information Centres (also referred to as Carnival Kiosks) at four malls in Southern California. Based on the positive effect on increased sales, the first Carnival Vacation Store appeared in Samsonite Travel Expo in the Palisades Centre Mall in Nyack, New York. The first freestanding Vacation Store was opened in June 2000 in Arlington, Texas. Others have opened since. The philosophy behind joint marketing the Carnival Corporation's brands is that one of the Carnival Corporation products is sure to fit the interest of any particular consumer.

In January 2000, Carnival Corporation took the joint marketing of its brands one step further. It began to honour past passengers with any of its cruise lines with benefits given to past passengers with any of the others in its family. As a result of the program, called VIP—Vacation Interchange Privileges, a past passenger with Carnival Cruise Line or Holland America Line can book a cruise with Seabourn Cruise Line or Cunard Line and be entitled to discounts reserved for past passengers of that line.

A marketing alliance of a different type was announced in late 2000 by Silversea Cruises. It joined forces with Relais & Chateaux, an international boutique hotel association, for an exclusive collection of land programs, culinary cruises, and reciprocal marketing. A cornerstone of the alliance will also be the culinary program found aboard Silversea's ships, featuring the chefs of Relais & Chateaux—Relais Gourmands. These chefs will offer entertaining and educational cooking demonstrations, host shopping tours in local markets, and create La Collection du Monde, a sampling of specialty dishes to be featured regularly on all Silversea cruises.

## Contests

Contests are one of the newest techniques for attracting new passengers. Contests are used to increase consumer awareness of cruises and of a particular cruise line. They also garner publicity by awarding free cruises. Examples of free cruises can be found by anyone who regularly "surfs the net." Premier Cruises had, for several years, given away a free cruise every month, from those who register at the web site.

Royal Caribbean International similarly gave away a free cruise on the inaugural sailing of the *Voyager of the Seas* from among persons who registered at their web site—the total number of entries was in the hundreds of thousands. Previously, they had run a contest in January 1998, to promote the merger of Celebrity Cruises with Royal Caribbean Cruise Line. Entitled "Cruise for Life", entries were taken at a special web site set up for the promotion. In the first two weeks there was an average of four thousand entries per day. The contest, which overlapped with Royal Caribbean's sponsorship of the Super Bowl's halftime show at a cost of $5 million, took entries for six weeks. The winner of the contest was awarded a cruise every year for the next fifteen years. RCCL was criticized in some of the trade magazines and by pundits. They simply posed the question of how Royal Caribbean knew that the winner of its "Cruise for Life" contest would live for only fifteen years. The faux pas was quickly forgotten.

Another contest that increased the visibility of a cruise line was Holland America Line's "I Love My Travel Agent" essay contest. Run in early 1999, the contest received more than 10,000 entries. It also received considerable free media attention. The winner of the contest was awarded a free cruise.

Princess Cruises has several times used contests to increase its visibility. In 1998, Princess Cruises ran a "Sea to Sea Search for Terrific Trios." The contest was used to call attention to the arrival of the *Sea Princess*, the third in a set of identical ships. The legendary trio, The Pointer Sisters, judged the twenty national contest finalists. The contest was open to amateur and professional trios throughout the U.S. and Canada. Contestants submitted a video performance, no longer than five minutes in duration, and a one hundred-word statement about why their trio is terrific. Twenty winning trios received an all-expense paid trip to Fort Lauderdale to participate in the inaugural festivities, including an overnight gala cruise and the naming ceremony of the *Sea Princess*; one trio was awarded a grand prize of a seven day Princess Caribbean cruise.

Princess' "Terrific Trios" contest followed on the heels of a promotion a year earlier in which two-for-one fares were offered to identical twins. In order to call attention to their twin ships, the *Dawn Princess* and the *Sun Princess*, the company offered two-for-one pricing to identical twins that booked cruises on one of their twins during Gemini— the astrological sign of the twins. The promotion was used to welcome the *Dawn Princess* to the fleet. It effectively garnered free media attention.

In 1999, Princess Cruises joined with Match.Com, an online dating and friendship service, to offer the "World's Largest Floating First Date" contest. Used to celebrate the debut of its newest ship, the *Ocean Princess* (also referred to as the cruise industry's first "millennium baby"), the contest awarded fifty couples an all-expenses-paid trip to Fort Lauderdale to attend a Valentine's Day gala aboard the ship in February 2000. To enter, a couple must have met through Match.Com, and submit a joint entry of up to two hundred words expressing why they would like to meet on the *Ocean Princess*. This contest, like others, is creative and is a way for a cruise line to receive media attention without the cost of paying for advertisements.

## Promotions Direct to Travel Agents

In addition to promotional pricing directed to consumers, cruise lines also offer a range of promotions to travel agents which provide incentives for them to book one cruise over another. The number of different schemes is difficult to track and to fully describe. It will suffice here to mention just a couple as exemplars.

In May 1999, Bob Dickinson offered a workshop to travel agents at the 17th Annual Travel Trade/CLIA CRUISE-A-THON conference, in Santa Clara, CA., and aboard Holland America Line's *Noordam*. For attending the workshop, travel agents were given coupons worth a total of $1,000 in commission bonuses from Holland America Line. These coupons were good for a $100 bonus commission per cabin, per cruise, over and above all regular pay and other bonuses earned for selling a variety of Holland America Line cruises, booked between May 10 and August 31.

Celebrity Cruises offered two interesting promotions in 1999, one to fill their European cruises, the other to increase booking of their millennium cruises. Announced April 1, 1999, and running for one month, Celebrity offered to travel agents who booked four cruises to Europe in the 1999 summer season, a European cruise for themselves and a guest at a special rate of $50 per person per night.

Celebrity's "Millennium Sweepstakes" offered prizes to passengers and to travel agents. Announced June 24, and running until November 12, the contest gave travel agents one entry for each stateroom booked. The prizes to travel agents consisted of one hundred and twenty-four U.S. Savings Bonds with values ranging from $50 to $10,000. This contest ran parallel to a drawing from all passengers on a Celebrity Millennium cruise, which awarded a grand prize of a Mercedes Benz SLK Roadster, and five first place prizes consisting of a seven-night Caribbean cruise onboard Celebrity's newest ship, Millennium.

The Cruise Line International Association offered an incentive in 1998 for travel agencies to renew their CLIA membership in 1999. In return for their membership renewal (which cost an agency $219), a travel agency received certificates worth $5000 in bonuses. The certificates, providing bonuses ranging from $50 for a three or four day cruise to $500 for a world cruise segment, were paid on specific types of cruises booked for 1999. One line offered a $50 bonus for five or seven night cruises during any season; another line offered a $100 bonus for any one of one hundred sailings to a dozen destinations; and another line offered a $200 bonus for ten and eleven day cruises to the Southern Caribbean, Panama Canal, Mexico, and Hawaii. These bonus certificates were in addition to the commissions normally paid (from 10% to 20%, though generally in the 14 %-15% range). To put the whole issue of commissions into perspective, Carnival Cruise Line as an example paid $150 million in commissions in 1998; they anticipated an additional $1 million to be spent for bonus commission certificates.

## Who cruises

There was a time when cruises were reserved for those in the leisure class. Many in the middle class could not see themselves taking a cruise: in some cases because of the perceived cost; in other cases because people felt cruises would be too regimented and didn't really offer a broad enough range of things to do that would interest them. In a February 1998 article in *Cruise Trade Magazine*, Rick James, Senior Vice President of Princess Cruises, suggests that it is from these objections that the cruise ships in the 1990s evolved. These new ships are targeted to the huge untapped market of those who have never been on a cruise ship. According to James, "These passengers will travel anywhere, and clearly do. They also are looking for less structure in their vacations and want many choices at the same time. These choices must cater to a wide range of ages, tastes, and interests—all within the same superstructure."

As Princess Cruises, like other lines, began to digest the research, their ideology of "what they want when they want it" began to emerge. It became apparent that cruise lines, to attract new passengers, had to include options for people that heretofore had been unheard of on cruise ships: things like ice rinks, wedding chapels, miniature golf courses, virtual reality centres, and twenty-four-hour restaurants. Combine these with the things that have been around for awhile— health spas, pizzerias, balcony cabins, expanded children's centres, and ever-larger and more elaborate show lounges—and the size of a ship quickly expands. In the case of Princess, to 109,000 tons; in the case of Royal Caribbean International, to 142,000 tons. In contrast, a typical ocean liner in the 1950s and 1960s was barely 20,000 tons.

The cruise ship of the new millennium is all about options. The lines expect to draw passengers from a wide range of backgrounds and demographic groups. New ships are being designed to accommodate this diversity of background, and passengers looking for different types of cruise experiences. According to Rick James, "Today, passengers can customize their cruise experience because one vessel can offer enough appeal to satisfy a widely diverse shipboard population." From this point, it is a small step to Princess Cruises' advertising "Personal Choice Cruising."

Along with these changes, the price of cruising has not increased over the past decade. In fact, adjusting for inflation, the cost of cruises has decreased for those in all categories.

So, how have these changes influenced who actually goes on a cruise? Perhaps the most significant change is in the number of people who cruise with their children. The 1992 *Market Profile* produced by the Cruise Line International Association indicated that 9% of passengers cruised with their children; in 1998, this had increased to 14% (an increase of more than 50%). It would also appear that these changes have attracted younger people to cruising—27% of cruisers in 1998 were younger than forty years of age.

While the cost of cruising does not appear to have increased, and cruise lines increasingly target those in middle income categories, it does not appear that the income demographics of those on cruises has changed significantly in the direction desired. However, this is difficult to judge with any certainty, given the absence of consistent statistics for comparing one year with the next.

*death by chocolate*

In 1986, the cruise industry identified, as its target, households earning more than $20,000. In 1992, adjusting for inflation, this same household would presumably be earning $26,000. In that year, 34% of persons considered new cruisers—those taking their first cruise in the previous three years—earned between $20,000 and $40,000 a year. The median household income in 1992 was $30,636 ($35,593 in 1998 equivalent dollars), about midway in this range. Six years later, only 20% of those taking a cruise had an income less than $40,000. The median household income in 1998 was $38,885, while the median income of those taking a cruise was $58,800

What has remained consistent is that the largest growing segment of the cruising population is the twenty-five to forty age category. In 1992, 46% of new cruisers were in this age range. In 1998, 27% of the more than 5 million people taking a cruise were younger than age forty; 45 % were between age forty and fifty-nine. Only 28% were at or near normal retirement age.

What all this suggests is that the answer to "who cruises" is "almost anybody." Cruises have made themselves appealing to a broad cross section of the population. Cost has increasingly been reduced as an impediment to cruising. In addition, cruise lines themselves have made it easier for those with young children and those with limited time (through short cruises) to take a cruise. If past patterns continue—85 % of those who cruise once will return to cruise again—it would appear that the cruise lines are being successful in creating demand for their expanding fleets.

These insights into who cruises are reflected in a press release issued by the Cruise Line International Association on October 19, 1999. The press release suggests that future cruisers fit into discernable categories. The categories say as much about expectations for who they think are their customers as they do about the advertising strategies that are likely to be used by cruise lines in the years to come.

The categories include:

*Family Folks.* These prospective cruisers are relatively young (average age forty), married, parents of children under eighteen, and watching their budgets. They're practical and down-to-earth, and more concerned with keeping their children entertained than pampering themselves. They find that many cruise lines offer a wide array of supervised children's activities, both on the ship and off.

*Want-It-Alls.* These are self-described workaholics with high expectations for their professional and personal lives, and that includes vacations. When they take a vacation, want-it-alls demand a tremendous amount of pampering and relaxation, two things they find in abundance on a cruise.

48

*Adventurers.* These sophisticated, well-educated travelers have a penchant for the exotic. On a cruise, they would find their fill of once-in-a-lifetime experiences in destinations as romantic and remote as Antarctica, the Far East, and Africa.

*Comfortable Spenders.* These well-off forty-somethings are well-traveled and active, and big fans of resort vacations. They, too, are perfect candidates for a cruise because, according to CLIA studies, people who have taken both cruises and resort vacations consistently rate cruises higher.

*Cautious Travelers.* These fifty-somethings prefer the simple things in life, and tend to opt for familiar experiences. Godsman believes a short cruise of three to five days is the ticket here, as it will provide cautious travelers with a bite sized taste of life at sea.

*Baby Boomers' Babies.* As freelance cruise journalist Anne Kalosh notes, "A large number of baby boomers are cruising with their kids. That means a whole generation is being raised on cruising. I can't imagine them growing up and not considering a cruise."

*Sophisticated Shoppers.* Given the high repeat factor in the cruise industry, frequent cruisers will become more discerning and sophisticated, and will demand new, highly specialized experiences, according to Joe Farcus, a ship designer for Carnival Cruise Lines. This growing sophistication will drive the production of more ultra niche vessels, designed around such themes as art or sports. For example, explains Farcus, a ship built around an art theme might feature an onboard museum rivaling those found in the world's largest cities, plus other activities to please the art lover's palate, such as lectures, art classes and museum visits.

---

[1] "Seabourn Head in Attack on Discounts," Lloyd's List, April 13, 1993, page 10
[2] "Seabourn Head in Attack on Discounts," Lloyd's List, April 13, 1993, page 10
[3] Wong, Betty. "Companies Are Entering New Waters With Theme Cruises,"
    Los Angeles Times, July 3, 1990, page D-7
[4] "Cruising Into Bank for a Vacation Loan," Los Angeles Times, March 9, 1997, page L-3

# 3 You Wouldn't Believe the Food!

For many, the highlight of taking a cruise is the food. This is reflected in the attitude expressed by many passengers. As one passenger was heard saying: "We're here to eat. That's what cruises are all about." Another was heard commenting that:"We paid for this; we're eating all of it. It makes you say 'I want one of this, one of this, and one of this." Observing passengers and their orientation to food, the executive chef of Royal Caribbean's *Sovereign of the Seas* commented: "I don't know where they put it. In a hotel, people will get pancakes. Here, it's pancakes and bacon and an omelette and French toast. And then the same thing at lunch and dinner. It goes on and on."[1]

The amount of food consumed on a cruise ship is amazing. Just consider. During a typical seven-day cruise of one of the smaller ships operated by Carnival Cruise Lines, carrying 2400 passengers, more than a half-ton of pasta will be consumed, along with 9000 hamburgers, nearly two tons of flour, 1400 pounds of prime rib, 6200 boxes of cereal, and more. With this level of consumption it is easy to see how 88% of passengers responding to a survey conducted by *Porthole Magazine* admitted to gaining an average of three to five pounds on a cruise. One passenger on a ten day cruise admitted to gaining sixteen pounds.

## Has It Always Been Like This?

While large amounts of food have always been associated with cruising—the midnight buffet was traditionally the crowning exhibition of the abundance of food—the growth in the size of the industry and of new ships has brought considerable change. While the quantity of food has remained somewhat constant, in the view of many the quality of the food has gone down. This change has accompanied a substantial increase in the number of passengers carried on a single ship. In the early 1980s, a large ship accommodated 600 passengers. By the mid-1990s, a large ship had a passenger load of 2000 passengers. Today, when one thinks of a large ship the image is of one that carries over 3000 passengers.

Larger ships have brought changes on a number of levels. First, in order to fill these ships, cruise lines have broadened their appeal to a larger consumer base. This means there are a wider variety of tastes among passengers. Different cultural and ethnic tastes are found, as well as differences in expectations for food.

A typical cruise ship will attract, at one and the same time, passengers looking for continental cuisine, passengers looking for ethnic dishes, and passengers looking for hamburgers, hot dogs, and spaghetti. Satisfying these diverse tastes is a challenge; a challenge to which most cruise lines fall short. Some have introduced food courts that have outlets serving different types and styles of food, however the food on most ships continues to be oriented to a narrow set of tastes. Even the food courts are designed to appeal to the lowest common denominator.

An insight into the challenge that faces cruise lines was provided one night on a recent cruise with Norwegian Cruise Lines. It was the fourth night of the cruise and I overheard a passenger expressing to her tablemates, when shown the menu, "Finally, something I can eat." She was referring to the fact that that night spaghetti and meat sauce was offered. The woman went on to explain that all that was offered each night before was French food and she expressed emphatically that she didn't like French food. The names of the dishes—Filet de boeuf roti Nouvelle, Coq au Vin, and Selle d'agneau au Romarin—were intimidating. It is possible that had the menu offerings been listed in plain English—roast beef, chicken stew, and lamb chop—they would have been quite acceptable. However, it is likely those wanting continental cuisine would be disappointed. Having overheard the passenger's comment, the waiter on subsequent nights brought the woman the children's menu. For the next three days, she had no problem choosing her meals.

A second change that has occurred with the increasing size of cruise ships is in food production. The galley on a typical ship in the mid-1980s produced meals for 600 passengers: 300 served at each of two seatings. Today, ships are serving six times the number of passengers: as many as 1800 per seating. This impacts on the methods of food production, the nature of the food served, and the quality of that food. It also has an effect on the food service. These will be discussed in some detail later.

## $350,000 per Week for Food

The food budgets for the large ships of today are staggering. The *Voyager of the Seas*, which can carry as many as 3800 passengers, consumes more than three hundred pallets of goods in a typical week. By comparison, the 1400-passenger *Song of America* consumed ninety. Many of the ocean-going ships of the 1980s, because they were half or a third the size, got by with proportionately less provisions. With the increase in size, the logistics of loading ships have changed considerably. While the amount of time allotted for loading provisions on a ship has remained the same, the methods have had to change to accommodate the increased volume.

With older ships, passengers could watch as food was loaded from the dock to the ship. A conveyer belt would be set up on the dock, going into the ship's loading area, and items would be loaded box-by-box, crate-by-crate. Quite often the executive chef and/or the food and beverage manager would open random boxes to check the quality of the produce or other food items. They would reject on the spot anything that did not meet their standards. Passengers with an interest could see the open-top boxes of oranges, tomatoes, cucumbers, etc. These older ships were built to be stored one case at a time.

Modern ships, in contrast, are built to be stored by the pallet. Ships are set up to have full pallets driven onto the ship from the dock and these are then transported to the ship's storage areas. To get a sense of the scale, consider the following list of some of the major items for a weekly provisioning of the *Voyager of the Seas*. They include 15,000 apples, 2800 pounds of bacon, 7000 pounds of bananas, 5000 gallons of beverages, 1600 pounds of breakfast sausages, 15,400 pounds of butter/margarine, 4500 bottles of champagne and wine, 13,200 pounds of citrus, 2000 pounds of coffee, 120,000 eggs, 15,000 pounds of flour, 1900 pounds of ham, 7600 hot dogs, 1400 gallons of ice cream and sherbet, 7500 pounds of lettuce, and 10,000 steaks. In a typical week, food costs alone can run as high as $350,000.

With this volume, quality control of items received is sometimes lost. I was on the *Statendam* for a sixteen-day cruise to the Hawaiian Islands. Halfway through the cruise, the bars stopped providing lemon wedges with mineral water or drinks. When asked, the bartenders said there weren't any on board. When I posed the same question to the hotel manager, I learned that they had opened several cases of lemons and found that most of what they had received was rotten. They used the few lemons on board sparingly for the remainder of the trip. On older, smaller ships this problem likely wouldn't have appeared—it would have been addressed before leaving port.

## All that Food for Ten Dollars a Day?

With the volume of food purchased, cruise lines are able to keep food costs relatively low. Per person expenditure for food has not significantly increased over the past six or seven years. In their book, *Selling the Sea*, Bob Dickinson (President of Carnival Cruise Line) and Andy Vladimir indicate that food costs on a per passenger basis range from $8 to $11 a day on economy and mass market lines, to as much as $18 a day on premium lines, and in the range of $25 to $30 on ultra-luxury lines. The fact is that expenditures by premium and ultra-luxury cruise lines have actually been reduced in the past several years. The *Radisson Diamond*, a ship in the ultra-luxury category, averaged $23 per day for food and $6 per day for beverages on its transatlantic cruise in 2000. Holland America Lines, whose ships occupy the premium category, spend between $14 and $15 a day.

Industry-wide, a survey of cruise line executives indicated that the average per diem for food in 1994 was $12 per passenger. This translates into a total expenditure by the industry of $354 million spent on food. An additional $184 million was spent on beverages in 1994. In the year 2000, food and beverage expenditures by the North American cruise industry could be as high as $1 billion.

While the per diem food cost per passenger sounds low, when the full volume of purchases is considered the amount being spent is quite significant. Take for example a report that food cost at Royal Caribbean Cruise Line in 1994 was $10.50 per passenger per day. Fleet wide, this translates to an annual expenditure for food of $54.4 million. Based on this same figure of $10.50 a day, Royal Caribbean International spent an estimated $135 million for food for its passengers in the year 2000. Including purchases for beverages, the corporate food and beverage budget for passengers easily exceeded $200 million. Carnival Corporation, which reportedly spends between 8% and 9% of its gross revenue on food and beverages, had an annual budget of over $300 million in the same year.

This volume of purchasing has allowed cruise lines to reduce or to keep food costs relatively stable. Through their ownership by Carnival Corporation, companies such as Holland America Line, Windstar, Costa, Cunard, and Seabourn have been able to reduce their expenditures for food and beverages. Radisson Seven Seas Cruises similarly enjoys advantages in purchasing power through its ownership by Carlson Companies, Inc. The Carlson Companies include Radisson Hotels, Regent International Hotels, Country Inns & Suites, Radisson Seven Seas Cruises, T.G.I. Friday's, Italianni's restaurants, and Carlson-Wagonlit Travel.

## The Art of Feeding More for Less

Purchasing power achieved through volume is only one way in which cruise lines have controlled the cost of food and beverages. There has also been an increasing shift to pre-prepared, ready to cook, and pre-cut foods. The advantage of these products goes beyond the material costs. Cruise lines achieve savings because pre-prepared, ready to cook, and pre-cut foods require less staff in the galley. This reduces salary costs, means fewer staff to feed, and it potentially frees shipboard space that would otherwise be devoted to crew cabins.

There are a number of ways that pre-prepared, ready to cook, and pre-cut foods have been used by cruise lines. Desserts are one area in which this is becoming more and more apparent. The desserts used are not unlike those found at the neighbourhood Price Club or Costco. Commercially mass prepared and frozen, these include such things as chocolate tortes, Mississippi Mud Pies, cheesecakes, and Black Forest cakes. These ready-to-serve products are used by, among others, Carnival Cruise Line and Holland America Line. Sadly, in some cases passengers are still told that everything is prepared fresh and on board. I first saw this contradiction while traveling with Celebrity Cruises. Kitchen supervisors told passengers on a galley tour that everything, including the ice cream, was made fresh on board. However, it was clearly stated by waiters that the ice cream (and other items) were bought ashore.

Cruise lines have also effected cost savings through the coffee served on many newer cruise ships. By the mid-1990s, many cruise ships were using instant espresso/cappuccino machines in their galleys. As well, the vast majority, including Holland America Line and Princess Cruises (among others), was using instant vending type coffee systems in the Lido Restaurants on some of their ships. These systems mix hot water with a canned concentrate that consists of 77% water and 23% "coffee based dry matter." The exact ingredients that comprise "coffee based dry matter" include coffee, but the United States Department of Agriculture also allows chicory and other ingredients. When traveling on most cruise lines, I have learned to stick with tea bags in which I know the ingredients. I avoid what looks like coffee because the taste is often far from "the real thing."

If a passenger wants a "real" cup of coffee they must go to the onboard coffee bar and in most cases —Holland America being an obvious exception—pay $1.50 or $2.00 a cup. Ironically, cruise lines do not advertise that they are using other than real coffee. In fact, on a cruise aboard Holland America Line's *Veendam* in 1999, the list of "Food Consumption During This Cruise" that was distributed at the end of the cruise indicated that 600 pounds of coffee had been used; however, none of the coffee dispensers in the Lido Restaurant used real coffee.

Real eggs have gone the same way as coffee. Cruise lines, particularly mass market and premium lines, are increasingly using "egg product" for omelettes, scrambled eggs, and other egg dishes. In some cases the difference between fresh eggs and "egg product" is not easily discernible; however, in others the difference is obvious. This shift is cost effective because "egg product" is not as perishable, does not risk breakage, and consumes less space.

Additional savings in food costs are achieved by purchasing meats that are pre-cut and frozen. The degree of preparation on shore varies. Some cruise lines, like Radisson Seven Seas, buys "boxed beef" which consists of large portions that must still be cut into individual steaks or filets. Others, such as the new ships being deployed by Royal Caribbean International, buy steaks that are already cut into exact, individual portions. These portions are ready to cook and take no further preparation by the ship's galley. On the other extreme, Costa Cruises still maintains butcher shops on its ships. They find that they can maintain a high quality product and make good use of most of the by-products in such things as soup stocks and consommés. Does the use of frozen versus fresh, processed versus not processed, make a difference? For the discriminating palate, the difference may be discernable and significant.

Other changes that are associated with cost savings include the use of fresh-frozen fish (rather than fresh), ready to cook shrimp, and ready to cook lobster tails. Each of these products reduces the amount of labour needed in food preparation, thus reducing the number of crew required in the galley. However, these changes also may impact on the final food product. Cruise lines claim that these changes all result in a better product when delivered to the dining room table. I would simply disagree. Fish that is fresh-frozen is never comparable to fish that is fresh.

Unfortunately, most passengers don't know that the "fresh fish" or "daily catch" has come out of the freezer. I recently had a friend, anticipating an Alaska cruise, who said he was looking forward to the fresh salmon, halibut, and crabs legs. Little did he know that the fish he would be served was not only frozen, but may not have even been caught in Alaskan waters.

I recall being on the *Norwegian Wind*, before and after the galley changed from fresh whole lobster to fresh-frozen lobster tail. There were two visible differences. While the portions of lobster tail were now consistent, the taste and texture was different. As well, the Lobster Bisque, which had previously been prepared with the shells and other leftovers from the whole lobster, no longer included these ingredients. It was a wholly different taste from the Lobster Bisque prepared when the ship received whole lobsters. The executive chef knew that the difference was unmistakable, but because purchasing was centralized in the corporate office he had only limited control over the product he served. No doubt, in future (like some of the soups already served on some lines) the Lobster Bisque may be from a can and merely given finishing touches by the ship's galley. I have been told that several cruise lines already rely heavily on soup bases that come from a can.

## The Best Food At Sea

All cruise lines claim to have the best food at sea. These claims are interesting when considered in light of the changes that the industry has undergone over the past fifteen or twenty years. For one thing, as galleys produce larger numbers of meals within the same period of time, the food is undoubtedly affected.

Few would disagree that there are significant differences between a restaurant that prepares meals cook-to-order, a galley that assembles meals-to-order (as is the case on most ultra-luxury cruise ships), one that prepares meals for 600 passengers divided between two seatings, one that prepares meals for 1000-1200 passengers divided between two seatings, and one that prepares meals for more than 3200 passengers divided between two seatings. Morton Mathiesen, Executive Vice President at Premier Cruises, suggests that, "On a mega-ship, you have more of a chance that the food will get cold before it's served...[You also] have more chance that the meat is cut too early and it's dried out when it's served."[2]

As the number of meals prepared increases, the food becomes increasingly standardized and there is greater chance that things will go wrong. When they do go wrong the impact can be monumental. On a recent cruise aboard Holland America Line, carrying 1200 passengers, the galley ran out of an entree. A couple hundred passengers did not receive the veal that they ordered. What they were served was whatever had already been prepared and was waiting in the kitchen (after all tables had been served) and was ready to serve. Because the galley didn't realize that they were going to run out in advance, those who had ordered veal generally received their chosen alternate after others at their table had already finished eating their entrees. Had this happened on a larger ship, the scale of disappointment and the ability to recover are difficult to imagine. Had it happened on a smaller ship, many more options for recovery would have been available to the galley.

When on Royal Caribbean Cruise Line's *Song of Norway*, this sort of embarrassing situation was avoided by the waiter each night recommending at the late seating dinner items that hadn't been ordered at levels that the chef had assumed would be the case. He would also dissuade passengers from ordering expensive items. He would warn that the lobster tails are dried out or the beef is tough. The items were never as he warned they would be.

As already mentioned, the move toward pre-prepared, pre-cut, and ready to cook foods has allowed cruise lines to reduce the number of staff needed in the galley. While this provides cost savings to the cruise line, having fewer staff can have some obvious effects on the food product. Shortcuts are increasingly used, because the person power just isn't there.

For example, breakfast, which may be one of the most difficult meals to prepare, is visibly affected on a number of cruise lines. Frequent cruisers become accustomed to poached eggs generally being overcooked. I have observed on both Norwegian Cruise Lines and Holland America Line times when the galley has poached a large number of eggs well in advance, sometimes days in advance. When an order for Eggs Benedict or poached eggs is received, they simply retrieve the already cooked eggs from the refrigerator, dip them in hot water to bring them up to serving temperature, and serve them to the passenger.

This trick was discovered because the eggs served on one cruise were hot on the outside, but still cold in the centre. Omelettes as well are often prepared in advance. They are kept warm in a steaming tray. While most passengers don't notice, there are always those who object to the texture change that occurs from the steam, and the discoloration sometimes caused by the eggs' contact with the metal of the tray. While fresh eggs will normally discolour, "egg product" is less likely to show the effects of being in the steamer. In either case, as a consumer, it is unattractive to have a greyish coloured egg, or one that is visibly saturated with moisture from sitting too long in the steamer.

## If You Don't Like Our Food...Talk To the Concessionaire

Cruise lines traditionally have used commercial caterers—a concessionaire— to provide their food service. Over the past ten years they have increasingly moved their food service to in-house operations. For most, as the cruise line grew beyond five or six ships, it became more cost effective for it to handle its own food service. Increased size brought economies of scale for both food products and for staff recruitment and training. Many cruise lines, particularly those with a small number of ships, continue to rely on concessionaires.

One alternative to moving food service to an in-house operation is seen in the strategy used by Costa Cruises. They bought their concessionaire, Zerbone Catering. Zerbone provides the food service on all Costa ships, but also provides services to other companies that contract for their services. For Costa, this arrangement allowed them to avoid the start-up costs of an in-house operation, but provided them with a specialist's expertise with the operation that was already on board their ships. As well, Costa enjoys the side profits of Zerbone's outside business.

Princess Cruises uses a slight variation of Costa's strategy. Rather than purchasing its caterer, Tiberio Corte, and bringing it under the P&O umbrella, Princess acquired in 1991, all the assets of the Tiberio Corte in the United States and appointed Giovanni Gallizio to the position of Corporate Director of Food and Beverage. Mr. Gallizio's family continued its ownership of Tiberio Corte and continued to provide service to other cruise lines.

Still one other variation is the partnership established between Celebrity Cruises and Apollo Ship Chandlers for the food service on Celebrity's ships. Through a joint venture called Celebrity Partnership Services, Apollo has responsibility for the food preparation and the food and beverage servers on all Celebrity ships. As with the other caterers, Apollo has other cruise lines as clients, Renaissance Cruises among them.

Most cruise passengers are unaware that the cruise line itself does not provide food service. This perception is reinforced by cruise lines, which, even though they use a caterer, will often tell passengers that the food operation is entirely in-house. On the galley tour during my first cruise with Celebrity Cruise, we were told in response to a direct question that all food and food service was an in-house operation —all kitchen staff and waiters were employees of Celebrity Cruises. I knew this statement was false, but the food manager conducting the tour was unwavering in his position. The easiest way to find out whether a concessionaire is being used is to ask a waiter or busboy. They know who employs them, and will normally tell passengers when they are asked.

Only rarely is there an obvious indication that a cruise line uses a caterer. For example, on the maiden voyages of the *Seawind Crown* in 1991, each dining room table had been set with packets of artificial sweetener carrying the logo of a competitor, Premier Cruise Line. The same Miami-based company catered both cruise lines.[3]

Whether a concessionaire prepares the food or it is an in-house operation makes no difference to most passengers. However, when there is a problem, the difference can be quite significant. Most passenger contracts—the small print that is included with the cruise ticket—provide that the cruise line is not liable for personal injury or death caused by any concessionaire unless the cruise line negligently retained such concessionaire.

Thus, in a case where I suffered a personal injury as a result of a shard of broken dinner plate in the food, the cruise line simply responded by saying, "Don't talk to us. That is between you and our concessionaire." I am prohibited from naming the ship or the cruise line as a condition of their agreement to pay my dental bills. Similarly, less serious concerns and complaints are merely passed on by the cruise line to the concessionaire, or the passenger is told to talk to the concessionaire about their concern or problem. Presumably, these occurrences may affect the renewal of a concessionaire's contract with the cruise line, but that still leaves the dissatisfied passenger dealing with a company from which he/she didn't know the food service was being provided.

## I Thought the Portions Were Getting Smaller

One way in which cruise lines have become more economical in their food operations is through volume purchasing. There are additional methods they have employed to reduce costs. A 1993 article in *Cruise Industry News Quarterly* observed that portions have been scaled down (perhaps as much in response to passenger eating habits as cost control) and that midnight buffets were not as elaborate as they used to be. These changes are not obvious to new cruisers or to those who are relatively new to the experience. They can be quite glaring to those who have a comparison point in earlier days of modern cruising.

Portion control is probably most visible with steaks. As cruise lines move more to pre-cut beef, portions are not only standardized, but the size is strictly controlled—usually to six ounces. While most cruise lines are quiet about their use of pre-prepared and pre-cut products, Royal Caribbean International's executive vice president of Total Guest Satisfaction indicated in trade publications that the Project Eagle ships (i.e., the *Voyager of the Seas* and *Explorer of the Seas*) would utilize a program of pre-cut steaks. To be clear, the quality of the product is not being sacrificed. It is simply more cost effective to use pre-cut, standard-sized steaks than to do the cutting in the ship's galley.

Cutting out certain expensive products also saves money. For example, upscale cruise lines used to consistently serve Beluga caviar, considered the highest grade of Iranian caviar. Today, because of escalated prices for Beluga, most, if not all, cruise lines have scaled back to the grade of either Oscietra or Sevruga. Stein Kruse, Executive Vice President and Chief Operating Officer of Radisson Seven Seas Cruises in 1995, suggested that the difference in taste quality is so minuscule that most passengers would not distinguish the difference between the three caviar brands. Radisson Seven Seas chose Sevruga, the least expensive of these.[4]

Another example of cutting out an expensive item is Royal Caribbean International's decision in mid-1997 to eliminate lobster from the menu on its three and four night sailings. As news of this change circulated, much fear was expressed on Internet discussion groups that it would also be made to seven day itineraries. The fear proved to be unfounded.

Adding pasta to menus is another method that can reduce food costs. In 1995, when Radisson Seven Seas Cruises added a pasta trolley for its deck luncheons, it not only proved very popular but also turned out to be a cost saver. Simply, pasta is less expensive to serve than a meat or vegetable-based dish. In this context, it is interesting that many of the alternative restaurants offered on cruise ships are Italian and include pasta as a major item. As well, Princess Cruises, Costa Cruises, and Radisson Seven Seas Cruises take pride in regularly offering pasta as an entree choice in the dining room.

The use of theme nights has also proven to save money on food by utilizing dishes that are less costly than traditional food items. Theme nights can also be used to increase the sale of drinks. Several years ago a cruise line shifted one night from a traditional midnight buffet to a country and western theme night held outdoors around the main swimming pool. They offered line dance lessons, food that was consistent with the theme, and special drinks to go with the occasion. The result was that more passengers attended the buffet. The actual food cost was significantly lower than the traditional midnight buffet, and the sale of drinks significantly increased.

With a minor change, the cruise line was able to significantly impact the bottom line of both the food and the beverage budget.

## Roast Pork Loin: Fourteen Grams of Fat and One Hundred Milligrams of Cholesterol

The diets of cruisers have changed over the years. Over the past decade and a half, Holland America Line has seen the choice of fish as an entree rise from 10% of passengers to almost 40 % of the passengers on the line's Caribbean cruises and 50 % on its Alaska cruises. This reflects an overall trend for people to eat more healthily.

This tendency toward healthy eating is reflected in two trends. First, more and more cruise lines offer vegetarian menus. Royal Caribbean has offered vegetarian selections at lunch and at dinner since 1992. Celebrity introduced a vegetarian menu in 1994. Holland America, which says it offers more than fifty vegetarian dishes during a cruise, and Princess Cruises, have both offered vegetarian options for several years.

The other trend toward healthful eating is reflected in each line's version of a light and healthy menu. Celebrity Cruises has Lean and Light options, Royal Caribbean International has a ShipShape menu, Norwegian Cruise Lines has Spa Cuisine, Carnival Cruise Lines has Nautica Spa fare, and Crystal Cruises has Lighter Fare lunch and dinner menus. The list can go on because there are few, if any, cruise lines that haven't followed the trend. The menus usually provide a breakdown of calories, fat, cholesterol, and sodium for the "light and healthy" choices. Most lines report that between 5 and 15% of their passengers take advantage of the healthful options, with many passengers mixing and matching meals with a light and healthy lunch and a traditional dinner.

## We Have Twenty-Four-Hour Dining, for Your Convenience... but No More Midnight Buffet

With the introduction of twenty-four-hour dining, many cruise lines eliminated the midnight buffet. Princess Cruises and Carnival Cruise Lines were the first in the industry to introduce the concept of twenty-four-hour dining. Princess Cruises inaugurated the idea in 1995 on the *Sun Princess* with introduction of the Horizon Court, an indoor/outdoor international food court. The Horizon Court appeared the next year on the *Dawn Princess*. Based on their success, the line quickly made plans to refit many of its older ships with a twenty-four hour Lido buffet. With food available any time of day or night, including a full sit-down dinner menu from 6:00 P.M through 4:00 A.M, the line was able to discontinue (without incident) the midnight buffet on those ships.

Carnival Cruise Line introduced twenty-four-hour dining in 1996, with its pizzeria, which is part of the "Seaview Bistro." On a typical cruise, Carnival Cruise Lines will serve 8000 pizzas each week. This is on top of the 9000 hamburgers served at its not-twenty-four-hour grill. Carnival also offers "midnight fare" at its Lido restaurant; however, it is not the traditional midnight buffet for which cruising has been associated.

As some lines begin dropping the midnight buffet—Disney Cruise Line never had one, saying it would interfere with the evening's entertainment—others have either cut back or changed their strategy altogether. For example, Celebrity Cruises has cut back its late-night spread to five nights a week. Other cruise lines have opted to produce a lavish buffet at lunch when the ship has a day at sea. Discontinuation of the midnight buffet, and the opulent display of food, is most assuredly a cost savings. While on Celebrity Cruises' *Meridian*, I was amazed at the volume of food (including whole fruits and vegetables) that was used for the sole purpose of the display. Much of the food was likely thrown away, or served in the crew mess, afterwards.

## So Many Options...Where Should I Eat?

In addition to the trend toward offering casual dining options, many cruise lines offer upscale alternative restaurants. Initially, these alternatives were extra tariff. For example, Royal Viking Line offered elegant dining in The Royal Grill on the *Royal Viking Sun* when it was launched in 1989. Meals cost $45. Similarly, dinner in the Palm Tree Restaurant on Norwegian Cruise Line's *Seaward* had an extra tariff of $35. The alternative outlets were short lived because passengers resisted additional costs to their "all-inclusive" vacation.

Crystal Cruises with its offer of Prego, an Italian restaurant, and Kyoto, a Japanese restaurant, began the move toward alternative dining without extra charge in 1990. Each of these restaurants has its own chef and its own galley. Not long after, Norwegian Cruise Lines initiated its Le Bistro, an alternative dining room that also has no additional charge. Passengers using the alternative restaurants on NCL and Crystal are encouraged to give a tip of $5 per person.

Today, many cruise lines offer alternatives to the regular dining room. For example, Orient Lines' *Marco Polo* has Raffles, Holland America's *Rotterdam* and *Amsterdam* has Odyssey, the *Radisson Diamond* has Don Vito's, and Radisson's *Song of Flower* has Angelino's. Norwegian Cruise Line's "free-style cruising", introduced after it was purchased by Star Cruises in early 2000, is based on offering a number of dining choices to all passengers. The company has eliminated assigned tables and assigned times for meals, and leave to passengers the decision of where and when they want to dine. The downside of this approach is that there are times when passengers must wait for an available table, and passengers who expect to have the same dining companions each night are often disappointed.

Princess Cruises followed Norwegian Cruise Line several months later with what it labelled, Personal Choice Cruising. As part of its Personal Choice Dining program, Princess Cruises offers passengers the choice between the traditional fixed seating times and fixed meal companions along with the option for flexible dining, either in a regular dining room or in one of the specialty or extra-tariff restaurants.

## Extra Tariff Restaurants Are Becoming Increasingly Common

Over the past several years there has been a re-emergence of extra-tariff alternative restaurants. There is no shortage of examples. The Painted Desert, the southwestern alternative restaurant on the *Grand Princess*, has a $3.50 reservation fee; Sabatini's, which serves Italian fare, has a charge of $15.00. The Italian alternative-dining restaurant on the *Costa Victoria* began charging a fee of $18.75 in December 1999; and, Celebrity Cruises' *Millennium*, which entered service in July 2000, has The Olympic Restaurant that has an extra charge of $12 per person. Royal Caribbean International included on the *Voyager of the Seas* both an upscale alternative restaurant, Portofino's, which charges $12 per person (though charges have varied from $5.00 to $15.00; the Potofino's on the *Radiance of the Seas* reportedly charges $26.00 per person), and a 50s-style hamburger-malt shop. The malt shop, a franchise of the Johnny Rockets chain, seats 259 and offers the same menu as Johnny Rockets anywhere in the United States. For the first six months, the Johnny Rockets on the *Vision of the Seas* charged on-shore prices. Based on passenger complaints, the company eliminated charges for food items, but has continued to charge for milk shakes and other specialty items.

This move toward extra-tariff restaurants is eroding the concept that cruises are an all-inclusive vacation. Though food is still included in the price of cruises sold in North America, there is increasingly delineation between the food that is included and that which is not. One cannot be sure where this is leading. Will cruises, like many land-based resorts, begin to offer different meal plans, or will the practice of offering a different set of dining choices to different classes of passengers become an element in choosing a cruise? Only time will tell.

# What Is the Best Food You Have Ever Had on a Cruise?

The question of the best food on a cruise ship periodically appears in discussions about cruises on the Internet. The answers provide insight into the changing tastes of passengers on cruise ships, and also give a sense of the disparity between the claim by cruise lines that their passengers want fine food and the actual tastes of those passengers being attracted to cruising.

There is little question that cruises attract a large number of passengers who are interested in fine dining, or at least in a continental cuisine. The menus on most cruise lines reflect this interest. They tend to include choices that are both contemporary and traditional. Steve Kirsch, Holland America Line's Manager of Onboard Services, described that line's menu selections (in 1994) as "American contemporary cuisine that places emphasis on high-flavour profiles and which are offered through innovative plate presentations."[5] The resulting menus have entree choices on one night which include: Grilled Supreme of Salmon, Seared Sea Scallops, Filet Mignon Oscar, Roast Duckling Bigarade, Medallions of Veal, and Roast Leg of Lamb; on another night, the offerings are: Pan Seared Gulf Snapper Fillet, Baked Stuffed Prawns del Ray, Broiled New York Sirloin Steak, Ballotine of Chicken, and Roasted Pork Loin.

Reiner Greubel, Holland America Line's Corporate Executive Chef, suggests that the line attempts to include into its menus "comfort food." Comfort food is food that people can relate to; they know what it is supposed to be. Examples include chicken pot pie with fresh vegetables and pasta with prawns or with chicken breast.

Presumably, the menu offerings provided by cruise lines appeal to most of their passengers. However, the menus are in stark contrast to the tastes of many of the new cruisers being attracted as the cruise lines broaden their appeal. Take for example the vignette above about the woman who finally found food she could eat when she was given the children's menu at each night's dinner. Her tastes are not unusual. They are reflected in a recent posting on the Internet that suggested the best bet for food on the Sea Princess is the beef burgers and the pizza.

This observation followed a query that asked, "What is the best thing you ate or drank on a cruise?" The question received a total of eighty-two responses. The largest number of responses referred to different types of alcoholic beverages (including tropical drinks with paper umbrellas, pina coladas, firecrackers, and lava floes), different types of chocolate cake, and two particular chilled soups (strawberry and pumpkin). Also popular were chocolate soufflé and Holland America Line's bread pudding. Some other items, mentioned by one respondent each, were: french fries, pizza, steak, lobster, cherry pie, peach pie, napoleons, warm buttery rolls at breakfast, and clam chowder. The only items reflecting continental cuisine were Beef Wellington, Lobster Thermidor, escargot, and rack of lamb. Each was mentioned only once.

Recounting this discussion helps put into perspective the wide variety of tastes that must be satisfied by cruise lines. There are those who are quite content with the traditional fare available in the main dining room of a cruise ship. Others have described the traditional food on a cruise as "French cuisine, interspersed with occasional dishes from other countries, as interpreted by French-type chefs," and have complained that the food on cruise ships simply lacks creativity. One person said he would prefer to be on a cruise with food from Popeye's, Bojangles, and the local barbecue joint. This explains the popularity of informal food courts. These informal food courts allow cruise lines to further reduce their food costs.

## Dining Cruise Ship Style: Images And Realities

As competition for passengers increases, with most North American cruise ships following nearly identical itineraries around the world, cruise lines have become keenly aware that it is a combination of the hardware and the software that sells a cruise and that ensures repeat passengers. On the hardware side, the major cruise lines have each devoted considerable resources to building new ships. While the ships may differ slightly in character, their differences are often not enough to attract passengers to one line instead of another.

What cruise lines have apparently determined is that passengers' perceptions of food quality are one of the fundamental components that sells a cruise and that brings repeat passengers. A second element in the food equation is food service. This is something to which cruise lines have not been as attentive.

With new ships and increasing passenger capacity, the size of waiter stations has increased from a normal maximum of 12 passengers per seating per waiter to as many as 18 or 20. This reduces costs associated with staff but has a potentially negative effect on service quality. Even with these larger waiter stations, cruise lines still must attract large numbers of staff to fill the positions in the dining room. Holland America Line graduates two hundred waiters a year from S. S. Jakarta, its training program for waiters. This barely keeps pace with the demands of new ships coming on stream. Royal Caribbean International estimates that it will need twelve thousand new hotel staff in the year 2000, and each of the five years thereafter, in order to staff their dining rooms and to have enough room stewards. This number is lower than anticipated because the company has succeeded in increasing its staff retention rate from 33% to 50%.[6]

Maintaining standards for food and for food service is obviously a challenge, particularly as the industry grows and the talent becomes more spread out. There is considerable variation among cruise lines in the way that they are meeting this challenge. However all are having difficulty.

Even though some cruise lines project images of having better food and for having better food service than others, the image is often inconsistent with what is actually provided. Even within individual cruise lines, there can be a wide variation in the food and food service on individual ships. A particular executive chef and maitre d' can account for wide differences such that the food on one ship belonging to a cruise line can vary considerably from that on another with the exact same cruise line. Food and service on the same ship can also vary widely depending on the executive chef and the maitre d' on duty during a particular cruise.

## Do You Wish to Eat or Do You Wish to Dine?

As already mentioned, all cruise lines claim to have the best food afloat. The expectations they create are that passengers will be treated to an endless experience of fine dining. Consider the following excerpt from a press release from the Cruise Line International Association (CLIA), a North American-based marketing and training organization representing twenty-five of the leading cruise lines and twenty-one-thousand affiliated travel agencies.

> *Mention a cruise vacation, and the first thing that usually comes to mind is the pleasurable experience of shipboard dining. Vacationers look forward to unlimited opportunities to enjoy the culinary talents of world-class chefs; and, at the end of a cruise, they reminisce about being able to select their heart's desire from menus that never had prices.*

> *According to James G. Godsman, President of Cruise Lines International Association (CLIA), "Dining is one of the most popular features of a cruise vacation. It's usually the first time travelers can venture into new food selections without fearing they have paid a fortune for an appetizer or main course they may not enjoy. On a cruise, diners can select whatever they want on the menu; and sample items they'd never try at home."*

> *Cruise vacationers are always amazed by the variety, abundance and quality of shipboard meals. And, as Godsman points out, part of the fun is the adventure of experimenting with dishes and menus created by some of the world's best culinary talent.*

The image produced from this text is one that leads the reader to believe that the dining experience in store for them on a cruise—any cruise—is going to be the epitome of fine dining. The advertising of individual cruise lines further reinforces this image.

## Like Dining at a Michelin-Starred Restaurant

A number of cruise lines advertise their cuisine as being prepared by world-class chefs who own restaurants that have earned Michelin stars. To the casual reader, one might easily assume that the food being served is the same as that which one would receive in that chef's own establishment. The fact is that these celebrity chefs are generally hired for their name and are used as consultants in menu development, and only in some cases do they visit the galleys on some of the ships. Contrary to popular belief, the food prepared on these ships is not being prepared by the celebrity whose name is attached, and it is never of a quality that would even be allowed out of the kitchen of one of the select restaurants that has achieved recognition from Michelin.

This is not to suggest that the food is not more than adequate. It is simply meant to balance the hype of advertising with the reality of the product. I recall meals on the now-defunct Regency Cruises. For a time, they listed special menu selections under the name of two chefs, prominently identified as former students of Paul Bocuse (owner and chef of a Michelin three-starred restaurant outside of Lyon, France). Amazingly, the recipes used margarine instead of butter. For those who are health conscious, this may be a positive; however, for those who have little regard about cholesterol the taste difference is staggering and anathema to what would be served by Paul Bocuse.

Celebrity Cruises projects an image of having fine food, referring to it as "gourmet Michel Roux cuisine." They suggest in their advertising that their food operation, including menu design and staff training, is overseen by Michel Roux. The Michel Roux associated with Celebrity Cruises operates the Waterside Inn, a Michelin-starred restaurant outside London; his nephew, also named Michel Roux, operates Le Gavroche in London and is often confused with his uncle. As any other passenger, I believed the advertising and expected the food on Celebrity Cruises to be significantly better than the competition. However, I was quickly disappointed. I experienced such things as a smoked salmon omelette in which the smoked salmon had been boiled before ("because that was the recipe") being added to the omelette; lettuce that was often served with rust marks; fruits at buffets whose bruises and discoloration would not have been seen had they been better trimmed; and chicken pieces that still had gristle and cartilage. Any one of these things would have been blasphemy in a restaurant having even one Michelin star. On the cruise they were laughed off as run of the mill and I was criticized for being too finicky. Michel Roux responded to my letter saying he would pass my comments on to Celebrity Cruises.

A different strategy used by some cruise lines, rather than using celebrity chefs as consultants, is to bring guest chefs on board. This is most common on ships in the ultra-luxury category. For example, in 1991, the *Sea Goddesses* hosted *Food and Wine* magazine's choices of America's 10 Best New Chefs on ten separate sailings; in 1993 they offered a series of "Epicurean Sailings" where the galley was staffed by world-renowned chefs. Crystal Cruises, Silversea Cruises, and the old Royal Viking Line have regularly offered cruises based around celebrity chefs. Perhaps the most ambitious effort was a week long Caribbean cruise offered on Norwegian Cruise Line's *S.S. Norway* where thirty-four Michelin-starred chefs were brought aboard to cook.

Silversea Cruises began an association in the late 1990s with Le Cordon Bleu culinary school in Paris, London, and Tokyo. Through this association, Master Chefs from Le Cordon Bleu were regularly brought on Silversea ships for special gastronomic sailings. Under the guidance of master chefs at Le Cordon Bleu, Silversea's then Executive Chef, Bernard Klotz, created a set of original recipes that were featured on menus throughout the year. They appear as "Silversea's Signature Series by Le Cordon Bleu." While passengers benefit from the line's association with the culinary institute, the on board chefs also benefit in that they receive ongoing support and training from the master chefs at Le Cordon Bleu.

Bernard Klotz became Corporate Executive Chef with Radisson Seven Seas Cruises in 1999. This followed Silversea Cruises not renewing its contract with V Ships—a concessionaire contracted to provide its hotel services. Silversea Cruises moved those activities in-house. Several years earlier V Ships had also contracted with Radisson Seven Seas Cruises to provide all hotel and ship services to that cruise line. Presumable, Mr. Klotz's move from one line to the other, facilitated for Radisson Seven Seas' recent association with the Le Cordon Bleu culinary school.

While Radisson Seven Seas Cruises develops its relationship with Le Cordon Bleu, Silversea Cruises has initiated an alliance with the international boutique hotel association, Relais et Chateaux. A cornerstone of the alliance is the culinary program found aboard the ships of Silversea featuring the chefs of Relais & Chateaux—Relais Gourmands. They will join Silversea's chefs to offer entertaining and educational cooking demonstrations, host shopping tours in local markets around the world (where feasible), and create La Collection du Monde, a sampling of specialty dishes to be featured regularly on all Silversea cruises. Additionally, visiting chefs will showcase the favourite dishes from their respective Relais & Chateaux.

## Our Chefs Are Members of the Prestigious Confrérie de la Chaîne des Rôtisseurs

In addition to using the names of celebrity chefs and strategic alliances to raise the image for their food, a proportionately large number of cruise lines have become associated as members of the Chaîne des Rôtisseurs. The Chaîne is an international gastronomic society devoted to promoting fine dining and preserving the camaraderie and pleasures of the table. It has members in more than one hundred countries. In the U.S., there are more than seven thousand members in nearly one hundred and fifty chapters across the country. Currently, ten cruise lines maintain membership: America Hawaii, Crystal, Cunard (and by association, Seabourn Cruise Line), Costa, Holland America, Norwegian, Princess, Radisson Seven Seas, Royal Caribbean, and Silversea.

A definite image is produced by a cruise line's association with the Chaîne des Rôtisseurs, and by its display of the Chaîne's plaque at the entrance of the dining room. Expectations are shaped for a degree of fine food and fine dining. While most passengers are satisfied with the food received, consider the following that have occurred in cruise ship dining rooms donning the plaque of the Chaîne des Rôtisseurs:

Caesar Salad prepared on Holland America Line's *Statendam* using iceberg lettuce rather than romaine;

Spinach Salad served on Holland America's *Rotterdam* with one spinach leaf on top of a bed of iceberg lettuce;

Sorrel Soup made on Norwegian Cruise Line's *Norwegian Crown* with no sorrel;

On most cruise lines, having soup regularly served with it spilled over the sides of the bowl;

Being told by the maitre d' on the *Norwegian Crown* that the rancid cheese in a cannoli was really fresh: "You just don't know the taste of mascarpone cheese." As it turned out, more than a dozen others also complained about the cheese being rancid.

The assistant maitre d' on Norwegian Cruise Line's *Norwegian Sea* assists passengers by removing their lobster tail from the shell. He goes from table to table, passenger to passenger, using the same knife and fork on almost one hundred plates. As he walks from table to table, he waves the silverware around, accidentally rubs it against his and other's clothing, and as he talks to passengers he frequently touches the seat backs with the knife and fork.

Several assistant maitre d's are setting up a champagne waterfall in the atrium of Princess Cruise's *Pacific Princess*. They have finished building the one-story high pyramid and have sprayed the glasses with champagne. As they are placing grapes in the glasses, a passenger comes by and asks to take a picture. One of the assistant maitre d's poses for the picture, placing a grape in his mouth as though it were an apple in the mouth of a pig. The picture is taken, the passenger turns and walks away, the assistant maitre d' takes the grape from his mouth and flicks it into a champagne glass.

Being served, in a special dining room for passengers occupying suites on Holland America Line's *Statendam*, on a table cloth that had crumbs and stains from already being used at two other meals.

Being served by the same waiters as a table of senior officers and VIPs on Radisson Seven Seas Cruises' *Radisson Diamond*. We watched as their mineral water is poured from a bottle wrapped in a white napkin, and our mineral water—the same brand—is poured without that pleasant touch. At the same meal, we watched as the same table of VIPs was served their entree: a whole sea bass weighing approximately four kilograms. The fish was brought out on a tray and carved at their table. A very nice touch, except that we had a fish head (with its open mouth and eyes) staring us in the face (no more than four feet away) from the time the fish was presented until the table finished their entree. We had the unpleasant experience of the extremely fishy smell, and had to watch as the assistant maitre d' cleaned the fish bones in front of our face, at the end pulling the full rib cage into the air from the tail and holding what was left vertically before being removed to the garbage.

On Seabourn Cruise Line's *Seabourn Goddess I*, having a waiter refuse to provide us food service for the remaining seven days of a cruise because we got our own water and wine after asking and waiting fifteen minutes. We were also told-off in a raised voice by the assistant maitre d' as we sat down for lunch one day because we expressed a discontent about the service received from a waiter the previous night.

## A Brief History of La Chaîne des Rôtisseurs

It was in the year 1248, under Saint Louis, King of France, that the Guild of Rôtisseurs was formed. Originally limited to roasters of geese ("Ayeurs"), the Guild expanded in scope and in numbers, and in 1610 it received the present coat of arms by royal warrant. The object of the Guild was to perpetuate the standards of quality befitting the Royal Table. Soon the craft of Rôtisseurs encompassed the preparation of all the various meats and fowls destined for the spit or rack. One of the most prosperous of the Guilds, La Chaîne comprised many members who were attached to the noblest of families of France. The activities of the Guild generally were under royal patronage. This proved less advantageous during the French Revolution, for along with most other Guilds, La Chaîne suffered significant loss of membership and was dissolved in 1789.

Gastronomically speaking, one hundred and sixty uneventful years passed until the revival of La Chaîne in 1950. Following recovery from World War II, three gastronomes and two professionals joined in Paris with a common goal—to restore the pride in culinary excellence which had been lost during a period of wartime shortages. In that year La Confrérie de la Chaîne des Rôtisseurs was officially incorporated, and the seal and coat of arms of the predecessor Guild were restored by an Act of the French Government.

Today La Chaîne des Rôtisseurs is the oldest and largest gastronomic organization in the world. More than ninety thousand persons participate annually in its activities throughout the world with seven thousand members, spread across one hundred and fifty local chapters, in the USA.

Underlying La Chaîne's growth is the organization's sense of purpose. A key criterion that distinguishes La Chaîne from other organizations involved in wine or food is the interrelation between amateur and professional. La Chaîne strives for balanced membership representing professionals involved in food preparation, service in hotels, private clubs and restaurants; wine, food and equipment suppliers and world-renowned lecturers, writers and critics, as well as knowledgeable laymen who, due to their interest in learning and/or well traveled backgrounds, are in a position to enjoy the pleasures engendered by good cuisine, good wine and good company.

Many would say that these are merely anomalies and that they do not reflect the experience of the majority of passengers. This may in fact be true, however they are things that are so incongruous with the image of being associated with the Chaîne des Rôtisseurs, that they stand out like a sore thumb. Sadly, the corporate offices of several cruise lines do not have sufficient concern for these sorts of mundane details. The obvious exception to this disinterest is Holland America Line, which consistently responded with appropriate concern and action.

To be fair, most cruise lines do work hard to provide the best they can, and they solicit passenger feedback in order to inform product improvement. However, there are also some cruise lines that take the tact expressed by the Corporate Executive Chef of one of the largest cruise lines (and a member of the Chaîne des Rôtisseurs) when he said: "I don't listen to passenger comments or feedback. I know best what the food should taste like." Arguably, this is not in the spirit of that line's association with the Chaîne des Rôtisseurs. However, at least he is being honest.

## The Actual Dining Experience

There is no way to summarize the actual dining experience across the industry. There is actually considerable variation depending on the size of the ship and on the particular cruise line. The dining experience on an ultra-luxury cruise line, where meals are generally served at an open seating and where they are assembled-to-order, is qualitatively different than that on a typical cruise line in the mainstream or premium categories. Within this latter group, there are wide variations between cruise lines and even between ships within a particular cruise line. I have had one of the best dining experiences and one of the worst dining experiences on the very same ship, but at times when the kitchen was under the direction of different executive chefs. However there are some common ingredients to dining cruise ship style.

## Time

The time allotted for meals is one element that directly impacts on the nature of dining on a cruise ship. Contrary to most restaurants where one's meal takes whatever time is necessary for its comfortable completion, on a cruise ship meals are made to fit into a definite time frame. On most cruise ships, one's lunch is given an hour. One's dinner meal is given an hour and one-half to an hour and three-quarters. This means that no matter how many courses are ordered, one must be finished within a predefined period of time. There may be a bit more flexibility for those at late seating for dinners, but given clean up schedules this flexibility is generally limited. As well, waiters are accustomed to the majority of passengers who believe that fast service is good service. Thus, the food is served as fast as passengers can consume it.

This limitation on time impacts the way in which a meal is served. In a restaurant, everyone at the table will be served the same course at the same time. All salads are served at the same time, and all entrees will be served at the same time. In dining cruise ship style, because of the pressure on time, only one course is generally served to everyone at a table at the same time: the first course. Industry-wide, it is common for one course to replace the next as each passenger finishes what is on a plate. Not uncommonly, one person at a table can be finishing their soup as another (who finished their soup already) is eating their salad and still another is finishing their appetizer and waiting for their soup. Each person eats in their own rhythm, but there isn't necessarily a table-wide rhythm.

Timing is also affected by the rhythm of the galley. Because modern galleys serve up to 1500 passengers at a time, there is a degree of order in how dishes are picked up. Different stations in the galley serve different courses, and the timing is such that entrees are ready later than first courses. Among waiters, there is competition to get into line in the kitchen. Those in the front of the line can get through faster and are more likely to get food at its prime—fresh and hot.

It is common that waiters will try to minimize the number trips to the galley. They will pick up all the appetizers and soups on one trip, the salads on another, and the entrees in another. These plates are brought from the galley based on the waiter's timing and that of the kitchen. If the passenger isn't ready for that item or course, the plate may sit atop the waiter's station until the passenger is ready, or it may be placed in a food warmer. In either case, the meal being served, because of the time it sits waiting until the passenger is ready, is not the same meal as that which left the kitchen. The food warmer will typically wilt any fresh garnish on the plate; the sitting and cooling off on the top of the waiter's station has its own negative effect. On a recent cruise with Holland America Line's *Statendam*, because it was on the same plate as a ham and cheese sandwich, a tomato-cucumber salad was put in a warmer for twenty minutes. The sandwich was kept warm, but so was the salad. By the time it was served it was limp and unappealing.

With growth of the industry, the level of service has deteriorated and the use of food warmers has by necessity increased. In an article in the summer 1993 issue of *Cruise Industry News Quarterly*, there is discussion of how the cruise product has changed in recent years. The article suggests that: "Food service has been affected by the scaling down of the number of waiters per passenger...The biggest shift is that most waiters serve 18 to 24 passengers per seating while a few years ago there was a maximum of 12 passengers per waiter....While food quality is still high, presentation has become more mass market."[7] Since 1993, both quality and presentation have continued to deteriorate.

## Ambiance

The timing of a meal is one element of ambiance. There are other elements as well. For example, the use of candles and/or the dimming of lights during a meal contribute to the feel of dining. Some cruise lines use candles at all meals, some at only formal evenings, and some at none at all. As well, cruise lines differ on the whether lights are dimmed. Norwegian Cruise Lines typically lowers the lights in the dining room fifteen minutes after dinner begins. In contrast, Holland America Line never changes the fluorescence of dining room lights, always keeping them on "high." It was suggested by a dining room manager on the *Statendam* that there were no dimmer switches installed for lights in the dining room, so the lights could not be dimmed during a meal.

The use of music is another element that can contribute to the ambiance. In the early 1990s, Holland America Line began having a string quartet, the Rosario Strings, play in the dining room at the start of meals. The music continues for the first twenty minutes or so, but then stops after people are seated and well into their meals.

Some cruise lines choose to have no music, while others play recorded music. I often recall cruises on Norwegian Cruise Lines' *Norwegian Crown* where the maitre d' chose to play something akin to Wagner's Greatest Hits played by a John Phillip Sousa marching band. The music was not attuned to fine dining, and it was generally played at an uncomfortable volume. The maitre d' on a different ship with the same cruise line was in the habit of playing peaceful and romantic classical music at a low listening volume. Despite both these maitre d's reflecting the same advertised product, the reality of dining was quite different with one versus the other.

The physical appearance of staff is one more element that may contribute to the ambiance. While most cruise lines draw staff from a variety of national backgrounds and with a range of different coloured skin, some lines are quite sensitive to the image produced by their staff. A number of years ago, one cruise line replaced their staff of Filipino wine stewards with European wine stewards, as I was told "because they believed that the Europeans projected a better image for their wine service." On another cruise line, a dining room busboy told me that he could never be promoted to waiter. The reason was simple: the company for which he worked—a concessionaire—did not put people with skin as dark as his in waiter positions.

Though the staff on any cruise ship is multinational and multiethnic, cruise lines can be quite conscious of the tone they set for dining by the staff they hire. Many lines have a preference for dining room staff from Europe because of their attitude about food and dining. As well, those who receive any training in Europe are generally well schooled in adherence to strict standards. However, there is difficulty in locating adequately trained staff. In an article entitled "The Challenges of Growth", Arne Baekkelund suggests:[8]

*In the years to come, hotel operations will have a harder and harder time finding qualified crew to service all the new vessels.*

*In the past, the industry has recruited from a number of regions: the Caribbean basin, Central Europe and Scandinavia, Korea, Indonesia, the Philippines, Malaysia, and India. Lately, lines have turned their attention to the old Eastern Bloc countries, with varied results. The lack of a mature service culture there has proven an obstacle difficult to overcome, however, several companies have had great success with Turkish crew.*

*It is obvious that the cruise industry must return to Central Europe for management and key positions in the coming years. The industry must also recruit more women, European or otherwise.*

The need to attract crew, and particularly crew that is skilled, is increasingly more of a challenge. It was mentioned above that Royal Caribbean International has to hire twelve thousand new hotel employees in the year 2000, and each year thereafter. Industry-wide, it is estimated that there is a need for one hundred thousand new hotel workers every year. The traditional training ground for these workers, the hotel industry, cannot support this level of growth. Some cruise lines have developed their own training centres for staff; others rely on on-the-job training, often broadening the category of workers who are judged appropriate for different jobs. Ultra-luxury cruise lines, which traditionally have employed European staff in the dining rooms and bars, are increasingly relying on Filipino staff. Unfortunately, many of these staff have been trained by mass market cruise lines, and as a result they do not have the skills or the demeanour to "fit" with the ultra-luxury product.

One factor that plays a major role in staff recruitment and retention is the salaries paid to staff on cruise ships. This is discussed in the chapter on ship society.

## It's The Little Things that Make the Difference

Part of the ambiance of a meal is the little things. This is an area where there have been changes in the industry over the past five or ten years. Glass crystal pitchers, which were common on some lines as recently as five years ago, have been replaced by stainless steel or sterling silver. Steak knives, which were part of the stock of most dining rooms up to the mid-1990s, are rarely being bought for new ships. In addition, cruise lines are not as prone to buying plates with their insignia. Some say that this practice is necessary in that it reduces pilferage—simply, some passengers will take anything that has on it a print of the company's insignia. The removal of insignias also has the side effect of making the kitchen and waiter's jobs easier. While most executive chefs will instruct staff in the design of food placement on a plate—orienting it to the insignia—in actual practice the placement of food in relation to the insignia is often given little attention. Even when the food is oriented to the insignia when it leaves the kitchen, waiters often ignore placing the insignia at the top of the plate as it faces the passenger. This is another area where there is a wide variation from ship to ship, and from one chef to the next. I have had this detail ignored on some ships with Holland America Line, but diligently respected on others. In my experience with Celebrity Cruises, this was a detail that totally escaped their attention.

Another little thing, which to many is something not even worth noting, is the tendency, more often than not, to be served soup on a cruise ship with the soup spilled over the bowl and onto the saucer. While it is obvious that this happens as the plates are brought from the galley, very few waiters take the time to wipe clean the sides of bowls and the rims of plates. This has a large impact on the ambiance of dining, is simple to do, but is often overlooked.

One other little thing is the table setting presented by a cruise line. Some cruise lines set a table "for show" before people are seated, clear the table once orders are taken, and then bring the needed silverware as each course is served. Others are more traditional and have all utensils for the meal at each place at the table. The waiter adds or takes away silverware as needed, but the utensils for each future course are always in place.

The question of which approach is preferred has been the subject of some debate among cruisers. Some say that they prefer to have all of the silverware, cups and saucers, and glasses set on the table as the meal begins because it looks more elegant and is like the days when cruises were a formal affair. Others prefer the more sparse approach, saying that it reduces confusion and that the table looks prettier when you sit down without all the extra silverware.

## Would You Like Some Song and Dance With Your Meal?

Part of the ambiance of dining cruise ship style is the entertainment offered by the dining room waiters and bussing staff. Though it varies from cruise line to cruise line, most cruise lines (except those in the ultra-luxury category) have the service staff in the dining room perform several or more nights during a cruise. There are standard things such as Baked Alaska on parade, where waiters march through the dining room with burning Baked Alaska on plates either on their heads or carried in their hand. There are commonly also nights where waiters sing a song, and where there are other forms of performance. To people who are new to cruising, these performances are an important part of the cruise experience. I recall one passenger who complained because the performances were not as numerous as she had heard they were on other ships of that same cruise line.

As much as new passengers appreciate these performances, they tend to be merely tolerated by most who have been on numerous cruises. To many, the performance detracts from the experience of dining, and the timing of the meal is directly affected because waiters and bus people have to time their work so that they will be free to perform. Meals that may already be rushed are rushed that much more.

## I Know You Are Eating, but Would You Like Your Picture Taken?

Another element in the ambiance of the cruise ship dining room is the photographers. On formal nights on a cruise, photographers go from table to table to take pictures of passengers dressed in their finest. Though viewed by some as an interruption in an otherwise fine dining experience, most passengers have no hesitation to stop in the middle of eating a course, stand up to pose, and have a picture taken.

It is also common to have photographs taken on other nights during a cruise. Sometimes a showgirl will pose at tables with passengers; other times a person dressed up like a pirate will go from passenger to passenger, posing with a plastic sword against the passenger's throat and holding a stuffed parrot. Despite being in the middle of eating, most passengers smile for the picture and then return to their meal.

Norwegian Cruise Lines, at one time, had pictures taken in the dining room by having a person dressed and acting as a "Mexican Bandit"—the Frito Bandito. The photo model would go from passenger to passenger, shouting "ariba-ariba", carry a gun, and of course be characterized as Mexican. The company cut out this particular theme following objections from the Hispanic community about the stereotype being reflected by the practice. However, the majority of passengers found these posed-for pictures as entertaining and desirable as any of the others.

## I'm Your Assistant Maitre d' and It Is My Job to....

One of the personnel in a cruise ship dining room is the assistant maitre d'. Most passengers are not quite sure what exactly is the person's role, but they do become accustomed to a nightly visit. While some assistant maitre d's are innocuous

—seen but not really heard—the majority take as part of their job chatting every day with the passengers at their station. The conversation may revolve around what the passengers did that day or what they are going to do tomorrow. Typical questions include: "Did you go ashore today?", "Did you go on a tour?", and "Did you go shopping?" While these questions lead to discussions with most passengers, they can be the beginning of an awkward couple of minutes for passengers who didn't go ashore, didn't go on a tour, or who are simply not interested in talking about their day with an assistant Maitre d'.

Most assistant maitre d's will initiate and go on with their visiting, regardless of whether people are eating and whether there is an ongoing conversation at the table. It is not uncommon to observe a five to seven minute conversation between passengers and an assistant maitre d' while food sits on the table, with guests being too polite to converse and eat at the same time. The ambiance of the meal is shifted from the food to the conversation with the assistant Maitre d'. And the food gets cold. Dining cruise ship style doesn't require this type of intrusion, at least for those who view it as intrusive. However a passenger being assertive and taking responsibility for the nature of their dining experience is the only way that one can prevent it. Most passengers are too concerned with hurting the staff's feelings and will simply endure the intrusion.

## You Want Some Wine? Let Me Get Our Sommelier... oops, I Mean The Busboy.

There was a time when cruise lines maintained a staff of trained wine stewards (a sommelier) for serving their wine. In modern times, the sommelier has disappeared—Holland America Line gave their last ones up in 1999—and the role has been filled by experienced bar staff (who are promoted to wine steward) or, in the case of Carnival Cruise Line, by the busboy. The result is that passengers no longer benefit from a person knowledgeable about wines and the wine list. In the case of Carnival Cruise Line, wine service is squeezed into the work of someone who already is stretched in what they need to do. In addition, the busboy is likely to have a very limited knowledge of wine and is unlikely to be able to provide effective advice for what to choose. The inconvenience of this set up quickly becomes apparent. On a recent cruise aboard the Carnival Destiny, wine orders were not taken until after bread (and often salads) had been brought from the kitchen. The busboy was rarely free to serve wine before the first course. Thus, a bottle of wine meant for the meal isn't served until the meal is already well under way.

The loss of trained personnel for wine service is consistent with the way that wine lists on cruise ships have changed in the past five or six years. The wine list for most cruise lines lacks information that, to many wine buyers, should be there. Vintages and wine producers (i.e., the chateau or vintner), which were regularly a part of wine lists a decade ago, are now rarely indicated. In addition, because the lists are made up by persons unfamiliar with wine, it is not uncommon to have wine indicated as coming from a different origin than it does (e.g., California rather than Chile), and there are the occasional humorous mistakes. Holland America Line at one point offered, fleet wide for several months, Don Perignon champagne. The correct name is Dom Perignon. This was only one of two dozen mistakes on the list.

Not only have the wine lists been cut back with regard to the information provided, but the selection of wines has also been severely curtailed. Ten years ago, most mainstream and premium cruise lines offered wine lists that included a mix of very fine wines and wines that were produced for mass consumption. Today, most cruise lines offer a small number of inexpensive but palatable wines, a large proportion of mid-priced wines, and very few if any fine wines.

The days of going on a cruise and having a list of bottles, which are indicated as "grand cru classe", are pretty much over. I saw three generations of wine list from Celebrity Cruises; the changes in quality was staggering. Even the ultra-luxury cruise lines have scaled back the wines offered on their wine lists. Undoubtedly, these changes are a reflection of the wines being purchased by today's passengers.

The ultra-luxury cruise lines commonly provide passengers complementary wines with their meals, which may make the wine list less important. This is certainly the case with Radisson Seven Seas Cruises and Silversea Cruises, both of which serve decent, palatable wines as their complementary selections. Oddly, Seabourn Cruise Line (in my experience) serves complementary wines that are poor by comparison. On the same itinerary within several months of time, the best wines served on the *Seabourn Goddess I* were barely as good as the worst wines served on the *Radisson Diamond*. The average wines on Seabourn Cruise Line were palatable, but then there were some that were totally unpalatable. One night the complementary wine was a Rioja that was purchased while in port. One passenger, commenting about the quality, said that the label was familiar—the wine was the same his mother bought in a milk carton and used as a cooking wine when he was a child growing up in Madrid. The wine list provided some alternatives, but not all that were listed were available.

## And Who Are Your Table Mates?

For some on a cruise, those with whom they share their dinner table is more important than either the quantity or the quality of the food. While dining room table assignments may appear seemingly random, there are some common tendencies in the industry.

The most common practice is to honour passenger requests for table size and location depending on the class of cabin one occupies. Passengers paying more for their cabin have their preference filled before those paying less. Cruise lines will also often group passengers from similar classes of cabins at the same tables and in the same area of the dining room. Those in suites will generally be seated with others in suites and those in inside cabins will generally be seated with others in inside cabins or in less expensive outside cabins.

One exception to this tendency is Carnival Cruise Lines. They give preferences in the dining room in the order that reservations are received rather than as a function of the class of cabin. Consequently, a passenger in a penthouse suite who books the cruise two months before the cruise will be lower in priority than a passenger in lesser accommodations who had booked earlier.

Table assignments on most ships are ultimately controlled by the maitre d'. Maitre d's often set up the initial seating chart for the dining room and can generally change this to accommodate individual special requests. Passengers dissatisfied with the dining assignment (either the table or the time) can often secure a change simply by talking with the maitre d'.

Because the maitre d' has access to the list of passengers and their cabin number, s/he can also consciously place particular passengers in certain areas of the dining room. I recall one maitre d' who sat single women booked in higher-priced cabins in an area of the dining room over which he was responsible and where he could regularly converse with these passengers. There was no mistaking his efforts to hustle these single women. Other staff members were quite vocal about the exploits of this particular maitre d'. Whether his is a common practice is open to question.

Aside from table placement, there is the whole issue of with whom one has been seated for the duration of the cruise. There are certainly cases where people at a table are matched quite well and end up having a good experience. In his article, "Fear and Loathing at the Dinner Table: What you eat when you're afloat may not be as important as who you are eating with," John Maxtone-Graham points to four couples who had been thrown together with stunning success. "Embarking as strangers, they became inseparable, for one of the great shipboard truths is that rewarding dining bonding extends throughout the vessel and even beyond. Those four couples re-met on deck, in the casino, around the pool and ashore, their table assignment having served as invaluable cruise catalyst." It is this experience to which many cruisers look forward.

However, there are also less than positive experiences. Consider the following:

> *Eight of us were thrown together, our six dining companions as follows: a young, liberal West Coast couple, new to cruising, and four hard-core reactionary adversaries—an Italian/American husband and wife in their sixties, a crusty Boston Irishman in his nineties and an arch-Republican widow in mourning. Acerbic political wrangling consumed every meal, throughout which my wife, Mary, and I served as uneasy referees. Since the vessel was full, we were glued together for that impossible fortnight. The worst shaped dining room table, incidentally, is a rectangle that seats four per side: General conversation, possible at a round table, is denied. But as our exchanges became increasingly argumentative, that rectangle worked to advantage, separating East from West Berlin.* [9]

One would like to think that this latter experience is uncommon and infrequent. It probably is. However, it helps illustrate that dining cruise ship style is not like going to the neighbourhood restaurant and being served a meal. Those looking for fine dining are undoubtedly going to be disappointed—the product of a galley serving several thousand passengers, no matter how organized and efficient, cannot compete with a restaurant that prepares each meal individually and specifically to order; even the galley on a smaller ultra-luxury ship is unlikely to be able to compete with a fine restaurant on shore. However, those wishing to partake in a pleasant and well-prepared meal, in a pleasant setting which has its own idiosyncratic pace, will likely be pleased with their on board dining experience.

[1] Goetz, Thomas. "When 9,000 Hamburgers Isn't Enough Despite Cruise Ships Efforts to Stress Health, Fitness, Passengers Just Pig Out," Wall Street Journal, December 18, 1998, page W8
[2] Miller, Greg. "Do Smaller Ships Have Better Food?," Cruise Industry News Quarterly, Spring 1998, page 43
[3] Slater, Shirley and Harry Basch. "Stirring Up a New Company for Sea Vacations," Los Angeles Times, August 18, 1991, page L-7
[4] Huie, Nancy. "Service Still Tops for Passengers," Cruise Industry News Quarterly, Summer 1995, page 43
[5] Huie, Nancy. "Cuisine with Broad Appeal," Cruise Industry News Quarterly, Fall 1995, page 89
[6] Niedermaier, Heinz. "The Future of F & B," Cruise Industry News Quarterly, Summer 1999, page 44
[7] Frey-Gaynor, Luisa. "Cruise Experience: As the Market Has Grown, the Product Has Changed. But has It Changed for Better or For Worse," Cruise Industry News Quarterly, Summer 1993, page 60
[8] Baekkelund, Arne. "The Challenges of Growth," Cruise Industry News Quarterly, Summer 1996, page 26
[9] Maxtone-Graham, John. "What You Eat When You're Afloat May Not Be As Important As Who You Are Eating It With," Los Angeles Times, March 28, 1993, page L-9

# 4 Ship Society

The movie *Titanic* turned out to be a major boom to the cruise industry. It is ironic that an earlier version of the movie had been proposed by Alfred Hitchcock in the 1930's, but had never been made, in part a response to lobbying efforts from the cruise ship industry. The industry feared that the movie would cause people to avoid trips aboard ocean-going ships. As it turned out, the version made in 1998, increased interest in cruising and was associated with increased bookings. Of course modern cruising is significantly different than the image presented in the movie. Among the most visible differences is that modern cruise ships (with only a few exceptions) do not have classes of passage. Everyone who books a cabin on a ship has equal access to all facilities and activities offered on board. However, it may be hasty to conclude that there are no class distinctions.

## You Mean There Are Classes on Cruise Ships

Modern cruise ships have a number of ways to distinguish passengers by class, without doing as in past and limiting access to one deck or another. Some distinctions are advertised in order to attract passengers to a higher category cabin. One of the most obvious distinctions is difference in cabin size. For example, a standard inside cabin on Holland America Line's Statendam-class ships measures 182 square feet, a standard outside 197 square feet, a mini-suite with a veranda measures 284 square feet, a suite measures 563 square feet, and a penthouse suite measures 1126 square feet. Of course, the cost for each increase in size has a corresponding increase in price.

Most cruise lines include upgraded amenities with their largest cabins. Increasingly, cruise lines are offering such things as a concierge, butler service, and a private lounge. In addition, they may provide higher quality soaps, shampoos, and other toiletries to those in their better cabins, and these items may be dispensed more liberally. There may also be bathrobes and slippers.

The nature of these amenities varies considerably from one cruise line to another. For example, Carnival Cruise Lines makes few distinctions between those in their penthouse suites and those in other classes of cabins. While suites may be provided bathrobes, they otherwise receive the same toiletries as any other cabin, until mid-2000 simply a bar of soap. In contrast, some others lines provide different quality products in their less expensive cabins than in their most expensive.

There are a number of subtle differences that also reflect a class distinction based on the cabin. The linens used in the upscale accommodations may not be the same as those used in mainstream cabins. The bed sheets may be higher quality and the towels are likely larger and more plush. As well, upscale cabins are likely to be accented with flowers and/or a plant, are likely to be provided with a fruit basket, and may have provided a "welcome aboard" bottle of champagne.

To the majority of passengers, these subtle differences are invisible. However, to those in the upscale accommodation, they serve as a reminder that all passenger accommodations, and perhaps all passengers, are not created equal. Carnival Cruise Lines is again a major exception. On a cruise on the Carnival *Destiny* in October 1999, though booked into the penthouse suite, I went for the entire cruise without a bedspread for the bed. The room steward said that none were available when the bed was converted to king size, even though some cabins with a king size bed were observed with bedspreads. Raising the matter to the hotel manager had no effect.

The nature of amenities provided curiously varies between ships within the same cruise line. For example, on a cruise aboard Norwegian Cruise Lines' *Windward* (now the *Norwegian Wind*) the robes provided to suites were removed the last day, so the one night that a robe would be most useful—the night that one packs all their clothes and leaves their luggage in the hall for pickup—one is not available. The official explanation provided was that the robes needed to be cleaned so they would be ready for passengers embarking the next day. The unofficial explanation was that the company wanted to prevent the robes from being stolen. However, on a cruise one week earlier, but in a different cabin, the robes were not removed the last night. It appears that standards of quality are left to the discretion of the room steward(ess); they are not maintained ship-wide by the ship's management, or company-wide by the cruise line.

I have also observed differences with Holland America Line. Their suites include a list of amenities provided to guests. On the *Maasdam*, complementary boutonnieres and corsages were on the list, but not provided. On the *Statendam*, the complimentary fruit basket, which is on the list and is advertised as an amenity, disappeared on day six of a sixteen-day cruise. The explanation given was that we hadn't eaten any of the fruit, so why leave it there. The flower arrangement, another amenity, also disappeared before the end of the cruise. While companies work to make their top end accommodations more attractive with selected amenities, they undermine their own goal by not fulfilling the expectations that they create.

# Are Amenities the Only Way That Class Distinctions Are Made?

Another way that cruise lines create and reinforce class distinctions on their ships is through special treatment. Ships with alternative dining rooms often give priority for reservations to passengers in suites and in other high-end cabins. As well, seating in the main dining rooms, whether it be by time and/or by table size, is often assigned with priority based on cabin category. Not only are preferences for seating time and table size given first to those in the most expensive cabins, but also those seated at a table are often drawn from similar classes of cabins. Rarely will passengers in a suite be seated with passengers occupying standard cabins. Simply, the class of cabin one occupies defines with whom they share their table.

One notable exception is Carnival Cruise Lines, which assigns dining room preferences in the order that reservations are made for the cruise and without regard for cabin category. Consequently, a last minute booking in even the highest category cabin is given the lowest priority for honouring stated preferences.

One's cabin can also influence who is assigned as one's waiter. Waiters with the highest passenger ratings tend to be assigned to tables with passengers occupying the most expensive cabins; those with the lowest ratings are assigned to tables with passengers from inside or standard cabins.

The cabin occupied is only one way that special amenities may be presented. Most ships maintain a VIP list, which often overlaps the list of passengers in top-end accommodations, but also includes others. A frequent passenger with the cruise line, a passenger who appropriately complained about a previous bad experience, and/or a high volume travel agent are each likely to be on the VIP list. It is from this list that people may be selected for the captain's table at dinner. It is also a list that is the basis for private cocktail parties, including private receptions with the captain and senior officers, hors d'oeuvres and drinks in the captains cabin, or a cocktail party for VIPs. Like the special amenities in cabins, many of these events go on without awareness from most passengers. However, to those invited, there is a sense of being special and different from others on board the ship.

An invitation to the captain's table is the most visible way that distinctions are drawn. Though there is no consistent formula for how passengers are chosen, it is common that a large proportion of invitations be given to travel agents and to people on board who are engaged in business arrangements with the cruise line: an inspector from the company's insurance carrier, a corporate executive negotiating the placement of ATM's on the cruise line's ships, an executive of a major supplier to the cruise line. Others may be chosen because of their cabin, their history of cruising with the line, or as in my case being recognized by the captain from a previous cruise, suffering an injury from a piece of broken dinner plate in my dessert, or simply because the maitre d' perceived us as a happy couple.

Regardless of how one gets to the captain's table, it is always an entertaining experience, though two experiences are never the same. Some notable memories include a woman who complained quite loudly that she wasn't seated next to the captain—she had always previously been seated at his side and was insulted that she had been displaced by someone else; a woman who tried to order a bottle of Chateau Y'Quem (a dessert wine that is normally priced at $400 per bottle) with her meal; political face-offs between passengers on opposite poles of the political spectrum; a hotel manager offering during the meal to show my wife, a physician, the scar from his appendectomy; a passenger asking my wife during the meal for advice on how to treat her hemorroids; and, the consistently asked questions of the captain that include such things as how fast the ship travels, how much fuel the ship consumes, and what is it like being the Captain.

The fact that there are these class distinctions does not detract from the experience of passengers not included. However, they do contribute to the positive experience of those included, and they serve to build loyalty to the cruise line. And if something goes wrong on a cruise, the passenger in upscale accommodations is more likely to have the problem addressed and corrected than the passenger in a standard cabin.


## A Dollar an Hour and Free Room and Board

While people go on a cruise to indulge in the luxury and glamour associated with cruising, most are unaware that those responsible for providing many of the elements that constitute the cruise experience are earning wages that are a small fraction of the U.S. minimum wage; less than one-quarter than received by the person flipping hamburgers at the neighbourhood McDonald's. Typical incomes of those working on cruise ships include:

> *A busboy on Celebrity Cruises who works sixteen to eighteen hours a day who earns a guaranteed wage of $50 a month (less than 10 cents an hour). If he receives the recommended amount in tips, he can earn an additional $1000 a month..*

> *A cleaner who spends eight to ten hours a day buffing brass is paid $81 a week, which works out to roughly $1.55 an hour.*

> *A janitor who has worked on Carnival Cruise Lines for five years, who works seventy hours per week and who receives a monthly salary of $372—less than $1.25 an hour;*

*A deck steward on Carnival Cruise Lines who earns $240 per month salary and an additional $400 in tips as a bellman on embarkation/debarkation days;*

*A waiter on Celebrity Cruises who earns a monthly salary of $50 and pays the company $7 a week for breakage (whether or not he breaks anything). If he receives the recommended tips, he can earn an additional $2000 - $3000 per month.*

*A cabin steward who earns $50 a month plus tips, which can amount to an additional $1500 - $2500 per month, depending on the number of cabins s/he is responsible for cleaning;*

*A head bartender on Carnival Cruise Lines, who started as a busboy thirteen years earlier earns $30,000 a year, primarily from tips.*

There are of course some variations. Cruise lines that do not allow tipping, or which discourage tipping, pay employees in service roles better wages. Holland America Line which has a policy of "tipping not required," reportedly, pays its waiters and room stewards $300 a month. While this is as much as six times more than similar workers receive on cruise lines that openly suggest tipping, most workers with Holland America Line will earn less after tips. A room steward once told me he earned half as much as his brother, after tips. His brother had the same job with a mass market cruise line on which tips were expected. His brother earned less in salary, but received much more in tips. When I asked why he didn't go to the other cruise line, the steward responded that he had much better living and work conditions with Holland America Line than did his brother.

Salaries among those who have no opportunities for tips are higher, though still relatively low by U.S. standards. Some examples, for seventy hour workweeks, include:

*A pantryman trainee receives $258 a month;*

*A galley utility worker receives $415 a month;*

*A pot washer receives $452 a month;*

*A cook receives $900 a month;*

*A deck hand receives $700 a month;*

*An engine room worker receives $700 a month.*

As can be seen, there are some variations in income based on role. Like workers who do not receive tips, the incomes of officers and of the cruise staff and entertainers are based on a different scale. However, most are paid wages that are lower than would be provided on land. A youth director on Premier Cruises, for example, received $1285 per month, plus tips and commissions.

There are also obvious differences by class of ship. Ultra-luxury cruise line such as Radisson Seven Seas Cruises, Seabourn Cruise Line, and Silversea Cruises pay their waiters and room stewards quite well. Waitresses working for Radisson Seven Seas Cruises, in 2000, earned $2000 a month. Waiters on Seabourn Cruise line report that they earn $3000 a month. Thus, waiters on these ships make as much as the mass market lines, and they don't have to vie for tips.

Generally speaking, it is difficult to get reliable figures for worker salaries for most onboard jobs. As stated by Carnival's spokesman: "We do not disclose employee compensation." Even if they did, these figures would not include bonuses provided to department heads for remaining under budget, nor would they include costs often required of room stewards, waiters, and busboys which are part of an on board mafia. These costs are discussed later.

## But...Isn't There a Minimum Wage?

An obvious question is, "how these companies are able to pay wages that are not at least minimum wage." The answer is simple. Those few companies (which together account for 1 or 2% of the cruise industry) that are registered as U.S.-flagged, must pay U.S. minimum wage; all the others operate free from U.S. labour law and U.S. labour policies. Thus, all workers on American Hawaii Cruises and Clipper Cruise Line's U.S. registered ships will earn at least the U.S. minimum wage.

In stark contrast, workers on foreign flag vessels can be paid whatever the employer feels is right. Workers may even have to accept arbitrary cuts in pay in order to keep their jobs. If they were to complain, they would undoubtedly be fired and returned home at their own expense. In the view of Paul Chapman, a Baptist minister who founded the Centre for Seafarer's Rights in New York in 1981, the typical cruise ship is a sweatshop at sea. "A ship owner can go any place in the world, pick up anybody he wants, on almost any terms. If the owner wants to maximize profit at the expense of people, it's a piece of cake."[1]

The requirement to pay minimum wage was extended to ships registered in the United States in 1961. However, Congress left intact the exemption for foreign ships. This exemption was further defined in a 1963 Supreme Court decision that held that U.S. labour laws, including the right to organize, do not apply to foreign vessels engaged in American commerce, even if the owners of these ships are from the United States. It is in this context that the modern cruise ship industry developed and took hold.

There have been some efforts by the United States Congress to extend the protection of U.S. labour law to the cruise industry, but they have been unsuccessful. The most concerted effort was made over a four-year period by William Clay, who at the time was Chairman of the House Labour-Management Subcommittee of the Education and Labour Committee of the House of Representatives. In 1989, Clay introduced legislation that would extend the National Labour Relations Act (NLRA) and the Fair Labour Standards Act (FLSA) to vessels that are "...regularly engaged in American commerce and not owned, controlled and crewed primarily by citizens of another country. The seamen employed on such vessels will then have the right to exercise the collective bargaining rights guaranteed by the NLRA and will be protected by the labour standards [including payment of minimum wage] established by the FLSA". [2]

At hearings in October 1989, the Committee was told of exploitation of sailors, who had no redress for grievances about their working conditions. Reverend James Lingren, the Director of the New England Seaman's Mission, specifically described conditions in the cruise ship industry:

> *We have discovered that on several of the largest cruise ship lines calling in U.S. ports a typical seafarer works one hundred hours each week with no days off during his one year of employment. Many of them work without benefit of anything resembling a true contract of employment. They often earn less than 75 cents an hour.*

------------

> *I personally saw the contract of...[a] seafarer who signed for $192 a month to work for seven days a week for one year. He was to be paid overtime for any hours over eight hours a day, and while he was required to work twelve hours a day, the company refused to pay the overtime. This meant he was effectively making 53 cents an hour. When he complained he was relieved of his duties and sent home.* [3]

The subcommittee approved the bill in the summer of 1990, though it never made it any further. It was reintroduced in the next Congress, on February 27, 1991. Congressman Clay introduced the legislation in the House of Representatives. At the time, he stated:

> *House education and labour subcommittees have heard testimony of [seafarers] being required to work eighteen to twenty hours a day for less than $1 an hour; of living conditions so unsanitary as to threaten life; of sailors being forced to provide kickbacks to labour contractors; [and] of sailors being abandoned in foreign ports and blackmailed from the industry for seeking to improve intolerable and inhuman conditions.*
>
> *Clearly this nation not only has the right but the moral duty to ensure that where such workers are engaged primarily in the commerce of the US such vestiges of 19th century servitude are eradicaed.[4]*

Claiborne Pell of Rhode Island introduced a similar version of the bill in the Senate. Though the Labour Standards Subcommittee of the Education and Labour Subcommittee held hearings in the House of Representatives, the act never went beyond the Committee's consideration. It lacked support from the Bush Administration and was actively opposed by the cruise industry.

Representative Clay again introduced legislation in the next Congress. On March 30, 1993, he introduced H.R. 1517. The hearings yielded no new information. However, for the first time the cruise industry, through its main lobbyist, the International Council of Cruise Lines (ICCL), threatened that if the House of Representatives passed the legislation, the cruise industry would be forced to relocate to non-U.S. ports. In his testimony before the Subcommittee on Labour Standards on May 13, 1993, the President of the ICCL, John Estes, stated:

> *Some have told you that we will not relocate. I am here to tell you that this industry will relocate if the bill is passed. It won't happen all at once, but it will happen.*

He pointed out the ease with which cruise ships can be moved from one homeport to another and that:

> *...in order to keep international costs competitive we do in fact on occasion move from country to country. International shipping will always seek a hospitable economic and political climate from which to operate.It would be an unfortunate failure of United States policy not to recognize that homeports are unimportant to passengers.*

Mr. Estes also pointed out the economic value of the cruise industry to the U.S. economy. In 1992, member lines accounted for 450,166 jobs, more than $14.5 billion was paid in wages to U.S. employees, and the industry generated $6.3 billion in federal, state, and local taxes.

The legislation made its way to the floor of the House of Representatives, but again failed to be heard. While some attribute the industry's threat as a factor in it becoming stalled, others suggest that its demise was a result of the measure's lack of sponsorship in the United States Senate—Senator Pell had not reintroduced his bill—and that the Clinton Administration had not extended its support for the legislation. In either case, the matter has remained relatively dormant since 1993. By keeping employee incomes low, cruise lines have been able to keep prices stable and at the same time increase their profits.

## What Difference Does it Make?

Some may question what difference it makes that workers are paid what they are. There are two sides to the issue. Those who argue that wages should be raised, base their position on humanitarian principles and on a basic belief that cruise lines based in the United States and selling to United States consumers should be bound to the laws of the United States. The issue, however, is not that straightforward. As will be discussed in chapter seven, most cruise lines operate under flags of convenience which allow them to not only be free of U.S. labour laws, but also free of U.S. taxes and other regulations designed to protect the health and welfare of the consumers they serve.

Those who are not concerned about wages argue that those working on a cruise ship know what they are getting into. Regardless, they are earning more on the cruise ship than they could or would in their home country. It is quite true that many workers on cruise ships earn incomes that are relatively high when compared to what they would earn at home. As pointed out in the *Wall Street Journal* in 1997, the average per-capita income in the Philippines is less than $1000 a year; an elementary school teacher in Romania earns just $70 a month. While the workers on a cruise ship may be paid poorly by U.S. standards, they are paid quite well by the standards they have when coming to the cruise ship. As overheard from many passengers, "if they don't like the wages, then they should go home from where they came."

As for the argument that employees know what they are getting into, it is questionable whether most workers fully appreciate the nature of their jobs or the expectations had for their work. Few workers expected to be working seven days a week, twelve to eighteen hours per day, for as much as a year at a time. Most also are led to expect that they will be paid overtime, and that their wages are guaranteed not to change.

There was a time when Panamanian law required ships registered in Panama to guarantee workers one day off per week. Interestingly, a number of years ago

Carnival Corporation was able to secure a change in Panama's laws (many of Carnival Cruise Lines ships are registered in Panama so are governed by Panamanian laws). The change left whether a day off would be given to the discretion of the employer. The six day work week on cruise ships is clearly a thing of the past.

In addition to surprises about the nature of the work, most workers are surprised by the very basic nature of their living conditions—on older ships sharing accommodations with as many as six to a room—and find inadequate the food they are served. Fresh fruits and vegetables are rarely available to them, and the food they are served may not correspond to their traditional diet. A European room stewardess on the Radisson *Diamond* confessed that for the five months she had been on the ship, she had eaten mainly pasta. The foods available in the crew mess catered to the taste of the Filipino crew. As she stated, "Most of the time, I'm not even sure what it is that is being served. Other times, I know it is fish, but not prepared in a way that I could eat it." A room steward with Royal Caribbean Cruise Lines also complained that he had no access to fresh fruit. He happily, but discretely, accepted fruit from a fruit basket that had been delivered to our cabin.

There is clearly a wide gap between worker expectations and the reality of work on a cruise ship. No doubt, this gap is a major factor in the fact that the average length of employment for a cruise line worker is just 5.8 months.[5]

## It Costs How Much to Secure a Job on a Cruise Ship?

The worker's income level is further clouded by the fact that most workers in third world countries must pay a fee to the recruiting agency through which they secure a contract, and almost all workers must pay for their travel to and from the ship. Paul Chapman, in his study of international seamen, provides some insight into the role of the recruiting agent:

> ...in many cases, seafarers view their recruiting agent, not the captain or the ship owner, as their employer. The agent becomes the seafarer's patron, someone to whom they remain loyal despite abuses. The others in authority are strangers; seafarers often do not know the ship owner, and the officers who give day-to-day orders are often from another country and speak another language. It is the agent with whom the seafarers negotiate the terms of their contract, in whose office employment agreements are signed, and the person who forwards allotment payments to their families. [6]

Using an agent increases the cost to secure employment on a cruise ship. For example, one newly hired cruise ship employee:

> *...had to pay a Croatian cruise ship agent $600 to confirm his hiring. Carnival then temporarily paid the $1400 for his ticket to the U.S. Suddenly in debt, Mr. Lukanov became, effectively, an indentured cruise line employee, obligated to work for months to pay off his loan.*[7]

Another employee, a cook on Carnival Cruise Line's Paradise:

> *...gave a Bombay agency $2000, which included airfare. That sum, much of which he borrowed from relatives, is almost a third of the $7000 he will make during his current ten month contract. The man, who supports five people including his wife and four-year-old son, has not received a promotion in five years.*[8]

Though it is technically not allowed that manning agents collect these fees—they are paid directly by the cruise line—these scenarios are common. Under such conditions, it is not surprising that a number of cases can be identified where an employee who was being fired has committed suicide rather than face the embarrassment of returning home and having to deal with the enormous debt accrued in order to acquire their job.

To avoid these types of occurrence (and as a basic management strategy), cruise lines generally do not notify staff that they are going to lose their job until the ship is safely in the port where the worker will be dismissed. I recall a food and beverage manager, after his first week on a ship, who told me he was firing thirty-two staff. As we were entering port, he said that he was up all night completing the travel arrangements to get these workers home. He now had to complete the second half of the job: let the workers know that they were fired and were heading home that afternoon.

There were explanations given for this strategy. First, a disgruntled employee can cause considerable unrest and difficulty if they know they have been fired and have nothing to lose. A manager does not want someone like this serving food in the dining room, or having responsibility for the cleanliness of a passenger's cabin.

The other reason given is to prevent people from harming themselves. For example, a twenty-eight-year old Turkish woman, learning that she was going to be fired, jumped overboard from Holland America Line's *Westerdam* as it was approaching Vancouver harbour in August 1998. It is hard to know how common suicides are among ship's crew because they are not regularly reported in the mass media. However, it is this type of occurrence that reinforces the practice of waiting until the last minute to notify an employee of their dismissal.

## It Doesn't Affect Me?

In one way or another, most cruise passengers can rationalize the wages being paid and dismiss the issue as not being of their concern. However, one by-product of the employment practices of cruise lines is that many workers suffer from fatigue. They work many hours, and are often unable to have sufficient uninterrupted periods of rest. Most workers, when asked how they will spend an upcoming two-month vacation from work will respond that the first month off they will sleep; the second month off they will begin to dread their return to the ship.

The effects of fatigue may be subtle as regards food service and cleaning of cabins. However, fatigue is not a problem unique to these workers. A study done by the International Transport Worker's Federation presents some insights that are cause for concern.

The study, entitled "Seafarer Fatigue: Wake Up to the Dangers", was based on a survey of two thousand five hundred seafarers representing sixty nationalities and sixty three flags of registration. Some of the most startling findings include:

*One-third of respondents reported daily working hours of twelve hours or more (5% reported working fifteen hours or more);*

*Two-thirds reported that their weekly hours of work averaged more than sixty hours (25% reported working more than eighty hours);*

*The longest hours being worked were by watch keepers and those in the highest ranks. The following are the proportion for each rank who report working more than eighty hours a week: 42% of masters, 44% of first officers, 26% of chief engineers, 17% of second engineers, 29% of deck ratings, 11% of engine room ratings, 13% of stewards.*

*36% of seafarers reported that they were unable to regularly obtain ten hours of rest in a twenty-four hour period. Half of these (or, 18% of the population) indicated they were unable to obtain six hours of uninterrupted rest. Broken down by rank, 50% of masters, 43% of first officers, and 42% of deck ratings indicate that they are unable to obtain six hours of uninterrupted rest.*

*17% of watch officers are on duty for twelve hours or more at a time.*

The study includes reports from respondents of two cases of watch keeping officers dozing off while in control of fast ferries; and, of a grounding that occurred after the deck officers had been working an average of sixteen hours a day, with no opportunity for sleep longer than three hours. One respondent, a first officer on a cruise ship, reported that on his previous ship he had worked twelve-to fifteen-hour days, never had six hours continuous sleep, and had worked eighty-seven hours a week for three months straight. He indicated that he regularly made errors in passage planning and execution, and that he did not dare sit down when he was on watch. Though many question how it was possible that the *Norwegian Dream* collided with a cargo ship in the early morning hours of August 24, 1999, with clear skies and with calm seas, these stories of fatigue suggest one possible factor.

Some will say that the hours of work and resulting fatigue are simply the nature of the job. However, others will argue that these types of statistics support the need for greater regulation of the work and the work environment on cruise ships. In either case, it is these people, fatigue and all, on which passengers must depend in an emergency situation. A tired waiter or deck hand may not raise much concern, but concerns may increase when this same person has a role of responsibility during a call for abandoning ship or if a fire breaks out. This will be discussed further in chapter five when we discuss safety at sea.

## Social Stratification

It comes as no surprise that there is a clear line of authority on cruise ships. The officers oversee the work of supervisors, who in turn oversee the work of those in front line positions. However, status among those working on a cruise ship is only partially based on one's place in the organizational hierarchy. There are a number of factors.

The income one earns is one source of status. Contrary to most work settings, those in mid level and supervisory positions do not necessarily earn more than those below them. I know of several cases where a headwaiter or assistant maitre d' have returned to working as a waiter because he could earn considerably more. In this case, the relative social status of the role (as a supervisor) is opposite that of what each earns.

The department within which one works, and one's role in that department also affects relative status. Those working at a purser's desk, though they may earn less than a waiter, have generally higher status. The status resides in the role they play in relation to passengers, but also is related to the degree of freedom of movement in moving through passenger areas of the ship. Workers who are behind the scenes are not allowed into passenger areas, and there are clear rules that prohibit interacting with passengers. Waiters and busboys are allowed interaction with passengers, but within certain parameters; they are prohibited from using passenger areas. Those who work at the pursers desk also interact within certain parameters, however they usually have more freedom regarding presence in public areas on the ship. The cruise staff is not only encouraged to interact with passengers, but also to be present in public areas and settings. In effect, the person's role, which is often associated with freedom of activity, contributes to status.

Race and ethnicity also define status on a cruise ship. A bellman on a Carnival Cruise Lines ship says:

> "We are black. Sometimes there is some kind of discrimination onboard." For example, he claims some light-skinned security guards act like prison wardens. "As soon as we put on reggae music [in the crew bar], the guards come and turn it off," he says. "They come and treat us like we're in jail or something. We're not making any trouble." Guards also hassle him when he is off-duty and passing through the hotel portion of the ship. "If I stand too long in the public area, the security guard comes along and asks, 'What you doin'?' A lot of bullshit goin' on," he concludes. "You have some crew members who don't like black people. You expect it from the passengers, but not from the crew."[9]

Similarly, on some cruise lines, skin colour is a factor in opportunities for advancement and in the job roles that are available. In one case, a cruise line disallowed "dark-skinned" people from positions as waiters; in another, a cruise line replaced their Filipino wine stewards with workers of European descent.

## Racial and Ethnic Tensions

As in any community with racial and ethnic diversity, there are tensions between different groups. There are occasionally fights between workers and there is the occasional stabbing. Likely the most extreme occurrence was a riot in the spring of 1994, when a crew galley ran out of rice. The cook was killed, and six others also died in the riot. This level of tension is uncommon. However, tensions between individuals and/or groups are not uncommon.

Several years ago, an executive chef on Norwegian Cruise Line's *S.S. Norway* was setting up a midnight Chocoholic buffet when a Filipino safety officer walked by, jabbed him in the ribs, and stated several ethnic slurs. This pattern was not new; the chef had endured it for weeks. On this occasion, however, he had had enough. He walked into the galley, returned with a fire extinguisher, and emptied the contents on the safety officer. The chef was fired from his job. The safety officer was reprimanded.

While ethnic and racial diversity may be a source of tension on cruise ships, it is also an effective means for undermining collective action by crew. It is uncommon for people with such diverse backgrounds to cooperatively join forces on an issue. When they do, the common practice of cruise lines is to simply send the workers home. For example, in 1981, two hundred and forty Central American workers went on strike aboard a Carnival Cruise Lines ship in Miami to protest the firings of two co-workers. The company ended the strike by calling the U.S. Immigration and Naturalization Service and the strikers were declared illegal immigrants, bussed to the airport and flown home, unemployed. Similarly, in January, 1986, Norwegian Cruise lines solved a sudden labour dispute aboard the *S.S. Norway* by loading fifty-five South Korean, Jamaican, and Haitian room stewards on buses at the Port of Miami and sending most of them back to their home countries. As stated by more than one source, "on cruise ships, supervisors often tell seafarers who complain, 'If you don't like it here, you can go home.' Since the seafarer has already paid for the return trip, the threat is real and the seafarers know it will be carried out at their expense."[10]

Between the mediating effects of diversity, and the threat that one will lose their job if they complain, there is a clear structure of social control on cruise ships. Staff know to do their jobs and not to complain. A worker with Carnival Cruise Line recently had his pay reduced, after five years, by $80. He was clearly upset, and was not sure what prompted the reduction, but he feared his supervisors would brand him a troublemaker if he complained. He'd rather endure the reduction in pay than to lose his job.

Subtle forms of control are also exercised in other ways. Holland America Line prides itself on its Indonesian staff and crew, who primarily serve as room stewards and dining room waiters. On a cruise aboard the *Veendam*, I asked a busboy handing out trays at the Lido what it was like working with a surveillance camera on him—there is a camera in the ceiling, like those in casinos, that monitors activity in the Lido. His response was simple: "The Dutchman is always watching." What became clear from the way that it was said is that the traditional colonial relationship between the Dutch and Indonesians was being replicated on these ships. The Indonesian staff were naturally reverent and deferential to the Dutch bosses, not just as their employer but also as the colonial power under which they grew up.

## Tensions Between Seamen and Hotel Staff

Another source of tension among staff on cruise ships is between those who are seamen, such as officers and crew, and the cruise staff and hotel staff. This tension became apparent in a conversation I had with a senior officer on a ship. He cautioned that if there were an emergency where a call was made to abandon ship, to find an officer and stick with him. He went on to distinguish between those staff trained to be at sea and to deal with emergencies at sea—officers and crew—versus staff that worked on the ship but who were not devoted to a life at sea. He suggested that many of the hotel staff would save their lives before helping passengers. This same view was subsequently expressed by senior officers on several other ships.

This tension was clearly illustrated one day when I was on the bridge of a ship and the fire alarm went off. Crew were dispatched to investigate and reported back within a minute or so that a dining room waiter was found in the sauna smoking a cigarette near the smoke detector. The officer on watch commented that this was a common problem with hotel staff: "They just don't appreciate issues of safety at sea."

Whether the perception of these officers is accurate is a question that I am unable to answer. Relevant here is that the perception exists and that it colours the way that some officers deal with staff.

## Gay and Lesbian Workers and Passengers

Considerable attention has been given the past several years to gay and lesbian passengers on cruise ships and whether they are welcome in certain ports. Several ships were refused government permission to stop in the Cayman Islands in 1998 because a group of gay passengers were aboard. In contrast to the Cayman Islands, where the government appeared to adopt an official anti-gay policy, private citizens protested the arrival of gays arriving on several ships in Bermuda and the Bahamas.

Hostility toward gays and lesbians is not limited to Caribbean ports. In 1992, a Greek Island cruise on the *Stella Oceanis*, chartered by the Oakland-based Olivia Company, was given a less-than-enthusiastic welcome when they landed on the island of Lesbos. One of the shore excursions took passengers to Skala Eressos, the legendary home of Sappho, the ancient Greek poet, professor, and political agitator:

> *One restaurant refused to serve* Stella Oceanis *passengers. The mayor, who was supposed to officially welcome us to Skala Eressos, "got sick" and sent a representative instead.* [11]

In the end, the group found that the majority of people were enthusiastic about their visit, but that there was a strong minority that didn't want them to be there.

The experience of a group of gay men visiting Kusadasi, Turkey in September 2000 was even more hostile. The cruise, organized by Los Angeles-based Atlantic Events chartered Royal Olympic Cruise Line's *Olympic Voyager* for what was billed as the largest gay cruise ever to visit Turkey. It carried 833 passengers on a seven day cruise with stops in Egypt, Israel, Turkey, and Greece:

> *On September 6, the* Olympic Voyager *docked in Kusadasi. Some of the men boarded buses for the tour of Ephesus. Police apparently realized that the tourists were gay, stopped at least two buses from leaving Kusadasi and chased after others. At least one bus was turned back at Selcuk, a town just outside Ephesus. More buses were sent back from the ruins themselves. Another group of men were ordered back to the boat from a shopping bazaar in the town of Kusadasi. According to at least one report, some men were explicitly told by police that they could not leave the ship because they were gay.[12]*

Because many of the passengers were Americans, the U.S. Government protested to the Government of Turkey, but the damage had already been done.

This sort of hostility toward gays and lesbians is not limited to ports. Many gays and lesbians remain "in the closet" when on a cruise to avoid uncomfortable situations. Officers, crew, staff, and other passengers are all potential sources for attack or sanction.

At the same time, there is a significant proportion of staff on cruise ships that are gay or lesbian. A hotel manager once told me that his career choice was related to his sexual preference. If he is at sea eight months of the year, then it is easy to explain to family why he isn't married and raising a family. He is not alone in this view.

There are several times that I have seen gay and lesbian officers and staff "come out of the closet," usually when there is a large number of gay and lesbian passengers. On one cruise I recall seeing notices in the daily program of meetings of Friends of Dorothy (similar to Friends of Bill W for alcoholics), which was a discrete way to bring gays and lesbians together. It is in these settings—a cocktail party or private reception—that officers and senior staff are most likely to let their sexual preference be known. But they remain quite discrete. They have concern about their employer finding out, and also about passenger reactions.

## The Nature of the Work

As already discussed, most workers on cruise ships work long hours. Most managers work four months and then have two months off. Those working in front line and behind-the-scenes positions work contracts ranging in length from six months to twelve. I met a Filipino deck boy on Holland America Line who said he had a contract for fourteen months. For many of us, it is difficult to imagine having a job that requires twelve or more hours a day, every day, and which provides no days off for a year or more.

The human side of this reality is visible in conversations with staff. A father working as a waiter who wasn't home for the birth of any of his four children, and who won't see his youngest son until he is nine months old. A young mother working at the pursers desk, to support her one-year old daughter who she left in her mother's care. She left her daughter when she was nine month's old, missed her first birthday, and will see her again when she is almost two year's old. The work is difficult enough, but the job is made that much more difficult by the separation from family. True, the income earned provides considerable status at home, but the emotional and personal costs are high.

Cruise ships as a workplace are unique in many ways. Workers do not leave their place of work and go home at the end of the day. They have little choice than to share their personal space, and to socialize with others who are part of the workplace. Intimate personal relationships among workers are common. As well, social status from work roles and work relationships carry over into recreational and informal relationships. Simply, the worker is rarely if ever free from "work," even when not on duty. Working on a cruise ship is described by former Carnival Cruise Lines Chef Luis Rodriguez as "...like jail, with a few more accommodations. You don't see your family. You don't see land most of the time." [13]

## The Passenger as an Intruder

As a passenger on a cruise ship, we are coming into an existing community formed by officers, staff, and crew. On most cruise ships this isn't even an issue. However, the situation is a bit different on small ships, particularly those in the ultra-luxury category where the ratio of passengers to crew is almost one to one. In these settings, the staff has a strong social system in place into which passengers come. The result is that the passenger is often viewed as an intruder into their community.

For most passengers this wouldn't be noticed or relevant. However, for the passenger who complains about serious lapses in service, or who speaks up when there is a problem, the feeling of being an intruder is created and reinforced. Going on a small ship is akin to visiting someone's home. It is impolite not to be appreciative of everything provided, it is crass to complain, and one is sanctioned if they do either. This is possible because of the small number of staff. There is less than fifteen bar/dining room staff on the *Seabourn Goddess I* and *II*; approximately twice that number on Seabourn's other small ships. The result is that staff members know one another and they support one another. Also, because they have to live with one another, they band together when there is a passenger who causes trouble for any one of them.

As one who has expressed concerns, I know first hand the risk one takes. On the *Radisson Diamond*, bar staff banded together and provided reduced service because one of their group got in trouble for his aggressive and inappropriate behaviour toward the passenger. On the *Seabourn Goddess I*, passengers were verbally assaulted and received a late-night telephone call that threatened their personal safety after they expressed dissatisfaction to the Maitre d' with dining room service provided by certain dining room staff. These cases are discussed in some detail later in the chapter.

## The Art of Working for Tips

A major feature of working in the hotel department (as a waiter, busboy or room steward) on a cruise ship is that one's income depends largely on generating tips. There is a certain attitude that must be maintained in order to generate a substantial income. At one and the same time, they need to assume a role of a humble servant, yet also be comfortable talking about their home and their family. The latter can be particularly stressful given the fact that workers commonly miss their family and loved ones and talking about them, particularly if it will be as much as eight or nine months or more until they see them again, can be very difficult. Add to this that there are as many as 40 new passengers every week, and a substantial number converse about the same thing, week after week. The stress of these conversations must be kept in check because cordiality and responsiveness are important elements in the size of tip they are likely to receive.

Another type of conversation to which workers must be tolerant is passengers who like to talk about themselves, their own family, and often their economic success. Cruise passengers tend to forget that workers are from third world countries, where many of the things that are taken for granted by cruisers are unavailable or too expensive to afford. Simply, there is a tendency for cruisers to forget that the economics and the social system from which these folks come is so different from their own.

The issue may be as fundamental as religion. On Holland America Line, like others, passengers traveling near Christmas tend to wish workers a Merry Christmas. They assume that the workers celebrate the holiday; even if the worker doesn't s/he is not likely to correct the misperception. The fact is that the majority of the Indonesian staff are of the Muslim faith. I conveyed good wishes to my waiter one year for his celebration of Ramadan. He was initially surprised that a passenger knew about the Muslim holy month. My statement of awareness of his culture and beliefs changed the manner in which he treated us through the remainder of the cruise. The point here is that workers become accustomed to playing the role into which passengers place them, and they tend to keep private many parts of their self. They discuss those things about which they know, from experience, passengers want to hear. Much of who they are remains hidden and private.

Also from experience, workers learn and adopt tricks to ingratiate themselves to those they serve. On many cruise lines room stewards lay out passengers' pyjamas or towels in the shape of animals when they turn down the beds for the night. This is something that many passengers like, and that they come to expect. It is not infrequent that individuals posting messages on Internet discussion groups express disappointment that their steward did not do this, or that it wasn't done as well as others had led them to expect.

Similarly, dining room waiters sometimes complement passengers about their choices for a meal. Curiously, passengers take these as positive statements about themselves as a person, and in turn view their waiter more positively. Waiters will often also bring passengers extra desserts, or a dessert with a scoop of ice cream. They have learned that these things produce positive reactions, and presumably result in larger tips.

## Where There is Money There is Greed

Although service personnel have developed a range of strategies to maximize the generosity of those they serve, few are able to keep all of the money they earn in tips. Workers quickly become aware of a "mafia" on board. They learn what they need to do for advancement, and what they need to do for the more lucrative stations in the dining room or the higher end cabins for cleaning.

A waiter wanting to maximize his/her income is likely to have to share tips with a number of different folks. By paying off the dining room manager, waiters compete (almost bidding against one another) for larger stations (12 passengers per seating versus 16 or 20) and for stations closer to the kitchen (which means food is warmer when it reaches the table). They may also need to payoff cooks, if they want their orders quickly, and the laundry if they want their uniforms cleaned in a timely manner. Similarly, room stewards often pay their housekeeping supervisor or the chief steward in order to be assigned more expensively priced rooms. They, too, will pay off the laundry in order to be among the first to receive fresh linens and to have their uniforms cleaned and pressed.

This system of payoffs doesn't necessarily affect the cruise experience of passengers, but it is a feature of the community on board the ship. It is another factor that defines the relationships among workers and between workers and their supervisors. It is also something that, with awareness, explains what one sees. I have found that I have received better service from waiters who are not actively participating in the "mafia." Service may be a bit slower, but the waiter normally has a smaller number of passengers to serve and consequently is more attentive. On the other hand, I have experienced waiters who are less than competent, but because they payoff their supervisors their mistakes and errors are overlooked.

On a cruise aboard the *Norwegian Crown*, we had a waiter who had a station of 18 to 20 passengers. Food was often served cool, or it was dried out because it was left too long in the food warmer at the waiter's station. Soup was served, slopped over the side of the bowl, and the waiter was quite belligerent when lapses in service were raised to his attention. Curiously, the supervisors did nothing to correct the situation. It became obvious that it was not in the supervisors' interest to interfere with this waiter because he was contributing to their own income. It is easier to dismiss a finicky passenger or two than to take on an individual from whom one earns, under the table, part of their own income.

Because it is something not openly discussed (except with the ship's physician and persons not affiliated with the company), it is difficult to get a clear picture of how far the payoffs go. I have been told of ships where the payoffs go as high as the hotel manager and the captain. Opportunities for advancement and for fair treatment are enhanced, if not guaranteed, by each level passing along to the level above a portion of the money they receive. Thus, while salaries may be modest, the "mafia" provides a source for substantially improving one's overall income.

This system of payoffs is most prevalent on ships where there are clear expectations for tipping. It is increasingly found less on ships that don't require or that don't allow tipping.

## And Then there are Cruise Lines Where Tips are Pooled, or Where Tipping is Not Allowed

An emerging change in the cruise industry is to charge onboard passenger accounts for tips. For example, with its Freestyle Cruising, Norwegian Cruise Line automatically charges each passenger $10 per day (though a passenger can alter this amount if they go to the purser's desk) to cover tips to all service personnel. With its Personal Choice Dining, Princess Cruises automatically charges each passenger $6.50 per day (and again this can be increased or decreased by request) to cover gratuities for the dining room. Because service workers are no longer dependent on receiving tips directly from the passenger, it is unclear whether service will be impacted.

If we take direction from the ultra-luxury cruise lines, which either disallow or discourage tipping, we can expect the quality of service to become even more inconsistent than it already is. As well, those who work particularly hard are given a disincentive in that they now need to toe the line for those other staff who receive the same gratuity regardless of performance. This isn't to suggest that service on ultra-luxury cruise lines is inadequate. However, service on these lines is very inconsistent, varying from ship to ship and from staff member to staff member. Unless management is willing to impose standards, staff take whatever liberties they can. There are no financial costs to them for doing this.

Take for example a conversation I had with a waiter on the *Seabourn Goddess I*. He had just returned from vacation and was telling me what a great time he had had. He stayed in nice hotels and didn't let anyone get away without providing him exemplary service. He knew the tricks and wasn't going to give those providing him service any slack. But then this same worker was laissez faire about providing service to those on the ship. He'd ignore passenger requests, he'd refuse to serve passengers he didn't like, and he let the other staff cover for his laziness. If management maintained standards he would be gone. But he assumed from experience that he could get away with it. With the dilution of trained staff for his position, he believed that the cruise line needed him more than he needed them. And of course the passengers were the ones who bore the brunt of his attitude.

## Would You Like to Come to My Cabin to See My Etchings?

There is a joke that was commonly used in the 1990's by cruise directors in their disembarkation talks. The cruise director begins the talk by saying that someone has found a diary on a deck chair and asking whether the owner is present. When no one responds, the cruise director begins to read the diary aloud:

It begins with a woman coming on board and meeting the captain when she walks up the gangway. That evening the captain sends a bottle of wine to her dinner table. The next night she is invited to the captain's table for dinner; she finds him to be a charming fellow. The next night the captain invites her to his cabin for dinner, two nights later she is invited to his cabin for after dinner drinks, and on the next night she is invited to his cabin for a private dinner and drinks. The story goes on, with proper ooos and aahs from the cruise director. Along the way, the captain propositions the woman a couple of times, but she declines. In her next to last entry, she writes that he has threatened to sink the ship if she doesn't sleep with him. The last entry reads: "On Saturday morning at 3:00 A.M. I saved the ship and the lives of 1500 passengers." Most passengers laugh, but some are still unsure whether it is a joke or whether it is true. Others are offended by the sexist nature of the joke.

Unfortunately, the joke is closer to reality than many would like to think. It is not uncommon to see officers, in their white uniforms, making a play for single female passengers. I was told of a maitre d' who would strategically seat single women, staying in high priced cabins, at tables in the dining room where it would be easy for him to flirt with them. Though many women are disinterested, there are always a few who respond to the overtures.

There is an interesting pattern to the dance played out between officers and the single women they target over a seven-day cruise. The initial play usually begins the first formal night, when officers and passengers are dressed in their finest. The nature of the contact between the officer and woman increases as the cruise goes on, however the contact is rarely intimate until the last night; sometimes the second to last night. As I have been told a number of times, this pattern is played out cruise after cruise. Intimate relations are delayed until the end of the cruise "so that the officer doesn't have to deal with the woman after having sex. She will disembark that morning, never to be seen again."

To be fair, not all officers play this type of game. It is also a game not played just by officers. There are passengers who come aboard seeking the affections of an officer. A woman discussed this openly on an Internet discussion group who knew, and who had observed, women who instigated involvement with an officer.

While on Royal Cruise Line's *Royal Odyssey*, I observed one of these situations. While going through the Panama Canal, I noticed on the bridge that the captain was being leaned on by a young woman. Each time she leaned into him, he would move away, which she would follow with another approach. This continued, on and off, for the better part of two hours. In the evening, I observed the same woman making her moves on the captain. But he was not interested and she didn't take the hint. Her efforts continued through the remainder of the cruise, but to no avail. When women are successful, it is not always clear whether the relationship is at their instigation or that of the officer.

These games are just one more feature of the society on a cruise ship. Awareness of the games provides those so inclined with another source of on board entertainment.

## The Art of Customer Relations

No one goes on a cruise expecting there to be problems. However, there are certain problems that are commonly encountered. Seating at dinner is one that is particularly common. Passengers may be given an assignment at a time they didn't request, they might be given a table of a different size than they requested, or they may be seated with tablemates from hell. If they express concerns, the usual response is that "we will do what we can to make the change," often adding the passengers' names to a wait list, but changes are not always forthcoming. The passenger can try to raise the matter again, and again, but there is no guarantee that the matter will be corrected.

The best way to avoid these problems is to be sure that one's requests have been conveyed before the cruise, in writing, to the cruise line. In the case of the dining room, there is often a corporate dining room manager who receives and addresses special requests. The passenger or their travel agent should fax, in very clear terms, the passenger's request and an explanation for why it needs to be accommodated. It never hurts to follow the request with a phone call to the person to whom the letter is faxed.

Even with this type of advance work, things still do not always go smoothly. In these cases, one quickly learns the ways that cruise lines use to control discontent and to manage their customers.

## Don't Promise What You Can't Deliver

Several years ago I was told by a hotel manager that his biggest struggle was with front line staff making promises that passenger complaints would be addressed to the passenger's satisfaction. Almost weekly, he reminded staff, "don't promise what you can't deliver." In other words, unless the staff person to whom the passenger is speaking can guarantee that the solution requested would be fulfilled, don't make the promise. This, of course, places the line staff (often those at the purser's desk, or in modern terms "guest relations") in an awkward position. They have an irate passenger who, in their eyes, has a valid concern or complaint, but they can't say that anything will be done. The two common responses are to say, "I will send your complaint to the appropriate department" or to deny that the problem exists. In neither case is the passenger led to believe that their concern has been heard or understood.

On five of the cruises I have taken, there have been problems with air conditioning. In one case there was no air conditioning at all, in the others the air conditioning was inadequate. In each case, when the matter was first raised to the purser's desk, the response was to say that they were unaware of any problem with the air conditioning. This includes a cruise on Regency Cruises' *Regent Sea*, which was now on its fourth cruise in a row without air conditioning—the staff had been sleeping on the outside decks for the past couple of weeks because of the heat in their cabins, but they were instructed to say that there was no problem. It also includes a cruise on Norwegian Cruise Line's *Norwegian Sea*—the air conditioning had been turned off, though the purser's desk reported that (despite the dozens of complaints they had received) there were no problems. The attitude displayed is that if we say there isn't a problem, passengers will believe us and leave us alone. In many cases the strategy works.

This denial that a problem exists was also observed on Holland America Line's *Rotterdam*. In its first year of operation, there was considerable discussion on Internet discussion groups, and some in the media, about problems with the air conditioning. Shortly after its first year anniversary, I was aboard and experienced a cabin, even after five repair visits, which never got cool enough for a comfortable night's sleep. When the matter was raised to the "passenger relations manager," she responded, "The ship has never had any problems with the air conditioning." Rather than argue the point, I moved along. Ironically, as I walked by the purser's desk I overheard a passenger from a suite, who had the same complaint, being told that "yes, there was a problem" and that it might help if they propped a trashcan in the doorway to the veranda. It was suggested that the air circulation, despite this being a cruise in the Caribbean, would help make the room more comfortable.

A year later, traveling aboard Holland America Line's *Statendam*, I again experienced problems with the air conditioning, this time while occupying a suite. It took four calls (and almost six hours) before someone was sent to check out the problem. In this case, the problem was a faulty thermostat. However, again, the problem was denied—that is why it took four calls to get a response. I have been told that there was a design problem with all of the *Statendam*-class ships and that the air conditioning was a habitual problem on each of them.

Though air conditioning problems are not the only difficulties one may experience, these cases illustrate how cruise lines tend to make passengers feel that they are the problem; not the ship. Passengers are made to question whether their senses are correct. I did until the air conditioning engineer brought a thermometer on his fourth repair visit on the *Rotterdam* and showed that the room got no cooler than twenty-two centigrade.

Passengers also begin to wonder whether their expectations, based on advertising and other promises, are too high. If at a land-based resort, some guests would move to another hotel. However, with the lack of choice, many cruise passengers settle for not having their concerns addressed.

## Please Accept Our Apologies And...

In recent years, cruise lines have tended to adopt an attitude that if they give the passenger something for free, the passenger will let go of their complaint. On some cruise lines, it may be a complementary bottle of wine at dinner. There is a problem with your plumbing? Have a bottle of wine on us. Your room isn't properly cleaned? Accept this gift of a bottle of wine. You found something in your food? Here's a bottle of wine.

The practice has become so routine, that some passengers have learned to scam the cruise line. An executive chef with Norwegian Cruise Lines indicated that almost once a week there is a case where a passenger puts something in their food, calls over the maitre d', and then asks for compensation. The chef indicated that sometimes what was found in the food, is clearly not something that could have originated in the galley.

Increasingly, cruise lines address problems by providing a discount certificate for a future cruise. They may not correct the problem, but instead say, "if you come back, we'll give you a 15% discount and we'll show you how good we can be." Carnival Cruise Lines and Seabourn Cruises (among others) have given these certificates while passengers are still on board, presumably to reduce the demand on their corporate customer relations department. Instead of a bedspread, I was given this type of certificate on the Carnival *Destiny*.

Customer relations departments at the corporate level are not much different than those on the ship. Letters addressed to corporate executives are commonly referred to "customer relations" for response. Sometimes the customer relations department will send a certificate for an on board credit or a discount for a future cruise, sometimes an appropriate explanation or apology. In any case, the typical written response, if one is given, reads something like:

> *Please be assured that a copy of your letter was directed to supervisory personnel in those areas mentioned, and corrective steps will be taken, wherever necessary, to ensure our passengers the most positive cruise experience.*

> *We value the opinions and observations of our passengers and wish to assure you that the situations cited were exceptions rather than the norm. For this reason, we invite your continued patronage, so we may demonstrate to you the high standards that have earned us the fine reputation we enjoy in the travel industry.*

Another type of response from cruise lines, when there is concern that the problem raised may have legal implications, is to respond that "your letter has been referred to the risk management department for their response." That response arrived from Royal Caribbean Cruise Lines after a letter was sent indicating grave concern that a bay leaf was found in a sandwich and was almost swallowed. The letter to RCCL didn't ask for anything, but simply suggested that there was need for greater care given the seriousness of injury that could result from swallowing a bay leaf—it can easily perforate the esophagus and one could bleed to death before medical assistance could be given. Four months later a letter arrived from risk management expressing delight that an injury was not experienced. The letter expressed Royal Caribbean's "concern for the safety and well being of our passengers," but made no comment about other concerns raised, including the health risks associated with the number of chipped plates used for serving meals. At least the corporate response was better than that received on board. When the matter was raised to the maitre d', his response was to shrug and to say, "She didn't swallow the leaf, so what's the problem?"

When a complaint is judged to have legal implications, then the response is different again. In those cases, companies may be equally as slow in responding, and in working out solutions. In a case where I cracked a tooth on a shard of broken dinner plate food, the company had as a condition for any settlement—even reimbursement for dental bills—that the case and the resolution be kept confidential.

## Two Case Illustrations

The discussion about customer relations has thus far been somewhat abstract and general. Following are two illustrations that may help in bringing the information to life. I have chosen to use two ultra-luxury lines because the cases illustrate both an attitude about customer relations and the nature of the community on small cruise ships.

### Seabourn Cruise Line

In October 2000, my wife and I took a cruise on Seabourn Cruise Line's *Sea Goddess I*. We embarked on the cruise the week after the company proclaimed in a press release that "we offer the best of the best on board," The press release also quoted *Stern's 2001 Guide to the Cruise Vacation*, noting the *Seabourn Goddesses'* "impeccable service, the finest cuisine, and unparalleled personal attention." We knew from experience that cruise lines are liberal in their use of superlatives, so embarked expecting service comparable to other cruise lines of the same quality. We did not take seriously that we would have "the best of the best."

Following the cruise we wrote to the company's chief executive officer because a number of the dining room staff treated us (and others) in ways that one wouldn't even tolerate at a Denny's or a HoJo's coffee shop. The letter began as follows:

> *We have just returned from a fourteen day cruise on the* Seabourn Goddess I. *We are writing to raise to your immediate attention an extremely serious and distressing incident that occurred the last night of the cruise. The phone rang, my wife answered it, and was subjected to a verbal threat to my safety and security.*
>
> *During the course of the cruise...I had cause to express concern when there were several serious lapses in service. The service often reflected a comment made to several passengers by two service personnel: in effect, they said: "we know everyone on this cruise is paying a discounted fare, so we feel justified in giving discounted service." They also said that with rebranding they are "paid the same but don't work as hard."*

Over the course of the cruise, we had orders for food that never arrived, we habitually had difficulty having water and wine glasses filled, and we were subjected to rude and crass service and behaviour. I had food dropped on me, a knife fall off a plate onto my head as the plate was being taken from the table, and a small bowl dropped on my back. Initially we wondered whether the problem was general or was it specific to us.

Our wonderment was answered the night we were invited to join the hotel manager's table for dinner. The service we received at his table was no better than we had had; in some ways it was worse. Several passengers at the table were not offered bread, most had water and wine glasses left unfilled, waiters reached over people to serve others at the table, and the staff attitude was about the same as we had experienced other nights. We concluded that if the hotel manager could tolerate the lapses we observed, there was little hope that the situation would improve over the next week.

In writing to the company, we raised these issues and, in addition to the threatening telephone call, an incident one day at lunch when the assistant maitre d' lit into us in a tirade, in a loud, raised voice because we had responded to his question by saying that the service the previous night at dinner was not good. When I tried to stop the verbal assault by pointing out in a calm voice that his behaviour was inappropriate, the assistant maitre d' continued by disagreeing with my statement, but finally stopped and moved on.

We received a telephone call on behalf of the chief executive officer as a result of our faxed letter and were told that they would investigate the situation and be back in touch. A week later we received a dismissive letter, with the usual "we hope we can have the pleasure of welcoming you onboard again in the near future." It did not deal with the concerns raised and it made no effort to ensure that we would keep reservations we already had for a subsequent cruise with the company.

After several efforts at finding a solution (our first letter was dismissed, two follow up letters were ignored), and after being jerked around by the chief executive officer's personal representative, we finally gave up and decided to cancel future plans with the company. The chief executive officer's representative actually told us that we were problem passengers, which apparently justified a senior manager raising his voice to a passenger, and it justified all of the other lapses (including having erroneous charges on our shipboard account which it took two requests onboard and five requests after arriving home to finally have corrected). The message: accept what you are given and in no circumstance ever complain.

We can't avoid contrasting our experience with that of a couple three doors down the hall from us (cabin 209). They complained about the sound of the hydraulic pump that operates the watertight doors on the deck below (which is part of the ship's design) and were given (without hassle) a certificate for $15,000 off a future cruise. Why the difference? The only explanation we can come up with is that a noise is real—it cannot be denied—but service is something that is individually judged and a passenger is easily dismissed as expecting too much.

In retrospect, looking back at the whole cruise, we came to realize that each time we raised a concern about service, service would get worse rather than better. We were told one day that everything about which we expressed concern was passed on to staff, along with who had complained. As a result, we were clearly being sanctioned for complaining that we weren't receiving adequate service. The service didn't even remotely approach "the best of the best" or "impeccable."

## Radisson Seven Seas Cruises

In May 2000, my wife and I cruised on the *Radisson Diamond*. The cruise was generally very good, however there was a minor problem that was a source of concern. It was a concern because we had a cruise booked on one of their other ships several months later.

The problem began the first morning when we went to the area around the pool, got comfortable, and became immersed in reading. As soon as the bar opened, music (at a higher volume than desired) was channelled over the speakers around the pool. Though we are relatively young (mid-forties), the passengers on this cruise were not likely to want to hear Madonna, rap, or similar venues of music. I went to the bar and asked that the music be turned down, which it was. However, each time a new bartender took over (every hour or so), the music would be turned up and I or another passenger would ask that it be reduced.

One afternoon, after three requests that the music be turned down or off (in the first two cases it was turned off), I was told that a passenger had asked that the CD currently playing be put on. Ironically, we were chatting with this passenger over a night cap that evening and he told us that he had taken the CD up and said, "If you insist on playing music, at least play something that I am willing to listen to." His preference was that no music be played at all. It appeared that the bar staff considered the music system at the bar to be their personal stereo system and that they were free to play, for consumption of all, the music that they liked. This was a struggle that seemed to never end.

The situation escalated when a bartender began saying under his breath, every time he saw me, "turn down the music?" One night we were seated with the staff captain at dinner. Believe it or not, he had the gall to make the same comment as he served my wine. At that point, my wife turned around and said, "That's enough of that!" and I continued by warning him that if he didn't improve his attitude I would be speaking with the hotel manager about his behaviour. His comments stopped, but he became passive aggressive in other ways. One evening, my wife went to the area around the Splash Bar after dinner to have a cigarette. The bar was closed and she was the only one there. It was perfectly quiet until I arrived to join her. Immediately, the bartender (who was cleaning the bar) turned the music on, loud enough to be bothersome. Rather than confront the situation we retreated to our veranda.

We raised our concerns to onboard management, but found that each time we complained, the passive aggressive behaviour would become more intrusive and troublesome. We had to resign ourselves to remaining captive to the musical tastes of the bartenders, all of whom appeared to be in their twenties.

When we returned home, we wrote to the company's chief executive officer. He responded by sending two certificates for $250 off a future cruise, but gave us no assurance that what we experienced was inconsistent with company policy. As we suggested in a follow up letter, the discount certificates were worthless if the company couldn't assure us that we would not be assaulted by unwanted music and if they couldn't control their own staff. That letter received a response that was described by my travel agency as arrogant.

We made one more attempt to clarify company policy, before cancelling our future cruise. We wrote a letter that had two questions:

1.    *When we go on deck the first morning at sea and get comfortable to read a book, will unwanted music be a constant feature of that setting? Please be clear about company policy on this matter!!*

2.    *Can you suggest how to deal with a staff person who is rude or abusive? Please provide advice as to how we should handle a situation, such as the protracted problem with the bartender on the* Diamond. *If this something over which the company truly has no control, please tell us.*

The response received indicated that yes, we would be subjected to unwanted music. It also confirmed that we shouldn't expect management to be able to deal with problematic staff.

In disbelief that a company would take this position, we wrote a final letter to the chief executive officer of the parent company to Radisson Seven Seas Cruises, the Carlson Companies. Though she did not respond, we received another letter from the chief executive officer of Radisson Seven Seas Cruises. First, he called us liars by saying that we hadn't given the company a chance to resolve the problem on the *Diamond* because we hadn't notified staff or management. Second, he claimed that the bartenders have no ability to control the music around the pool.

We responded with a letter that documented the close to two dozen complaints made to bartenders, the bar manager, and the food and beverage manager (who was also the assistant hotel manager). We also pointed out his misinformation about the way his own ship is being run. That letter was totally ignored. Again, the message given is that as passengers one takes what they are given, and they should not complain unless they are willing to endure the consequences.

To be fair, one shouldn't assume that these experiences are representative of all cruise lines and of all dealings with a cruise line's customer relations personnel. They are offered here as an example of my own experience. They may help shape your expectations for how a customer relation issue is handled, but the fact is that each company handles complaints differently. In our experience, Holland America Line stands well above other lines in dealing with customer concerns. Other passengers, however, may argue that their experience with Holland America Line is quite different.

## From The Stranger-Than-Life Archive

In closing it may be worth mentioning several odd cases around customer relations that have been reported in the media. They provide some insight into customer claims.

In 1994, a passenger filed a lawsuit after a cruise line failed to provide compensation for false teeth that had been inadvertently thrown in the trash by a cabin steward. The passenger had taken his teeth out before going to bed, wrapping them in tissue paper and placing them on the dresser in the cabin. He did not put the teeth in again before leaving the cabin the following morning and the steward threw them in the trash as rubbish. In a newsletter published by the company's insurers, it was stated, "The managers are at a loss to advise how the prudent ship owner might prevent this kind of claim and invite ideas."[14]

In 1997, a couple traveling on Royal Caribbean Cruise Lines had placed clothes out to be laundered. They were told, when asking about the return of their clothing, that the clothing had accidentally ended up in the ship's incinerator. Several months of correspondence between the passenger and the cruise line followed after the cruise. The passengers claimed that the clothes had a value of approximately $1500, but they were told that the ship's insurance limited compensation to a payment of approximately $150 per person. A newspaper consumer-help column ended up intervening on the couple's behalf.[15]

In December 1998, Royal Caribbean International's *Monarch of the Seas* ran aground off St. Maarten, tearing a hole in the hull and necessitating an emergency, night time abandoning of the ship. Passengers were assured that their personal belongings would be packed for them and would follow later. One couple rushed to their lifeboat, but in the chaos left behind a box containing the ashes of the man's grandfather. The couple had planned to scatter the ashes in Barbados, the deceased's native island. When their belongings were finally returned to them, the ashes were nowhere to be found. The company's spokesman indicated, "he did not believe the company would be liable for the loss of the ashes. Before they board cruise ships, passengers sign forms releasing the company from claims for lost goods." [16]

[1]  Reynolds, Christopher and Dan Weikel. "For Cruise Ship Workers, Voyages
        Are No Vacations," Los Angeles Times, May 30, 2000
[2]  House of Representatives, Coverage of Certain Federal Labour Laws to Foreign Documented Vessels (House
        Report #103-818), Washington, DC: GPO, 1994, page 1
[3]  House of Representatives, Coverage of Certain Federal Labour Laws to Foreign Documented Vessels (House
        Report #103-818), Washington, DC: GPO, 1994, page 3
[4]  Glass, Joel. "House Subcommittee Reviews Bogey of Maritime Labour Law," Lloyd's List,
        October 10, 1992, p. 4
[5]  Reynolds, Christopher and Dan Weikel. "For Cruise Ship Workers, Voyages
        Are No Vacations," Los Angeles Times, May 30, 2000
[6]  Chapman, Paul K.  Trouble On Board: The Plight of International Seafarers," Ithaca, NY: ILR Press, 1992,
        page 32
[7]  Prager, Joshua Harris. "For Cruise Workers, Life is No Love Boat," Wall Street Journal, July 3, 1997, page B1
[8]  Nielsen, Kirk. "The Perfect Scam: For the Workers Life Is No Carnival, Believe It Or Not," Miami New Times,
        February 3-9, 2000
[9]  Nielsen, Kirk. "The Perfect Scam: For the Workers Life Is No Carnival, Believe It Or Not," Miami New Times,
        February 3-9, 2000
[10]  Chapman, Paul K.  Trouble On Board: The Plight of International Seafarers," Ithaca, NY: ILR Press, 1992,
        page 56
[11]  Van Gelder, Lindsy and Pamela Robin Brandt. "Cruising Greek Isles with Daughters of Sappho," Los Angeles
        Times, March 28, 1993, page L - 7
[12]  "Gay Cruise Fiasco in Turkey," Daily News - Yahoo.Com, September 8, 2000
[13]  Reynolds, Christopher and Dan Weikel. "For Cruise Ship Workers, Voyages
        Are No Vacations," Los Angeles Times, May 30, 2000
[14]  "A Cry For Help From The UK P&I Club Whose Loss Prevention Newsletter Can Sometimes Throw Up The
        Most Extraordinary Puzzles," Lloyd's List, February 11, 1994, page 5
[15]  "Royal Caribbean Cruise Line Appears To Have Come Up With A Novel Way Of Dealing With Dirty Laundry,"
        Lloyd's List, May 19, 1997, page 5
[16]  Reuters News Service, February 10, 1999

# 5 Safety at Sea

The last thing that one thinks about when embarking on a cruise holiday is safety and security. According to the industry, a cruise is among the safest choices for a vacation. While this claim may be relatively accurate, and in fact was echoed in a 1995 report by the U.S. Coast Guard, the reality is cruises are not without difficulties in terms of passenger safety and security. Between 1980 and 1992 the U.S. Coast Guard investigated seventy-three accidents involving large cruise ships. These included thirteen collisions, sixteen fires, twenty-two equipment or material failures, and twenty-two groundings.

Unfortunately, these types of events are as common today as they were then. Consider, for example, that in a two month period in 1995, two ships grounded and two others experienced crippling fires. Or, in the Pacific Northwest alone, twenty cruise ships grounded in the three year period from August 1996 through August 1999. More recently, Norwegian Cruise Line's *Norwegian Dream* was involved in a major collision in the English Channel in August 1999, NCL's *Norwegian Sky* was grounded a month later in the St. Lawrence River, and a month after that, in October 1999, Carnival Cruise Line's *Tropicale* experienced a disabling engine fire that caused the loss of electrical power and left the ship adrift. Power was eventually restored, but the ship's arrival in port was delayed for two days by a combination of reduced engine power and the need to avoid a tropical storm. This was the fourth major fire on a Carnival Cruise Line ship in as many years.

The fact is that "events" on cruise ships —whether they be minor accidents, engine problems, groundings, fires, or collisions—are much more common than we tend to think. They are certainly more common than the cruise industry would like us to believe. These events on cruise ships provide information that is ultimately used in efforts to increase shipboard safety. For example, the sinking of the *Titanic* in 1912, when more than 1500 lives were lost, drew considerable attention to safety issues related to passenger ships. These issues were dealt with to some extent under the framework of the League of Nations, with the 1929 *Convention on the Safety of Life at Sea*.

The first organization focusing exclusively on improvement of safety at sea was established by the United Nations in 1948. Initially called the Inter-Governmental Maritime Consultative Organization (IMCO), and later renamed the International Maritime Organization (IMO), the organization now includes in its mandate both safety at sea and the prevention and control of marine pollution. Control of marine pollution is covered under agreements referred to as the International Convention for the Prevention of Pollution from Ships (MARPOL). These will be discussed in the following chapter.

## The International Convention of Safety of Life at Sea (SOLAS)

Anyone who has been on a cruise is likely familiar with the "SOLAS" acronym, though many of us have limited knowledge about what this means and how it affects us. The Convention of Safety of Life at Sea is an international treaty that sets minimum standards for shipboard safety. It is the responsibility of each of the one hundred and thirty-eight nations subscribing to the International Maritime Organization to ensure that vessels sailing under their flags comply with the treaty's requirements. However, in reality, not all countries equally enforce these standards for their ships. Consequently, the U.S. Coast Guard inspects all ships using U.S. ports, regardless of the country in which the ship is registered, four times a year to ensure their compliance with the standards under the SOLAS convention. Cruise travelers outside the U.S., on cruise lines that don't utilize U.S. ports, are not guaranteed these same protections. In contrast, the few passenger ships registered in the U.S. must meet U.S. standards, which are higher than those under the SOLAS convention.

## What Are Some of the Things Covered by SOLAS?

SOLAS regulates a wide range of elements on a cruise ship. Early regulations required that passenger ships have twice as many lifeboat seats as potential passengers, and that they have 25% more life jackets than would be needed for the passenger capacity of the ship. In addition, it was expected that lifeboats would be partially covered in order to protect occupants from hypothermia caused by cold or wet conditions.

The SOLAS Convention also requires that a passenger ship must be able to be abandoned within a maximum of thirty minutes. While this thirty-minute limit was realistic when ships were smaller, there is increasing concern that an efficient and timely evacuation of the larger mega ships would be difficult if not impossible. There is a large difference between evacuating 600 or 1000 passengers and the evacuation of a ship like Carnival's *Destiny*-class ships, or Royal Caribbean International's *Eagle*-class ships, which have as many as 5000 occupants, including passengers and crew. These ships are as much as seven times larger than the large ships afloat when the thirty-minute limit was put in place. On these larger ships, it is possible that it will take thirty minutes for passengers just to find the muster station for their lifeboat. Concern about evacuation in a timely manner is voiced most strongly by the insurance consortiums that are financially liable if there were a disaster at sea.

SOLAS conventions also cover methods for fire safety. Early agreements focused on such things as the materials used in ship construction and ship insulation. The fact that there is an agreement, however, does not guarantee that safety requirements are met. Safety inspections are generally the responsibility of the nation in which a ship is registered.

Because countries such as the United States, Great Britain, Norway, and Sweden (among others) make stringent inspections of ships using their ports, we gain insight into some of the slackness by nations offering flags of convenience in their ensuring adherence to SOLAS regulations. For example, a 1988 Coast Guard inspection of a cruise ship, which had passed its inspection by its nation of registry, found blue Styrofoam insulation around the overhead ventilation ducts. Because Styrofoam insulation is flammable, and emits a toxic gas when it burns, the ship was not allowed to leave port (thus requiring cruises to be cancelled) until proper insulation was installed.

A United States General Accounting Office analysis of cruise ship safety examinations conducted between 1990 and 1992 by the U.S. Coast Guard, found in every examination sampled that there was at least one deficiency in three of the six safety related categories: structural fire protection, improper storage of flammable materials, inoperable fire safety equipment, poorly executed fire or lifeboat drills, improper documentation, and missing or inoperable lifesaving equipment.

Some of these problems have been solved by the introduction of newer ships that are constructed to higher safety standards. For example, as part of the 1974 SOLAS safety standards, a sprinkler system or system of heat detectors has been required on new ships since 1980. But older ships continued to be able to operate without sprinklers at least until 1997, and if given an exemption by their nation of registry they could operate without sprinklers until 2005, or in some cases 2009.

Starting in 1994, all new ships had to come out of the yard with both sprinklers and smoke alarm systems, but again a long phase-in period was allowed to accommodate older ships. Since that time there has been continuing debate about whether smoke alarms should sound in passenger cabins and hallways, or whether (as the requirement is written) it is sufficient to have the alarm heard only on the ship's bridge. The U.S. Coast Guard and National Transportation Safety Board have argued strongly since the early 1990's, based on fires that took human lives, that the alarms should be heard in cabins and hallways.

As recent as July 2000, the National Transportation Safety Board renewed its call for smoke detectors and fire alarms that would be heard at the source of the fire. They pointed to the fact that fire is the number one safety concern on cruise ships, and that passengers are every day placed in danger because the ships lack a local sounding alarm. The cruise industry, through the International Council of Cruise Lines (ICCL), opposed the NTSB's position, claiming that individual smoke detectors produce numerous false alarms that could result in mass panic aboard ship. They took the position that smoke alarms should only be heard at a central location on the ship's bridge.

In November 2000, the ICCL dropped its opposition to local sounding smoke alarms. It announced that its sixteen members unanimously agreed to install the alarms on all their ships. No time frame was given for the installation.

As solutions to older safety problems are found, new construction designs have introduced new issues. The popularity of atriums is one of those designs that, according to the National Transportation Safety Board chairman in 1990, present a severe challenge to fire control and safety. His warning however had no effect on ship design. An atrium may be less than ideal from a safety standpoint, but they attract passengers and have become internationally accepted, if not expected. The *Carnival Destiny* has not just one atrium, but two. Cruise ships have introduced designs for fire control and confinement, given the chimney effect introduced by an atrium, but to date these systems have not been tested. Unfortunately, as we will see later, it is often through system failure or system breakdown in an emergency that changes in regulations have been adopted.

## The Convention on Standards of Training, Certification and Watchkeeping for Seafarers (STCW)

Because safety on a ship ultimately rests with the crew rather than with the ship itself, the International Maritime Organization convened in 1978 a conference that adopted the first ever Convention on Standards of Training, Certification and Watchkeeping for Seafarers. This Convention, which entered into force in April 1984, is part of the requirements under SOLAS. It established, for the first time, internationally acceptable minimum standards for training and certification of crew. It was not intended as a model on which all States would base their crew requirements, because in many countries the requirements are actually higher than those laid down in the Convention.

The Convention was revised in 1995. Apart from bringing the Convention up to date from a technical point of view, the revision also gave the International Maritime Organization the power to audit the administrative, training and certification procedures of parties to the Convention. These amendments, which entered into force in 1997, established requirements for basic safety training for all crew members, and advanced training requirements for crew members with assigned safety or pollution prevention duties. The Standards of Training, Certification and Watchkeeping for Seafarers amendments also specify minimum standards for crew competence and set criteria for evaluation of crew training by the flag administration.

## International Safety Management (ISM) Code

One additional convention under SOLAS, passed in 1994 and brought into effect July 1998, is the International Safety Management Code. The purpose of this Code is to provide an international standard for the safe management and operation of ships and for pollution prevention. It specifically focuses on the role which onboard crew management and shore side management play in maritime safety.

The objectives of the Code are to ensure safety at sea, prevention of human injury or loss of life, and avoidance of damage to the environment, in particular to the marine environment and to property. This includes safe practices in ship operation and a safe working environment; establishment of safeguards against all identified risks; and continuous improvement of safety management skills of personnel ashore and aboard ships. Personnel are required to prepare for emergencies related both to safety and environmental protection.

The International Safety Management Code requires cruise lines to develop a safety management system. The functional requirements under this system include: 1) articulation of a safety and environmental-protection policy; 2) instructions and procedures to ensure safe operation of ships and protection of the environment; 3) clear definition of levels of authority and lines of communication between, and amongst, shore and shipboard personnel; 4) specific procedures for reporting accidents and non-conformities with the provisions of the Code; 5) formal articulation of procedures to prepare for and respond to emergency situations; and 6) a set of procedures for internal audits and management reviews which ensure that the Safety Management System remains current and effective.

The International Safety Management Code may provide passengers some sense of security, however it needs to be kept in mind that certification under the Code is left to the country in which a ship is registered. Consequently, given the large number of ships registered in Panama, Liberia, and the Bahamas, it is the practice of these countries on which we depend. As well, the fact that regulations or procedures exist does not guarantee that they will be followed. For example, it was determined in the collision involving the *Norwegian Dream*, that contrary to Company policy which requires two officers to be on watch only one was on the bridge at the time. This will be discussed in greater detail later.

## The Occurrence of Events at Sea

Many of the regulations covered by the SOLAS Convention are based on knowledge gained through accidents or events at sea. As already mentioned, the sinking of the *Titanic* brought to the forefront the need for adequate numbers and space in lifeboats. More recent problems have focused attention on the need for such things as the competence of crew to effectively communicate in English, and the installation on the bridge of ships of "black boxes" similar to those use on commercial aircraft.

There is a range of events that can happen on a cruise ship. Some are simply an inconvenience to passengers and are minimally disruptive. However, others are quite disruptive and can be potentially life threatening.

## What are The Most Minimally Disruptive Events?

The least disruptive events include cruises that are cancelled or delayed, or cruises in which there are problems with air conditioning or plumbing. These events are inconvenient to those affected, and would be considered quite disruptive to those who have a cruise cancelled at the last minute. However, in the grand scheme of things, they are relatively minor.

Beginning in the late 1990's, cancellations and delays began to become common due to new ships simply not being delivered on time, or being delivered with mechanical problems. For example, in 1997, the inaugural voyage for two ships were cancelled: Holland America Line's new *Rotterdam* was delayed six weeks, and Radisson Seven Seas *Paul Gauguin* was delayed one week after experiencing engine problems during its sea trials. A year later, the *Disney Magic* was delayed almost four months, Princess Cruises' *Grand Princess* was delayed two weeks, and the *Sea Princess* was delayed four weeks, all because of delays in delivery. The pattern continued in 1999, when Holland America Line's *Volendam* was delivered ten weeks late, the *Disney Wonder* had its delivery delayed several months, and the *Carnival Triumph* began service two weeks late. In the first half of 2000, Holland America Line's *Zaandam* was one month late, and Celebrity Cruises' *Millennium* was delivered two weeks late.

This problem with new ships is not limited to ships that are newly built. There are cases, such as the *Big Red Boat III* which had its maiden voyage cancelled at the last minute because its refit was not completed on time, the *Norwegian Majesty* which experienced a number of mechanical problems on its first voyage after being stretched—the problems reached public attention through demonstrations by passengers at the pier in Bermuda, and Cunard Line's *QE II* which has sailed more than once with work still being done while passengers were aboard. In 1994, the *QE II* actually left 190 passengers at the pier because renovation of their rooms had not been completed. Those who did board the ship complained loudly about the construction that was going on around them throughout their transatlantic crossing.

The delay of ships appears to be decreasing, as cruise lines learn to build additional time into planning for the arrival of a new ship. However, other problems appear to be on the increase. Celebrity Cruises' *Millennium*, delivered in June 2000, two weeks later than planned, was plagued with engine problems during its first summer at sea. It was pulled from service in November 2000 for remedial repairs, causing the cancellation of several cruises. It was pulled from service again April 2001 for two weeks to repair an under-performing electric motor that operates the ship's two propulsion units.

A similar situation was experienced with Royal Caribbean International's sister ships several years before: the *Grandeur of the Seas* and the *Rhapsody of the Seas*. Both had engine problems shortly after leaving the shipyard. These problems caused itineraries to be changed, ports to be missed, and necessitated the ships being dry-docked for major repairs.

Similarly, Carnival Cruise Line's *Paradise*, which entered service in 1998 as one of the first ships to use an Azipod propulsion system, was pulled from service for two months in the summer of 2000 to address engine problems. The *Elation*, which has an identical propulsion system to the *Paradise* was also taken out of service for two weeks in the fall of 2000 in order to complete preventative maintenance. P&O's *Aurora* had its maiden voyage cancelled eighteen hours after it began because of problems with a propeller shaft.

What all of this suggests is that those booking maiden or inaugural voyages need to be aware that there is considerable potential for delay and inconvenience. However, inconvenience is not limited to these situations. Ships may experience mechanical difficulties at any time in their life, resulting in delayed or cancelled cruises. As well, as seen in Appendix A, problems with insufficient or nonexistent air conditioning are not altogether uncommon—air conditioning has been a problem on four of the cruises I have taken.

There are also unforeseen events that cause cancellation of cruises. In the year 2000, Premier Cruises' *Island Breeze* was pulled from service after being struck by a tugboat while docking in Houston; earlier that year the World Cruise Company's

*Riviera I* had its world cruise cut short, leaving passengers stranded, when the ship was seized in Tahiti for unpaid fuel bills and the company went into bankruptcy; a year before Royal Olympic Cruise Line's *Stella Solaris* was delayed in leaving Galveston, Texas because of crew member complaints about unpaid overtime and poor working conditions; and in 1998, Princess Cruises' *Pacific Princess* was detained for several weeks at Piraeus after Greek inspectors found twenty-five kilograms of cocaine on board. There are also occasional cases where ships are detained in port because they do not meet basic safety and fire codes.

The simple fact is that cruises are not problem-free, nor should one expect that everything will be perfect. I have experienced minor engine failures on four cruises. On another cruise the ship ran out of fresh drinking water and was admitted to a port during an extended storm for humanitarian reasons following two days with limited to no water supplies. However, I was spared the inconvenience experienced by the thousands of passengers stranded by the bankruptcy in 1996 of Regency Cruises, and have not been affected by freak accidents such as a rogue wave that struck Holland America Line's *Rotterdam* in 2000 and which damaged almost anything not bolted down, or a freak wave that hit Fred Olsen Cruises' *Black Prince* as it was leaving Dover and which smashed three windows on the bridge and caused electrical equipment to fail. In none of these cases were there any serious injuries.

## If These are Minor Problems, What are Major Problems?

There is something of a continuum in the seriousness of problems experienced by cruise ships. As already indicated, minor engine or power failures are not uncommon. Less common are major engine problems that disable a ship. However they do happen. For example, in the first half of 2000, Carnival Cruise Line's *Paradise* experienced engine problems that caused the itinerary of its millennium cruise to be significantly altered, and later that year the propulsion system failed entirely as it was leaving Miami, causing the cancellation of that and a series of subsequent cruises; and also in 2000, the *Carnival Destiny* was adrift for twenty-seven hours off Turks and Caicos because of propulsion problems. Several months later it missed a cruise and changed the itinerary of another because of mechanical problems while in Boston Harbour. At roughly the same time, Sun Cruises' *Sundream* had no air conditioning and limited power for two days because of failing generators—crew members reported that these problems began several weeks before and had affected several cruises; and, the World Cruise Company's *Ocean Explorer* had its world cruise end midway through because of engine failure.

Less frequent, but perhaps more frightening to passengers, are the occurrence of events such as running aground, fires, and collisions. These will be discussed in turn.

## Running Aground

Though Carnival Cruise Line would likely prefer it be forgotten, the maiden voyage of its first ship, the *Mardi Gras*, ran aground while leaving Miami Harbour and remained stuck for almost twenty-four hours. Unfortunately, grounding of cruise ships is not uncommon, even today. In the ten-year period from 1990 through 1999, twenty-nine ships were reported by the popular media as running aground (see Appendix A). In some cases, as with the *Radisson Diamond* running aground near Stockholm in the Summer of 1999, the ship was freed and the cruise continued. In other cases, the grounding caused damage to the ship, though passengers were able to remain on board until the ship reached port. In still other cases, the grounding required evacuation of the ship—as was the case with Royal Caribbean International's *Monarch of the Seas*, which struck a charted reef at St. Maarten and was holed, requiring a night-time evacuation of almost 2600 passengers in December 1998.

In some cases, damage to the ship pales in comparison to the damage caused to the environment. In 1996, Cunard Line's *Royal Viking Sun* collided with a reef in the Red Sea and was holed. While damage to the ship was in the millions of dollars, the cruise line was fined $23.5 million for the irreparable damage to the reef and its fragile ecosystem. Also that year, Holland America Line was fined by the Cayman Islands after the *Maasdam* dragged its anchor over more than one thousand meters of Soto's Reef, just off the coast at Georgetown. A year later, Norwegian Cruise Lines' *Leeward* was fined $1 million after damaging 460 square yards of the Great Mayan Reef near Cancun Mexico.

Environmental damage is also caused by oil spills when a ship is holed. In the Spring of 2000, Sun Cruises' *Carousel* leaked 50 tons of oil when it ran over rocks at Calica, Mexico. Light pollution was caused by the grounding in Southeast Alaska of P&O's *Star Princess* in 1995, and Holland America Line's *Nieuw Amsterdam* in 1994. Perhaps the most serious spill by a cruise ship in Alaskan waters was from Clipper Cruises' *Yorktown Clipper*, which ran aground in the ecologically-sensitive Glacier Bay, and which spilled 28,000 gallons of fuel.

The obvious question is how, with advanced navigational aids, it is possible that a ship would run aground. In some cases, the problem is in part due to outdated charts (as in the case of the *QE II* running aground off Nantucket in 1992), with failure of navigational equipment (as was the case in the grounding of the *Royal Majesty* off Nantucket in 1995), or with reliance on a buoy that had drifted out of place (as was the case when the *Hanseatic* ran aground in the Northwest Passage [Simpson Strait] of Canada in 1996). However, more frequently, grounding is caused by human error. In each of the cases just mentioned, human error was a contributing factor. Human failure includes failure to correctly set a course, failure to correctly navigate a course, failure to keep a vigilant watch, or simply someone not doing their assigned job.

## Fire on Cruise Ships

Fire is the greatest threat to a cruise ship. There are many safety systems and safety precautions in place, but fires still happen. Some of these fires are spectacular and lead to the loss of a ship. For example, Starlauro's *Angelina Lauro* sunk at St. Thomas in 1979 following a fire that began in the crew galley, Holland America Line's *Prinsendam* sunk one hundred and forty miles off the coast of Alaska in 1980 after an engine fire necessitated a middle-of-the-night abandoning of the ship, and engine fires led to the sinking of Starlauro's *Achille Lauro* in the Indian Ocean off the Seychelles in 1994, New Paradise Cruises' *Romantica* off Cyprus in 1997, and Sun Cruise's *Sun Vista* (previously the *Meridian* with Celebrity Cruises) off the coast of Malaysia in 1999. Miraculously, only in the fire and loss of the *Achille Lauro* was there any loss of life: four people died and eight were injured.

For most of us, however, the image of fire on a cruise ship is not quite as spectacular. It is likely reflected by the television pictures we saw when Carnival Cruise Line's *Ecstasy* caught fire shortly after leaving Miami in 1998. The fire, caused by a worker's blow torch igniting lint in laundry vents, was extinguished within several hours and no one was seriously hurt, but the pictures showing the soot-covered back of the ship and passengers waving signs and placards from the upper decks was beamed into every household with a television, and shown on the front page of most newspapers. We likely read the stories with interest, but assumed that fires on cruise ships were relatively uncommon. To the contrary, as shown in Appendix A, there were forty-three media reports of major fires on cruise ships between 1979 and 2000.

Most of these fires were extinguished without much event and, though in some cases the cruise was prematurely ended, resulted in more inconvenience than actual harm. In cases when the ship was at sea, the ship was able to make it to port—sometimes under its own power and sometimes requiring to be towed—and passengers disembarked. However, there are also cases, other than those mentioned where the ship sunk, where fire at sea necessitated evacuation of the ship. For example, Regency Cruises' *Regent Star* twice had fires that required evacuation: in 1990, while on the Delaware River on its way to Philadelphia, and in 1995, while in Prince William Sound in Alaska; and Carnival Cruise Line's *Celebration* evacuated passengers in 1995 after drifting for two days, three hundred and seventy miles south of Miami, following an engine room fire that resulted in loss of all power.

Unfortunately, some fires on cruise ships have resulted in casualties among passengers and among crew. One of the most deadly fires on a cruise ship occurred in 1990 when the *Scandinavian Star* caught fire while in the North Sea and 159 passengers perished. Though the cause of the fire was suspected to be arson, there were complaints by passengers of rotten lifeboats and of missing or insufficient fire alarms. Curiously, this same ship had two prior fires. In 1988, it sustained a fire that required evacuation of the ship and which caused more than $3.5 million in damage. Four years earlier, under the name *Scandinavian Sea*, the ship was evacuated because of fire, and it took more than forty-five hours to put the fire out. This same ship, sailing under the name *Discovery I* in 1996, again experienced an engine room fire that disabled the ship. It was towed to Freeport, Bahamas, the port from which it had just left. There were no injuries in this case.

The same company that operated the *Scandinavian Star* also experienced a deadly fire in 1984 aboard the *Scandinavian Sun*. The fire, which killed one crew member and one passenger and which injured 62, was attributed to human error. According to the report issued by the National Transportation Safety Board:

> *...the probable cause...was the crew's failure to tighten a threaded pipe fitting...which allowed the fitting to vibrate free and oil to spray from the line which ignited when it contacted the hot exhaust manifold of the engine. Contributing to the spread of the fire...was failure of the crew...to keep closed the watertight door and self-closing fire door between the engineering spaces and the accommodation spaces. Also contributing to the spread of the fire was a delay in closing the automatic fire doors and stopping the ventilation system because a watch was not maintained in the pilothouse where the alarms and fire detection cabinets are located.*

The most serious fire on a cruise ship in U.S. waters occurred in 1996 aboard Commodore Cruise Line's *Universe Explorer* while en route from Juneau to Glacier Bay, Alaska. Though the cause of the fire was never determined—leading some to speculate that it was a case of arson— it began in the main laundry. Dense smoke and heat quickly spread upward to a deck on which crew quarters were located, leaving some seafarers trapped in their cabins for up to five hours. They had to wait until they heard rescuers in the passageway and then pounded on the door to attract attention. Five crew members died from smoke inhalation, and 55 crew members and one passenger were injured.

An investigation by the United States Coast Guard found that passengers were left unattended at abandon-ship stations for up to seven hours, and many complained they were not informed of what was happening. It also found that there appeared to be "no coordinated search plan" for passengers or seafarers, and that crew members searching for missing crew apparently did not have breathing apparatus to protect them while entering smoke-filled passageways.

A subsequent investigation by the National Transportation Safety Board attributed the cause of the accident to a lack of effective oversight by the cruise line and V-Ships—the company contracted to manage the ship. The NTSB suggested that the companies allowed physical conditions and operating procedures to exist that compromised the fire safety of the *Universe Explorer*. Factors that contributed to the loss of life and injuries include: the lack of sprinkler systems, the lack of automatic local-sounding fire alarms, and the rapid spread of smoke through open doors. The Board also raised as major concern the adequacy of shipboard communications, and the ability of crew to effectively communicate in English with passengers.

Two issues raised by the fire aboard the *Universe Explorer* continue to be current today. In several of the recent emergencies on Carnival Cruise Lines' ships, passengers have complained about the adequacy of crew members to communicate clearly and effectively. They have expressed concern about confusion, but also simply about the ability to understand information being given by crew. This is an area that has continued to receive attention in inspections by the United States Coast Guard. In June 1998, Coast Guard inspectors cancelled two cruises of Commodore Cruise Line's *Enchanted Isle* because they found the crew was unable to communicate effectively. Inspectors also cited crew members' failure to effectively conduct fire and boat drills, and that the public address system was inaudible in several locations and several fire screen doors did not work.

Fire and smoke alarms is the other matter that continues to be controversial. The fire on the *Universe Explorer* renewed calls by the National Transportation Safety Board for alarms that sound in passenger cabins. Only recently has the cruise industry dropped its opposition to smoke alarms that sound in passenger cabins.

Agencies of the United States Government have been successful on other issues. Following a 1991 fire that broke out in a lounge on the Royal Caribbean Cruise Line vessel *Sovereign of the Seas* while docked at San Juan, the U.S. Coast Guard presented eight new proposals on passenger ship safety to the International Maritime Organization. The proposals were based on testimony heard from passengers and crew. Particular criticism was directed at problems with the on board self-contained breathing apparatus oxygen bottles used by fire fighters, failure of the ship to notify the Coast Guard or the fire brigade in San Juan until four hours after the fire broke out and only after passengers had abandoned ship, and failure to have passengers evacuated quickly and by taking their place at their assigned abandon-ship stations.

It is unfortunate, but it is only after accidents that sensitivity is raised to the full range of safety issues and safety concerns. This is not to suggest that cruise ships are unsafe, nor that cruise lines do not value safety. It does suggest, however, that safety is a goal which has economic cost to achieve, and that cruise lines, because they are in business to earn money, attempt to find a balance between the ideal of safety and the reality of costs associated with reaching this ideal.

## Collisions and Near Misses

The least frequent type of accident, but potentially the most devastating, involves a collision. As with other accidents, these events are often associated with human error.

There have been a number of very minor collisions where a ship has struck a pier. In 1997, Regal Cruises' *Regal Empress* ran into the pier at St. Andrews, New Brunswick (near St. John) causing a large gash in the hull and damaging an onboard water tank, and in 1998, Royal Caribbean Cruise Lines' *Rhapsody of the Seas* hit the pier in Curacao causing a seven meter hole above the water line. In neither case were there any injuries. Temporary repairs were made on the spot and the ships continued on their planned itinerary.

There have also been minor collisions attributed to weather conditions or equipment failure. In 1989, the *Viking Princess* rammed a Navy vessel in port when its steering mechanism failed. In 1991, Regency Cruises' Regent Sea and Princess Cruises' *Island Princess* collided in strong winds while both were at Skagway, Alaska. The Regent Sea had the steel hull plating on its stern ripped. The *Island Princess* suffered a fifty-foot gash thirty feet above the water line, causing eleven cabins to be exposed. And in the summer of 2000, the *QE II* suffered some scratches and dents in a three-ship incident in New York harbour. The collision was attributed to high winds.

Unfortunately, there have also been some serious collisions. In 1989, Carnival Cruise Lines' *Celebration* collided with a Cuban cement freighter twenty-five miles northeast of Cuba. While no one was injured on the cruise ship, three on the Cuban vessel died and thirteen were injured. Though it was unable to complete a full investigation because of noncooperation from Carnival Cruise Lines, the National Transportation Safety Board did find that no one was monitoring the radar on the bridge of the *Celebration*.

In 1992, there were two collisions involving a cruise ship. In April, Hapag Lloyd's *Europa* collided with a containership one hundred and eighty miles off Hong Kong. No passengers were seriously hurt, but both ships were disabled. Blame for the accident was shared by the officer on watch on each ship. An inquiry determined that they had failed to maintain sufficient safe distance from one another and that they had drawn erroneous conclusions from data provided by their radar. Later that year, the *Royal Pacific*, while cruising in the Indian Ocean, collided with a fishing vessel and sank from the damage. Two were confirmed dead in the accident, but between 30 and 100 people were declared missing.

A year later, Holland America Line's *Noordam* collided with a freighter in the Gulf of Mexico. There were no injuries but there was substantial damage. The National Transportation Safety Board did not undertake a full investigation of the accident because (like the collision involving the *Celebration* several years earlier) officers on the Holland America ship refused to cooperate, claiming that the accident occurred outside U.S. waters and the U.S. therefore had no jurisdiction.

Several years later, in 1997, Carnival Cruise Line's *Jubilee* was involved in a middle of the night near-miss with a fishing vessel off the California coast. While there were no injuries, passengers complained of being awakened at 2 AM by a severe jolt—most likely the evasive action taken by the ship.

There had been another near-miss one year earlier, but this one had the potential for a much more disastrous outcome. The event involved Holland America Line's *Statendam* and its near-collision in 1996 with a barge carrying eighty thousand litres of propane and pallets of dynamite. The barge was traversing Discovery Passage on the west coast of British Columbia as the *Statendam* entered the Passage from Johnstone Strait on its voyage back to Vancouver. According to an investigation by the Transportation Safety Board of Canada, if not for evasive action taken by the barge, the two vessels would have undoubtedly collided.

Cause for the incident was attributed to several factors. Because it was running behind schedule, the *Statendam* was traveling at a higher rate of speed than allowed and as a result took a wider turn than was normal as it moved from Johnstone Strait to Discovery Passage. In addition, the Board faulted the pilot for his lack of familiarity with the navigational systems on the *Statendam*, and faulted those on the bridge for failing to share the workload and tasks of navigation and communication in accordance with accepted principles of bridge resource management. Most disconcerting is that the officer on watch did not challenge the pilot's handling of the vessel when it became apparent that the *Statendam* was not turning quickly enough to follow her preplanned course, and no member of the bridge team gave continuous undivided attention to the approach of the barge to determine the risk of collision, even though the information was available through navigational aids.

The reality of collisions was likely brought to the awareness of many in the summer of 1999, following the collision in the English Channel between Norwegian Cruise Line's *Norwegian Dream* and the containership *Ever Decent*. The collision caused considerable damage to the *Norwegian Dream*, resulting in it being pulled from service for two months for repairs, and a fire broke out among the containers, some including dangerous cargo, on the *Ever Decent*. It took more than thirty-six hours to contain the fire and the toxic smoke it produced. No one was seriously hurt on either ship, but passengers on the *Norwegian Dream* were quite shaken, being awakened by the crash in the early morning hours of the day they were to disembark.

As with other accidents, the cause of the collision between the *Norwegian Dream* and *Ever Decent* was attributed to human error. According to an investigation completed by the Bahamian Government—they were responsible for the investigation because the *Norwegian Dream* is Bahamian-registered—much of the blame is given to the officer on watch on the *Norwegian Dream*. As stated in the report: "It seems that during the period immediately before the collision he became confused about the exact situation around him," and his bridge practice fell short of the ideal in several areas. While he relied heavily on the use of radar for his anti-collision work, he did few visual checks and did not make the most effective use of the radar data provided. In addition, he appeared to ignore warnings of the collision, contrary to company policy he was the only officer on watch at the time, and he was given responsibility for a series of clerical tasks that were in addition to his responsibility as the only officer on the bridge. Perhaps the clearest picture of the situation is provided by the recommendations made to Norwegian Cruise Lines by the Bahamian authority:

> The [officer on watch (OOW)]of the Norwegian Dream *at the time of the collision should undertake further training in radar usage. Norwegian Cruise Lines should ensure that this is carried out as soon as possible, they should also ensure that other watch keepers within their fleet are fully familiar with the bridge equipment with which they will have to deal.*

> The master of the Norwegian Dream *should draw up more explicit standing orders in accordance with the company procedure manual to clarify when the OOW should call for assistance on the bridge. Norwegian Cruise Lines should ensure that satisfactory masters orders are drawn up for all ships.*

> *Norwegian Cruise Lines should take steps to enforce and monitor the guidelines contained in their procedures manual about when watches should be doubled.*

A potentially serious accident resulting in loss of many lives was without a doubt narrowly avoided. As in the case of other events discussed above, the main cause is reduced to human error. There is no way to know whether fatigue, as discussed earlier in relation to a study done  by the International Transport Workers

Federation, was a factor. It is immaterial whether or not it was. As passengers and crew on cruise ships, we need to be aware of the risks associated with traveling on a cruise ship and do what we can to ensure that lapses in enforcement of policy and in unsafe practices or situations be raised to those responsible for ensuring that passengers and crew remain safe.

## Cruise Ships and Security

Just as the sinking of the *Titanic* directed attention to the need for adequate lifeboats for passengers on a ship, the hijacking by terrorists of the cruise ship *Achille Lauro*, when an elderly American in a wheelchair was murdered and thrown overboard, raised awareness to the need for greater security. A year later, in 1986, the International Maritime Organization adopted "Measures to Prevent Unlawful Acts Against Passengers and Crews On Board Ships." However, these measures were not part of SOLAS, so they were totally voluntary and they had no legal force.

In 1987, the United States Coast Guard put forth its own "Voluntary Guidelines for Cruise Ship and Terminal Security," which were patterned after the measures adopted by the International Maritime Organization. However, based on a perception that many of the measures were being ignored or only partially implemented, the Coast Guard proposed in 1994 its plans for a set of mandatory regulations on security for passenger vessels and passenger terminals. The position taken by the Coast Guard was that cruise ships and cruise lines should maintain the highest level of security at all times. Despite the high cost associated with its proposal, the Coast Guard asserted that the benefits would far outweigh the costs. Regardless, the cruise industry opposed the guidelines on the basis that they were "too stringent and inflexible," and expressed its concerns through formal comments to the U.S. Government.

Opposition to the initial proposal led to a revised set of rules that were implemented in 1996. The Coast Guard conceded to a system where three different levels of security would be imposed based on assessment of the level of risk. At the lowest level were nine mandatory standard measures for all cruise ships home ported at, or calling at, ports in the United States. These include denial to boarding of unauthorized visitors, photographic identification cards for seafarers, metal-detector screening of all boarding passengers, random inspection of hand-carried baggage and ship's stores, and restricted access to the ship's bridge, engine room, and radio room. When there is medium risk of a terrorist attack, cruise lines are required to search at least half of all ship's stores and embarking passengers and their carry-on baggage, and must also provide passengers with photo identification cards. At the highest level of risk, all passengers and their carry-on baggage must be checked, as well as all luggage that is checked-in. In addition, the targeted cruise ship could bypass any scheduled port of call where terrorists were expected to strike.

While these rules were developed in accordance with guidelines from the International Maritime Organization, they were mandatory rather than voluntary. Anyone who has been on a cruise in the past several years will recognize many of the provisions that have been implemented. Most notable is the introduction of the A-PASS or a similar system on almost every cruise ship. The A-PASS was first introduced to North American cruisers by Princess Cruises in 1998, and since that time it has been adopted by other cruise lines.

A-PASS (Automated Personnel Assisted Security Screening) is an electronic vessel access security system that provides high speed, interactive photo identification and access control screening of passengers and crew as they enter and exit a ship. Prior to entering a ship, passengers stop at a kiosk and insert their combination room key, shipboard credit card, and identification card. A camera within the kiosk will take their photograph and will store the photo in the ship's computer. Each time a passenger exits or enters the ship, they insert the card into a kiosk located near the ship's gangway and their time of entry or exit is recorded. As well, the safety officer stationed at the gangway confirms that the card belongs to the person using it by matching the photograph on the computer with the person as they enter or exit the ship. The system also allows the ship to know, at any point in time, who is on board the ship and who is off. In concert with the automated locks on cabins that record each entry to and exit from a cabin, and the increasing use of surveillance cameras throughout the ship, a cruise line is able to maintain current knowledge of the comings and goings of most passengers.

These sophisticated systems however are still at the mercy of human error. For example, in July 2000 a nine-year old autistic boy wandered onto Carnival Cruise Line's *Sensation* while it was visiting New Orleans as part of a seven day cruise from Tampa. He was somehow able to get past customs officials and ship employees, boarding the ship with a woman who had a group of children. The woman showed her identification card, said the children were with her, and they were allowed to pass. It wasn't until midnight that crew realized that the youngster was not part of any group and they began the process of trying to identify him. This was made more difficult because he was uncommunicative, was carrying no identification, and the missing person report filed with the New Orleans police had been misplaced. The child was taken into custody by authorities when the ship reached Tampa, two days later, and was reunited with his mother the following day.

Two months later, a woman was reported missing from Princess Cruises' *Dawn Princess* on its Alaska itinerary. The room steward, who found when he entered to clean her room that she likely hadn't slept in the bed, reported her absence. Because the A-PASS system did not show that she had disembarked, the Coast Guard was noti-fied and a search was undertaken with the presumption that she had fallen overboard between 4:30 PM the afternoon before and 8:30 AM that morning. A day later she had been found at her home in Michigan. She had left the ship when it was in Juneau because of a disagreement with her traveling companion. While this case, and that with the autistic child, are likely anomalous events, they demonstrate that security systems, like ship safety, is dependent on the work of people as much as technology.

## How About the Security of Individuals Once They Are On Board?

The focus on security has tended to be more concerned with the security of the ship and of passengers as a group. However, there does not appear to be the same vigilance with the security of individuals once they are on a cruise ship. This is reflected in the frequency of reports of sexual (and sometimes physical) assaults on cruise ships. Though Tim Gallagher, a spokesperson for Carnival Cruise Line, has stated numerous times over the past decade the belief that "cruise ships are as safe an environment as you can find," this is small consolation to the victim of a sexual assault. The statement is also troubling because while passengers are likely to be cau-tious in dealing with other passengers, they are not likely to consider the need to pro-tect themselves from employees of the company they have paid for their vacation.

The issue of sexual assaults on cruise ships reached public awareness in 1999, when Carnival Cruise Line admitted—as part of the discovery process in a law suit involving an alleged rape—that it had received one hundred and eight com-plaints of sexual assaults involving a crew member in the five-year period ending August 1998. This number includes twenty-two rapes—sixteen rapes of passengers by crew and six rapes in which one crew member assaulted another. There were fifty-eight sexual assaults reported on Royal Caribbean Cruise Line's ships during the same five-year period. In none of the twenty-two cases involving forcible rape on Carnival Cruise Line has the perpetrator been successfully prosecuted. The reasons for this will be discussed later.

Unfortunately, it is difficult to get a full picture of the problem because cruise lines keep a tight lid on the information, and victims who have settled with cruise lines are generally required to keep silent about the incident. However, it appears that sexual assaults were at least as common in the late 1980s as they are today, and that children are among those who are at risk. In a statement made in 1990, a spokesper-son for the Major Crimes Section of the U.S. Attorney's office indicated there was a pattern: those at greatest risk are "...women under twenty-one, alone and outside their cabins when attacked, on cruises less than a week long. Most passenger complaints involve a crew member, though not an officer."[1] These comments reflected complaints received by the FBI office in Miami. In 1988 and 1989, it had received twenty-eight complaints alleging violent crimes (involving all cruise lines). Seventeen complaints led to a formal investigation by the FBI, including twelve into reported rapes. In 1995, U.S. Justice Department figures indicated that one in three crimes reported at sea is the crime of rape.

## Children Are at Risk

Though it wasn't the first incident in which a complaint of rape was raised to Carnival Cruise Line, the first time a crew-member actually went to trial was in February 1990. The case involved the rape in August 1989 of a fourteen-year-old girl on the *Carnivale*. According to testimony at the trial, as the ship was returning to Miami from the Bahamas, the fourteen-year-old girl went to the family's cabin (while other family members remained on deck) at 5:30 A.M. to check on a suitcase. While she was in the elevator, a male crew member—a cleaner on board the ship—kissed and fondled her. He then dragged her from the elevator to a cleaning closet and raped her on the floor. The thirty-two year old crewman, a Colombian national and father of two, was picked out of a line up by the girl, and was ultimately found guilty of the charges and sentenced to thirty years in prison.

At the time, the case received considerable attention because it was the first to actually go to court. As stated by Thomas Fitzgerald of the U.S. Attorney's Major Crimes Section, "Very few of these cases occur in U.S. jurisdiction, and very few develop into prosecutable cases." The simple fact is that because all major cruise lines sailing from U.S. ports are foreign registered and largely are staffed by foreign officers and crews, once the ship is at sea the passengers are essentially in foreign territory.

Though there are some safeguards in place—the FBI and Coast Guard have the authority to investigate and prosecute alleged crimes in international waters involving U.S. citizens, and the International Maritime Organization's "Measure to Prevent Unlawful Acts Against Passengers and Crews on Board Ships" requires that the operator of a vessel report each unlawful act—until 1999 there was ambiguity about the definition of "unlawful" and cruise lines tended to avoid reporting physical and sexual assaults. In addition:

> *Cruise ships are required to report only crimes and other incidents that result in serious physical injury, which does not necessarily include rape. "Unless otherwise required to do so, Carnival leaves it to the individual to decide to report to authorities," said Curtis Mase, a lawyer for Carnival.* [2]

Since the case in 1990, there have been additional cases reported in the media that have involved children. In 1991, a twelve-year-old girl was fondled in the elevator of Carnival Cruise Line's *Jubilee*. The perpetrator was never found. In 1992, a fifteen-year-old girl was raped on Windjammer Cruises' *Fantome*. At the time, none of the cabins had doors that locked, so the crewman easily gained entry. An article in 1995 reported an incident in which a crewman who broke into the cabin they were sharing raped two girls under the age of ten. A year earlier, in 1994, a crewman on Dolphin Cruises' *Seabreeze I* molested a thirteen-year-old boy. In both the latter cases, the offender was identified, but it is unclear whether they were ever prosecuted for the crime.

Between 1995 and 2000, the media reported at least eight other cases involving children: a sixteen-year-old girl celebrating her birthday was raped on Royal Caribbean Cruise Line's *Monarch of the Seas* after striking up a conversation with a bartender who later was her attacker; a fourteen and a sixteen-year-old girl were both raped, in separate incidents several weeks apart in 1996, by the same crewman aboard Carnival Cruise Line's *Fascination*—the latter case only came to light because of publicity from the first; a thirteen-year-old child was the victim of an attempted sexual assault by a thirty-year-old passenger in 1997 aboard Premier Cruises' *Atlantica*; a fifteen-year-old boy was molested in 1998 by a bartender on a Royal Caribbean Cruise Line ship after he was served more than a dozen glasses of champagne and then taken to an empty cabin where he was stripped and sexually assaulted; and in 1999 a thirteen-year-old girl was assaulted by a waiter aboard Celebrity's Cruises' *Galaxy*, and a twelve-year-old boy was molested by a kitchen steward aboard a ship belonging to Norwegian Cruise Lines. In October 2000, a thirty-year-old youth coordinator on Norwegian Cruise Line's *Norway* was arrested and charged with sexually assaulting a twelve-year-old girl who had come with him to his cabin.

As can be seen, these attacks on children are not limited to any single cruise line. Though insensitive as a line of defence, in the case involving the sixteen-year-old raped on her birthday, Royal Caribbean Cruise Lines suggested that the girl's parents were to blame because they had failed to exercise reasonable care in protecting their daughter. While this comment is actually somewhat instructive, it is inconsistent with Royal Caribbean's "New Adventure Ocean Dining Program" which was introduced in December 2000. Children sailing on any Royal Caribbean International ship (of which there are 120,000 per year) can now eat dinner with their favourite youth staff. The service is offered three times on a seven day cruise.

Many parents let their children run free when they are on a cruise ship, feeling there is nothing to fear. However, the reality is that they must treat the ship much as they would any urban setting. As expressed by an FBI agent in Miami, "Even out at sea, you can't let your guard down." It isn't a matter that assaults of children are overly common, but they do happen and children and parents must use caution. There is certainly greater risk than is suggested by a comment made in 1999 by Carnival Cruise Line's attorney Curtis Mase:

> *If you look at the statistics, what they really bear out is that you have an incredibly diminished or smaller number of instances on the ships than you do just out in the world.*[3]

## It Isn't Just Children

Sexual assaults are not limited to children. Though as with children, it is difficult to get a clear picture of the problem because it is so well concealed. The admissions by Carnival Cruise Line and Royal Caribbean Cruise Line to one hundred and sixty-six sexual assaults between them—an average of 33 per year—are an indication that they happen. But there are only a few cases that have been reported in the media.

An early glimpse of the problem is found in a letter to the editor of the Los Angeles Times in 1991. Written by a forty year old woman who had recently returned from a cruise with her mother, she warns single women about what is in store for them on a cruise.

> *The second day of our cruise I went to our cabin to get a sweater...While on the way to our cabin, our room steward saw me and opened the door for me. He was pleasant and talking to me and came into the cabin. He asked if we could meet for drinks and to talk. To avoid the issue, I told him I would have to think about it. I made a point of never going to my cabin alone again.*

> *At dinner the same evening a waiter from another table came over to talk. He told me he walked each evening at a certain place and at a certain time. The implications were so clear that my mother and another diner at our table who had heard him were amazed.*

> *Every day my mother and I had our lunch at the same buffet. The young man handing out the trays on the third day of the voyage asked me if I was busy that night. I said yes. He asked every day after that.*

Sometimes it is just harassment, but sometimes it goes further. In 1990, a passenger with Carnival Cruise Line accused her cabin steward of entering her cabin while she was asleep. He climbed on top of her and fondled her, but was scared away when the woman and her roommate both began screaming. The woman reported the incident to the safety officer, but nothing happened. In 1992, a thirty-one year old woman traveling on Carnival Cruise Line's *Festivale* claimed that a waiter had snuck into her cabin while she was getting dressed in the bathroom. According to a report the woman filed with the police in Barbados:

> *I asked him what he was doing in here. He pinned my back against the closet and then started kissing me. I told him 'Don't,' and he continued kissing me. The next thing I knew...my pants were down.* [4]

Nothing came of the investigation by the Barbados police, and neither the woman nor Carnival contacted the FBI. However, the woman did launch a suit against Carnival Cruise Lines. It would appear that the case was settled out of court.

In June 1997, a thirty-five-year old woman aboard Royal Caribbean Cruise Line's *Majesty of the Seas* complained she was raped after returning from the night-club at 4:00 A.M., where she had consumed only a non-alcoholic beverage. She testi-fied in court that: "I put my key into the slot to open the door. I put one foot in and was pushed from behind." She had been attacked by a member of the cleaning crew, and picked him out of a line-up conducted by the ship's security officers. Questioned by the ship's security officer and a company lawyer who had flown in, the worker "...denied being anywhere near a passenger, saying he had been washing decks at 4:00 in the morning. When asked about scratches on his body, he said they were from minor work accidents." He was indicted, and as his trial approached DNA evidence linked him to the assault. He switched his story and his lawyers argued that the woman had consented to sex. They also brought out the fact that the woman had filed for bankruptcy just before going on the cruise and suggested that the suit against Royal Caribbean Cruise Line had been planned. A jury acquitted the alleged attacker after four hours of deliberation.

In 1998, there were two cases reported against Carnival Cruise Lines. In one, a woman on a Caribbean cruise with her husband accused a waiter of drugging their dinner drinks and later raping her in their cabin as her husband lay unconscious. The couple complained to cruise officials, who responded in part by moving them to a better cabin for the remainder of the cruise. The case was settled just before it was set to go to trial. In another case, a woman named Mary, from Georgia, claimed she had been raped. She was traveling with her mother, Janice, shortly after her father's death and shortly after experiencing a miscarriage. According to her story:

> On the night the ship left port, a cabin steward...carried the women's bags to their room. He questioned Janice about Mary. "He asked if she was married and did I think she liked him," Janice recalls. "He kind of gave me the creeps." Later [the steward] returned and knocked. He said he needed some papers signed so the women could use the room's safe. Janice left to explore the ship.

> Then, Mary claims...[he] made his intentions known. Violently. She asserts...[he] pushed her down on one of the beds and raped her. She reported the incident immediately to ship personnel, who questioned [the steward]. He denied the charge. [5]

The disposition of that case is not known.

In 2000, two young women on separate cruises reported being raped by the same 30-year-old employee on Premier Cruises' *Seabreeze*. In one case, the passenger was returning to the disco from her cabin. She asked a crew member for directions and he proceeded to lead her down a dead end and sexually assaulted her. Though the crew member was immediately fired and confined to his cabin, he was not turned over to U.S. authorities when the ship returned to Boston. Also in 2000, a forty-year-old woman was raped in a restroom aboard the *SeaEscape* by another passenger. Her attacker was not found.

There are also cases that have more severe outcomes. In 1993, a sixty-two year-old woman on the Seawind Cruise Line's *Seawind Crown* was strangled to death following a failed rape attempt when she was using a public toilet at 9:00 AM. The two crewmen were caught because they were seen throwing the body overboard as the ship left the harbour in Aruba. They were detained and went to trial in Aruba.

In 1997, a twenty-nine-year-old woman on Celebrity Cruises' *Galaxy* was pursued by an engineer and eventually became involved in an affair with the man. Within seven months, she separated from her husband and in August 1998, she moved to Greece to live with the man. In January 1999, she was murdered and dismembered following an argument in which she threatened to return to the United States. Though this type of event is quite uncommon, it does point to a culture on cruise ships with regard to crew and officer attitudes about female passengers.

Though cruise lines have policies that prohibit crew from fraternizing with passengers, there are not similar policies as regards officers and staff. In fact, officers are in many cases urged to socialize with passengers. However, "socializing" is subject to different interpretations, and in many cases it isn't limited to a drink and dance. According to a woman who had worked for five years on a cruise ship:

*Some officers were notorious womanizers. In my first weeks at sea, I was so naive that I actually visited an officer's cabin and admired his photos of his beautiful blond sister—before realizing that she was really his wife.*

*I got wise. Others didn't. One passenger had been swept off her feet, on an earlier cruise, by a chief engineer...and though he was no longer with the company, she always insisted on being seated, for nostalgic reasons, at the chief [engineer]'s table in the dining room.*

*Officers usually relished female attention, but a few had to dodge unwanted advances. One engineer locked himself in his cabin for an entire cruise to avoid a young woman he had wooed on a previous sailing; she had returned with her mother, who was talking marriage. As an escape trick, some officers would arrange in advance to be paged at a certain time. "My beeper," they'll tell a lovesick lady as they dashed off the dance floor. "Duty calls."*[6]

Despite policies prohibiting crew from socializing with passengers, they are often ignored. There are many cases of consensual relationships involving passengers and crew. Only when there is an attack or a complaint are policies prohibiting these contacts apparently enforced. According to a musician who worked for both Carnival Cruise Line and Royal Caribbean Cruise Line, "Sex between crew and passengers happens all the time. Every cruise, every day. Crew go into guest cabins and guests go to crew cabins. Both seek it out, passengers and crew."[7] A bartender employed by Carnival Cruise Line suggests that crew members make a sport of having sex with passengers. It is simply part of the game.

## Female crew are also victims

The case that brought attention to sexual assaults on cruise ships involved a twenty-seven-year-old nurse who had been employed by Carnival Cruise Line for three years. She had claimed that she had been raped and sodomized in August 1998 by the ship's engineer, allegedly an experienced sexual predator, while working on the *Imagination*. She immediately reported the incident and the engineer was promptly fired. However, his firing was not because of the rape, but instead because he had been drinking within six hours of going on duty and for being tardy. He was sent back to his native Italy as soon as the ship reached the Port of Miami, even before the FBI had initiated an investigation. The nurse filed a suit against Carnival Cruise Line. The case was settled fifteen months later, less than two weeks before its scheduled trial.

Unfortunately, this woman's case is not altogether uncommon. What is uncommon is that she had the ability to speak up. Very often, the victim is among those crew with the least ability to speak up or to risk their employment. Consider the following account from a woman working as a bar waitress:

> Nick, the bar manager, turned out to be nothing but a constant source of trouble. On the second night aboard, he approached Barbara about going to bed with him. She tactfully declined his crude advances—Nick kept up his disgusting pursuit of Barbara. We had a rough time. He was a disgusting creep who just wouldn't leave us alone, and he was our boss.
>
> When I left that ship, I finally had a phone conversation with the owner. He only laughed at me and said I was wasting his time....
>
> I was very lucky that I had the money to get myself out of the rotten situation, but there are many who are not as fortunate. They have to stay and make the best of it because they have families to support and that is the weakness which this disreputable cruise line exploits.

In an article based on her five years at sea, a young woman whose job it was to produce the ship's daily newspaper tells similar stories. She recounts an officer who refused to take no for an answer, and who chased a female crew member so relentlessly that she signed off in tears at a remote port in Alaska.

A fifty-four-year-old woman who worked at the ship's gift shop on Crystal Cruises' *Crystal Harmony* tells similar stories. In 1998, she initiated a lawsuit against Crystal Cruises, claiming that the company allowed a sexually charged atmosphere and that she had been fired for refusing the captain's advances. She says that from the start, she saw that parties and love affairs were common among crew members:

> But more disturbing, she said, was how the ship's top brass hit on stewardesses and other lower-ranking crew members....One ship stewardess confided....that she was "stressed" over sleeping with thirty-one crew members. And she heard that an officer tried to hang himself after finding his girlfriend in bed with the ship's doctor...She also said she once encountered the captain and a stewardess in a sex act below deck.[9]

*The woman claims that she was forced to engage in sex with the captain, for fear that if she refused she would lose her job. She characterized the cruise ship as a more blatant sexually promiscuous environment than she had ever seen, and suggests that, "The officers and captain think they can take liberty with anyone....It's quite amazing....Nobody wants to complain, because they would lose their job."*

## How are Complaints of An Assault Handled?

As already seen, there are cases of sexual assault that are disclosed. As well, there has been recent attention to how cruise lines have dealt with these assaults. This attention led four companies (Carnival Corporation, Royal Caribbean Cruises Limited, Crystal Cruises, and Princess Cruises) to sign a letter, under the auspices of the International Council of Cruise Lines, that pledged zero tolerance of crime on cruise ships and a commitment to report all crimes involving U.S. citizens to the FBI. Time will tell the degree to which this pledge changes practices that appeared to be common.

A 1998 New York Times article describes the pattern that was common at that time. Based on examination of court records and on interviews with cruise line employees, law enforcement officials, and passengers and their lawyers, the article suggests:

*...a pattern of cover-ups that often began as soon as the crime was reported at sea, in international waters where the only police are the ship's security officers. Accused crew members are sometimes put ashore at the next port, with airfare to their home country. Industry lawyers are flown to the ship to question the accusers; and aboard ships flowing with liquor, counterclaims of consensual sex are common. The cruise lines aggressively contest lawsuits and insist on secrecy as a condition of settling.[10]*

According to a former chief of security for Carnival Cruise Line:

*You don't notify the FBI. You don't notify anybody. You start giving the victims bribes, upgrading their cabins, giving them champagne and trying to ease them off the ship until the legal department can take over. Even when I knew there was a crime, I was supposed to go in there and do everything in the world to get Carnival to look innocent.[11]*

Once a crime is reported, there are problems with preserving evidence—cabins are routinely cleaned twice a day, so much evidence is destroyed very quickly, and there is often a delay between an attack and a landing at a U.S. port. Rape experts suggest that cases reported within seventy-two hours provide the best forensic evidence, but this time frame is often difficult for attacks on a cruise ship. In addition, many victims are likely to delay making a report as long as they are aboard a ship because of fear of reprisal and because there is no independent investigator or rape-treatment centre. Simply put, rapes on cruise ships are often not reported until it is too late for criminal investigation.

The fear of reprisal may sound unrealistic to many. However, it is quite real. Though not anything as serious as a sexual assault, on a transatlantic cruise in 2000, I approached a bartender on the *Radisson Diamond* about the type and volume of music being played around the pool, all day, every day. I politely asked that the music be turned down, or in the case of rap music it be turned off. For the next fourteen days on the ship, I was subjected to aggressive and abusive behaviour from this bartender, including snide remarks every time he would walk by. I also experienced reduced service from those who were his friends also working at the bar. I raised the matter to senior management, and was told that this employee had been a problem in the past, but the behaviour not only didn't stop, it became more passive aggressive. This reprisal was simply for asking that I not be subjected to rap music while sitting by the ship's pool. Similarly, on Seabourn Cruise Line's *Seabourn Goddess I*, my wife and I received an explicitly threatening telephone call in our cabin following expression of service concerns to the ship's management. The management conveyed our concerns, but also told the offending crew exactly who had expressed the concerns. It is difficult to imagine the potential harassment that would have been forthcoming had either of these situations been as serious as an assault. In my situation, the basic attitude of both cruise lines appeared to be that it is easier to find a new passenger than it is to find a new bartender or a new dining room waiter.

In those cases where a sexual assault is reported in a timely manner, victims and prosecutors are faced with the common practice of cruise lines to immediately send the accused back home, purportedly because they have violated company policies that prohibit fraternizing between passengers and crew. Reporters for the *Miami New Times* found that in each of five lawsuits against Carnival Cruise Line they reviewed, the employee was swept out of the country immediately after the ship arrived in port. In one case, the employee, Hitesh Panchal, was later rehired by the company, and was subsequently served with a summons while at the dock in Los Angeles. However:

> *Carnival's lawyers continued to protect Panchal. They filed a motion arguing the Indian couldn't be sued in U.S. court because American laws do not apply to him; not only is he a foreigner, the company argued, but the alleged crime took place in Barbados on a ship registered in Panama. The move was successful. Although Palm Beach County Circuit Court Judge Kathleen Kroll denied Carnival's motion to dismiss, the Fourth District Court of Appeal overturned the decision and dismissed the case against Panchal....Although the suit against Carnival remained: the company later settled the case for an undisclosed amount.* [12]

It remains to be seen whether these patterns continue under the new "zero tolerance" pledge. Regardless, each of these cases suggests that passengers need to protect themselves and to treat a cruise ship like any other unknown environment. They need to be aware of risks, and take precautions so that they are not left alone and vulnerable.

## Sometimes Security is Also The Responsibility of The Passenger

One additional security concern is with prevention of accidents involving an individual. Because only the most extreme incidents appear to be reported, it is very difficult to get a picture of the problem. For example, in 1994, a fourteen-year-old boy on Royal Caribbean Cruise Line's *Majesty of the Seas* drank himself to death. He became involved in a party with eight others—six of them under eighteen, one eighteen, and one twenty-four years of age—and in two hours drank six tumblers of tequila and rum which had been supplied by the twenty-four-year-old passenger. The boy returned to his cabin at 5:00 AM. His parents called for medical assistance when he stopped breathing six hours later. Resuscitation efforts failed and the boy was pronounced dead. His blood alcohol level was 0.29, between three and six times the legal threshold for intoxication.

There have also been some freak accidents, sometimes involving crew and sometimes involving passengers. For example, in 1991, two crew members were killed and five were injured on Regency Cruises' *Regent Sun* when the cable holding a lifeboat broke during a drill and the men were thrown into the water. The following year, a similar accident occurred on the *Regent Star* when a lifeboat fell and killed one crewman. Investigators ruled that the lifeboats were unsafe and that the death constituted homicide. And in 1998, a lifeboat fell twice while being raised aboard Celebrity Cruises' *Zenith*, killing one crew member.

There have also been freak accidents involving loading ramps. In 1994, one passenger was killed and 5 injured when the gangway leading to Clipper Cruise Line's *Yorktown Clipper* broke from its supports and fell. And in 1999, a loading ramp on the *Queen of the West* fell, killing one passenger.

More commonly, accidents involving tenders occur when passengers are transiting from the ship to a port. In January 1998, former baseball star Eddie Mathews filed suit against Carnival Cruise Line, claiming permanent disablement after falling from one of the cruise line's tenders.

> *Mathews broke a hip, fractured his spine and had more than one stroke as a result of the accident which happened when the tender moved away just as Mathews was stepping on to a pier in Grand Cayman....[He] fell between the pier and the tender and, while hanging between them, was crushed when the tender swung back toward him. Carnival is contesting the suit, alleging the accident was Mathews' fault.*

Eddie Mathews died February, 18, 2001.

In September 1999, a seventy-nine-year-old man filed a similar suit against Royal Caribbean Cruise Line after he fell into the water when going from the *Legend of the Seas* to the tender. The passenger claims he sustained serious and permanent injuries in the fall, which occurred when the tender moved away from the gangplank just as he was stepping on to the tender.

These two cases give a clear sense of why cruise lines have become increasingly cautious about the use of tenders and about passengers' use of the tender service. They also underline the need for passengers to use their own caution and good judgment when having to rely on a tender to get to port.

Still another type of accident involves the pools on cruise ships. Though most cruise lines have a policy of placing safety nets over outside swimming pools during the night, this precaution is not always taken. In January 1997, a passenger on Dolphin Cruise's *Island Breeze* died when he dived or fell into an empty swimming pool at 4:00 A.M. In December 1997, a nineteen-year-old woman drowned in the pool on Holland America Line's *Rotterdam* during a night time swim. It is assumed that the young woman bumped her head on a ladder in the darkness while swimming, lost consciousness, and drowned. Though the pool is normally covered at 9:00 P.M., on this night there had been a pool party that went later than the quitting time of the employee whose job it was to cover the pool, so he left without shutting down the pool and putting on the cover.

The distress experienced by the woman's family was increased by the way the situation was handled by staff on the cruise ship. They said that:

>...*employees on the cruise ship intentionally inflicted emotional distress by asking whether Erica had been drinking and why she had been swimming alone...[Further,] the head of security for the cruise line asked the family to sign a statement that released the company from liability in the incident. When the family refused, the head of security became upset....[In addition,] cruise line officials said [Erica]...had been diving when diving wasn't allowed....[but the family] came to find out later (from an eyewitness employed on the cruise ship) that she didn't dive into the pool.* [13]

This case is just one more instance that illustrates the need for passengers to be cautious and to look out for their own safety and security.

## Code Oscar—Person Overboard

Some of us have been on a cruise and heard "Code Oscar," which means that a person has gone overboard. Though this is not an uncommon occurrence, it is not always clear whether it is accidental or intentional. For example, in March 1996, a twenty-three-year-old college student on Carnival Cruise Line's *Celebration* fell overboard, as the ship was steaming away from San Juan, as he was urinating over the side of the ship. Fortunately for him, he was able to swim the four miles to shore. In contrast, a year before a fourteen-year-old boy jumped overboard from Princess Cruises' *Regal Princess* following an argument with his parents. He left a suicide note behind.

Between 1997 and 2000, there have been at least twelve reports of passengers and two reports of crew overboard or missing. In one of the cases involving crew, a twenty-eight-year-old woman jumped overboard because she was about to be fired; she died from her injuries. In the other case, a casino employee jumped overboard from Celebrity Cruises' *Meridian* after a fight with his lover. The attempted rescue by the ship's personnel actually failed when the lifeboat got stuck and couldn't be lowered. A young passenger jumped into the water and held the man above water until the lifeboat arrived. Passengers on the ship were upset by the incident because the well-meaning passenger was reprimanded by the ship's captain for interfering in the rescue attempt. In the first case, the woman died; in the second, the employee was successfully rescued.

The cases of passengers overboard reflect a range of backgrounds and ages. In 1998, a thirty-five-year-old physician fell over the aft railing after losing his balance while sitting or standing on a table at the outdoor restaurant on Carnival Cruise Line's *Fantasy*, and a seventy-seven-year-old man went missing from P&O's *Victoria* as it cruised off Bonaire. In 1999, a twenty-two-year-old man disappeared from the *Carnival Destiny* after he left the nightclub, and a middle aged man fell over the railing on his private balcony on the *Grand Princess* while on a cruise of the Mediterranean. In the first seven months of 2000, six men and two women, in separate incidents, jumped or fell overboard. Only in the case of a twenty-year-old man who went overboard from Royal Caribbean Cruise Line's *Nordic Empress*, twelve miles from St. Thomas, was the person successfully rescued. In the other cases, which included ships belonging to Carnival Cruise Line, Royal Caribbean Cruise Line, and Radisson Seven Seas Cruises, the passenger died. In two of these cases a body was recovered.

Perhaps the most curious case of a missing person involved a twenty-three year-old woman who disappeared from Royal Caribbean Cruise Line's *Rhapsody of the Seas* in March 1998 while vacationing with her family. According to Royal Caribbean Cruise Line, the case is undoubtedly one of suicide. However, the missing woman's parents believe otherwise. They suggest that she was happy, not suicidal, and that she was physically fit, so it is unlikely that she would have accidentally fallen overboard. The family believed that she had been abducted and was either still on the ship or she had been smuggled ashore. They suggest as support for their claim that she was last seen at 4:30 A.M., sleeping in a lounge chair on the balcony of the cabin she was sharing with her family. There was a pack of cigarettes on the table next to her and the door from the cabin to the balcony was closed. At 6:00 A.M., when the woman's father awoke, she was gone, the door was open, and her cigarettes were no longer on the table. A thorough search of the ship, and of the waters through which it traveled, turned up nothing. The family initiated a lawsuit against the cruise line. The suit was dismissed by the court as without foundation.

## Cruise Ships and Crime

Aside from the incidence of sexual assaults, crime on cruise ships tends to be quite limited. There is the occasional case of a fight between two passengers, but these generally involve younger people who are intoxicated. The most visible exception is a gay man who was badly beaten by two straight men during a Halloween cruise aboard Carnival Cruise Line's *Jubilee* in 1999. The cruise was comprised primarily of gay and lesbian passengers. The gay man claimed the beating was a hate crime, and he planned a civil rights lawsuit against the cruise line, saying that the cruise line was partly responsible because it had not warned him or other members of his group that it wasn't a totally gay cruise.

Because of their travels in the Caribbean, drug smuggling is not an uncommon crime involving cruise ships. Sometimes a crew member on board the ship hides the drug. Other times, drugs have been found in containers welded to the hull of the ship below the water line. This was the case with Regency Cruises' *Regent Sea* following its circumnavigation of South America in 1993. However, it is more common that drugs are discovered during an inspection—as was the case in 1994 on the Fiesta Marina when the captain found four kilograms of cocaine in a routine inspection of the ship, and in 1998 when twenty-five kilograms of cocaine was found on the *Pacific Princess* by inspectors at Piraeus.

Drugs are also discovered as they are being smuggled and sold ashore. In 1997, two passengers and four kitchen staff aboard Celebrity Cruises' *Century* were caught trying to smuggle twenty pounds of cocaine and forty-six pounds of hashish at Key West; in 1998, two crew members from Carnival Cruise Line's *Inspiration* were arrested at San Juan with seven and a half pounds of heroin; and in 2000, three members of the crew from Royal Caribbean Cruise Line's *Splendour of the Seas* were arrested by undercover police in Grand Cayman when they tried to sell cocaine.

A wholly different type of crime led to a seventy-three-year-old woman being arrested by police in Ketchikan, Alaska. According to Alaska Sightseeing/Cruise West, the woman was unruly and disruptive and was a potential danger to other guests. According to a local news account, the woman complained about paper napkins and accused the crew of fabricating whale sightings. She was charged with criminal trespass when she refused the Captain's orders to leave the ship. Though she was put in jail, the cruise line arranged for her bail and paid her way home. Interestingly, other cruise lines contacted by *USA Today* indicated that they would do the same in a similar situation.

Several companies in 1997 initiated policies to deal with rowdiness and unruliness of younger passengers, particularly college students during spring break. Carnival Cruise Line and Royal Caribbean Cruise Line ban passengers under twenty-one, unless they are accompanied by someone twenty-five or older. The requirement is waived in the case of a married couple. Norwegian Cruise Line and Princess Cruises require at least one person twenty-one or older in each cabin. Disney Cruises requires that persons under eighteen must bunk with someone over twenty-one.

These policies were cheered, at least until June 2000, when a twenty-four-year-old man learned at the last minute —when he read the cruise contract on the ticket—that he and his fiancée could not embark the surprise cruise he had planned to celebrate their engagement. His fiancée was twenty-years-old. The couple filed a complaint with the Miami-Dade County Equal Opportunity Board, claiming discrimination based on age and marital status. Though they lost the $2100 they had paid to Carnival Cruise Line, they changed their plans and took a cruise with Disney Cruises instead.

## How about Petty Larceny?

Though humorous at first blush, another common crime on cruise ships is the pilfering of anything not tied down. There is a case of a maid who was caught with a suitcase of silverware as she walked off the gangway of a ship, and I have watched as a passenger accumulated over the course of a cruise an entire set of napkins. However, these are somewhat petty in contrast to the descriptions given in a 1996 article appearing in the Orlando Sentinel entitled "Cruise Lines Bear Brunt of Guests' Sticky Fingers." The hotel manager aboard Carnival Cruise Line's *Sensation* is quoted as saying that disappearing towels are so common that when staterooms are prepared each Sunday for newly embarking passengers, steward captains just reflexively will put two more towels in each cabin. The company eliminated logos on its towels because these only increase the likelihood that passengers will take home souvenirs.

Royal Caribbean Cruise Line's *Sovereign of the Seas,* for example, once had Villeroy and Boch tea ware bearing the cruise line's logo. They all disappeared within two weeks.

> *For obvious reasons, virtually every line has ditched putting logos on items used on board. But being without logos doesn't make items any safer...On a Cunard trans-Atlantic voyage two elderly passengers ordered all their meals from room service, served on clearly marked fine Rosenthal china. Guess what was missing after each meal? But Cunard didn't wish to embarrass the ladies and, instead, notified customs officials. At disembarkation, a tipped-off official examined the women's suitcases. On finding the full set of china, the official asked: "And where did you buy these madam." Cunard got its china back.* [14]

The article also discusses pilfering even stranger items. For example, a melon sculpted into a chicken shape disappeared from a gala buffet, a certain body part disappeared from the replica of Michelangelo's statue David aboard Royal Caribbean Cruise Line's *Splendour of the Seas*, three of the twelve telescopes mounted in the observation lounge of Celebrity Cruises' *Century* disappeared during its inaugural voyages, and the Hollywood look-alike mannequins on Carnival Cruise Line's *Fascination* routinely had wigs or clothing removed until they were permanently fastened. More recently, in the summer of 2000, Celebrity Cruises' *Millennium* was introduced with a music library containing thousands of CD's for passengers to use. After the first couple of cruises, more than a hundred CD's were missing. Celebrity was forced to change to a more controlled lending policy.

Admittedly, much of the pilfering is innocent—though it is still stealing—but it has an impact on the cruise experience. I have wondered why most cruise lines no longer use steak knives, and I have wondered why plates and towels are increasingly nondescript. The "five finger discount" appears to partially answer my curiosity.

One of the most bizarre crimes on a cruise ship took place on the Holland America Line's *Veendam* in December 2000. As it arrived in Fort Lauderdale at the end of its Christmas cruise, crew found that all of the teak deck chairs on the lower promenade deck had been thrown overboard sometime during the night. The U.S. Coast Guard and the cruise line undertook an investigation, but no explanation for the vandalism was ever found.

## Cruise Ships and Health

Oversight of health and sanitary conditions on cruise ships visiting U.S. ports is the responsibility of the Centres for Disease Control (CDC), a division of the U.S. Public Health Service. Through the Vessel Sanitation Program, the CDC evaluates water systems, food preparation and service areas, general hygiene facilities, and waste management equipment and facilities. The CDC also issues health advisories, when necessary. For example, in 1992 when two Filipino crew members on Regency Cruises' Regent Sea were found to have active cases of tuberculosis, health officials sought to contain the spread of the disease, and they issued guidelines to cruise lines for pre-employment and annual screening of employees.

In 1998, following rubella (German measles) outbreaks among crew on two cruise ships, the CDC cautioned women planning to take a cruise and who were pregnant or of childbearing age to make sure they were immune to rubella. At the same time, the CDC recommended that all cruise lines administer rubella vaccine to all crew without documented immunity, but that recommendation was generally ignored because of the potential cost. The medical director for Holland America Line suggested that it would cost $600,000 to inoculate all crew on Holland America Line and Windstar Cruises.

While sanitation and the health of ships visiting U.S. ports are monitored by the U.S. Government, there is no government regulation or oversight of medical care and services on board cruise ships—there is not even a U.S. or International Maritime Organization standard that doctors be on board passenger vessels. The Standards of Training, Certification and Watchkeeping for Seafarers (SCTW) Convention does require that certain crew members have various levels of first aid and medical training, but that is all that is legally required.

In 1996, the International Council of Cruise Lines (ICCL) adopted industry guidelines for medical facilities and personnel on cruise ships. These guidelines were in large part due to pressure from the American Medical Association which had that year called on Congress for the development of medical standards for cruise ships, and called for greater awareness of the limited medical services available aboard ships. The AMA's position was based in part on the results of a survey administered by two Florida doctors to eleven cruise lines.

> *[The] doctors found that 27 % of doctors and nurses did not have advanced training in treating victims of heart attacks, the leading killer on ships, and 54 % of doctors and 72 % of nurses lacked advanced training for dealing with trauma. Fewer than half of shipboard doctors—45 %—had board certification, an important credential that is granted after three to seven years of residency and a written examination in a specialty or its equivalent....As for equipment, the survey found that 63 % of ships did not have equipment for blood tests for diagnosing heart attacks, and 45 % did not have mechanical ventilators or external pacemakers. "What we found was that the quality of maritime medical care was less than adequate, from the medical facilities to nurse and physician credentials..."* [15]

The American Medical Association's call for regulation of health care on cruise ships was also based on a number of cases of disease on cruise ships, including a recent outbreak of gastroenteritis on Carnival Cruise Line's *Jubilee* on its weekly cruise from Los Angeles to Mexico. 52 passengers became ill and one person died. The American Medical Association has continued to lobby for government regulation of health care on cruise ships, but with no success.

## What is the Vessel Sanitation Program?

The Vessel Sanitation Program (VSP) is administered by the Centres for Disease Control. It provides oversight of safety and sanitation of cruise ships. It was established in 1975 as a cooperative activity with the cruise ship industry in response to several major disease outbreaks on cruise vessels. Its primary goal is to lower the risk of gastrointestinal disease outbreaks on cruise ships. The program ceased operations for several months in 1986/1987, during a period of cutbacks in Government spending. It resumed operations in March 1987, and in 1988 user fees were introduced in order to reimburse the government for the costs of the inspection.

The Vessel Sanitation program conducts twice-yearly surprise inspections of cruise ships visiting U.S. ports. The inspection focuses on the ship's water supply, the ship's food, the potential for contamination of food and water, the practices and personal hygiene of employees, the general cleanliness and physical condition of the ship, and the ship's training programs covering general environmental and public health practices. A ship is scored for its compliance on forty-two items. A score of eighty-six points out of one hundred is the threshold for determining a ship's compliance. When a ship fails its inspection, it is reinspected within thirty to sixty days. There were more than three hundred reinspections in the six-year period 1988 through 1993. In the six-year period that followed, the number of reinspections were reduced by two-thirds; less than one hundred and ten cruise ships received scores less than eighty-six.

Regardless of score, each ship is required to document a corrective plan to address any deficient items identified by an inspection. Even ships that pass are likely to require some corrective action. For example, I was recently on a ship that had received a score of ninety-six, but it had had serious problems with its water purification system and there were clear requirements for corrective action by the ship. Information on all recent inspections of cruise ships is available at the Vessel Sanitation Program's web site (http://www.cdc.gov/nceh/vsp/vsp.htm). The site provides the scores received, and provides access to the full written report, item by item.

The work of the Vessel Sanitation Program has had positive results. In the 1970's and 1980's, twelve to fifteen outbreaks of gastroenteritis (or similar illness) occurred each year aboard cruise ships. By the early 1990's the number had decreased. In 1997, there were ten reported outbreaks, and in 1998 there were nine. While VSP data indicate a significant decrease in the number of outbreaks of gastrointestinal illness aboard cruise ships, they show that an increased proportion of outbreaks has been caused by contaminated food or water (rather than by person-to-person contact). While the proportion of bacterial outbreaks caused by agents such as salmonella and shigella remained constant, the percentage of outbreaks caused by Norwalk-like viruses has increased to one-third of all cases.

Cruise lines are required to notify the Centres for Disease Control any time an illness strikes more than 3% of the passengers on a ship. In these situations, the CDC is likely to undertake an investigation to determine the cause of the illness. From

1994 to 1997, the CDC investigated eighteen outbreaks of disease on cruise ships, including an outbreak of Legionnaire's Disease and numerous outbreaks of gastrointestinal illness.

## What Types of Illnesses are Common on Cruise Ships?

Before going further, there are two things that must be kept in mind. First, incidents of gastrointestinal illness are not directly related to whether a ship has or has not passed its sanitation inspection. There are certainly cases where a ship having an outbreak of disease failed its sanitation inspection immediately following the outbreak. But there are also cases where a ship has had an outbreak within weeks of passing their inspection with a particularly high score. Thus, inspection scores are not generally a good warning. Second, these incidents are not something about which most cruisers need to be concerned. Though disease outbreaks are relatively frequent —six to ten times a year—any single cruise is highly unlikely to be affected. The statistical risk in 1997 was 2.1 outbreaks in every ten million passenger days. Between 1975 and 1979, the risk of outbreak was four times higher—8.1 outbreaks per ten million passenger days.

Gastrointestinal illness is the most common outbreak on cruise ships. In most, if not all cases, a virus or bacteria in the food or water cause the disease. Several different agents can cause these food borne illnesses.

## Norwalk Virus

The most common cause of gastrointestinal disease on cruise ships is the Norwalk virus. The Norwalk virus (or Norwalk-like virus) is part of a family of unclassified, small, round-structured viruses, and is named after Norwalk, Ohio, where the first outbreak was documented. It is associated with a mild and brief illness that includes nausea, vomiting, diarrhea, and abdominal pain. A headache and low-grade fever may also accompany this disease. The disease develops twenty-four to forty-eight hours after contaminated food or water is eaten and lasts for twenty-four to sixty hours. It can be transmitted through the water, shellfish (ingestion of raw or insufficiently steamed clams and oysters poses a high risk for infection with Norwalk virus), salad ingredients, and by anything prepared by an infected food handler.

There are several ships, which in recent years have had serious Norwalk Virus outbreaks. In 1997 there were outbreaks on three successive cruises of Norwegian Cruise Line's *Royal Odyssey*. Following the CDC's "Recommendation Not to Sail" the ship was pulled from service a week earlier than planned and was sanitized and refit as the *Norwegian Star*. In 1998, Princess Cruises' *Regal Princess* had three successive cruises with gastrointestinal illness traced to Norwalk virus. The ship was pulled from service for a week and was completely sanitized. In 2000, Clipper Cruise Line's *Nantucket Clipper* was taken from service following an outbreak on two cruises. It was cleaned, returned to service, and had another outbreak on the first cruise requiring it to be pulled from service again, and again sanitized.

## Bacteria Such as E. coli, Shigella, and Salmonella

There are also several bacteria that have been implicated in food borne illness on cruise ships. For example, in 1994, Royal Caribbean Cruise Line's *Viking Serenade* had an outbreak of gastrointestinal illness caused by shigellosis. Approximately 600 of the 1700 passengers aboard were struck by the disease and one passenger died. The bacteria were likely to have been transmitted by a food handler not properly washing his/her hands.

Salmonella is not a common problem on cruise ships. This is in large part because there are fairly clear guidelines for handling fresh eggs. In addition, cruise lines (like many commercial kitchens) have increasingly turned to commercial egg products. These products not only remove the problem of breakage, but they can be pasteurized, thereby greatly reducing the risk of disease.

Enterotoxigenic Escherichia coli (E. coli) is a bacteria that is of increasing risk to those on cruise ships. According to an April 2000 article in the *Journal of Infectious Diseases*, which studied outbreaks of gastrointestinal disease on three cruises in 1997 and 1998, contaminated water taken on the ship in foreign ports appeared to be the source of E. coli in each case. The 1300 passengers collectively affected were infected by consuming beverages with ice cubes or by consuming unbottled water. Though cruise ships have water treatment plants that are designed to avoid these problems, it was believed that the water treatment system "had briefly failed" on the ships where these outbreaks had occurred.

There are also cases where unknown bacteria cause what comes to be simply labelled as food poisoning. For example, in 1996, Greek authorities quarantined Costa Cruises' *Costa Riviera* after 800 of the 1400 passengers became ill. After twenty-four hours, it was determined that passengers were suffering from chronic food poisoning and were not infectious. A common source of the disease was not identified. In 2000, there was an outbreak of food poisoning from contaminated shrimp, affecting 200 passengers on Disney Cruises' *Disney Magic*. The shrimp were isolated as the cause, but the Centres for Disease Control was unable to isolate the source of the contamination.

Because bacteria and viruses are sensitive to heat, they are not generally a problem when food is properly cooked and when it is properly stored. This fact is the basis of the Vessel Sanitation Program's recommendation in 1994 that all cruise lines advise passengers that, "Consuming raw or undercooked meats, poultry, seafood, shellfish, or eggs may increase your risk of food borne illness." A few cruise lines, including Norwegian Cruise Line and Seabourn Cruise Line, place this statement on their menus. Others scoffed at the recommendation, criticizing the VSP for trying to further regulate the industry, and not incorporating any warning to passengers.

As passengers, we can feel fairly secure if the food we are served is cooked fresh. However, when food is held for reheating, we can never be sure. Almost two-thirds of cases involving food borne illness have as a contributing factor inadequate cooling and cold handling of an item. It is at this point, where human error is certainly an element, over which we have no control.

## Are There Airborne Illnesses?

Also not uncommon on cruise ships, particularly in cooler weather when passengers are more likely to stay indoors, are influenzas and colds. During the 1998 season, more than twenty-one hundred cases of flu were reported among cruise passengers and crew in the Alaskan market. There are also reports of large outbreaks on cruise ships. Some of these have received media attention, such as an influenza that struck passengers on successive sailings in 1997 of Holland America Line's *Westerdam* on an itinerary between New York and Montreal. Others are more anecdotal and are discussed on Internet news groups. People appear to be continually surprised that the same influenza being passed around at home is also being passed around on a cruise ship during their winter vacation. The cruise ship is in many ways an ideal incubator for the flu. It provides a confined area, and people are engaged in almost non-stop socializing. It is no wonder that flus and colds are quickly transmitted among passengers.

Some of these flu outbreaks receive attention. The flu outbreak on the *Westerdam*, like the gastrointestinal outbreak on the *Regal Princess*, was initially given a very careful look because of fear that the case may have involved Legionnaire's Disease. There have only been two reported incidents involving Legionnaire's Disease on cruise ships. In 1994, there were sixteen confirmed cases, and thirty-four suspected cases, of Legionnaire's Disease among passengers aboard ten cruises of Celebrity Cruises' *Horizon*. One person died from the disease, and four persons required intensive treatment on ventilators. The source was traced to the outside whirlpool spa. Current regulations pertaining to water temperature and filtration systems are an outgrowth of that event.

In 1998, there were two cases of Legionnaire's Disease traced to Direct Cruises' Edinburgh Castle, which was operating in the U.K. In this case, the problem was in the water purification system. The system was disinfected before the ship was placed back into service.

Legionnaires disease was initially suspected in two passenger deaths on P & O's *Fair Princess* in September 2000. Health officials in Australia ruled out legionella as the source of the illness. The exact cause of dozens falling ill remains a mystery.

There is only a small chance that you would become ill while on a cruise. In cases when one does become ill, there is medical care available on most cruise ships. However, as already mentioned, the nature of this medical care can vary widely from one cruise line to another. There are no binding international regulations that govern medical care on cruise ships

## Medical Care on Cruise Ships

Most of the cruise lines marketed to North Americans are members of the International Council of Cruise Lines (ICCL) and they subscribe to ICCL guidelines for medical facilities and medical staff. These guidelines are entirely voluntary, and as the ICCL policy statement explicitly states, "they are not intended to establish standards of care for the industry. They simply reflect a consensus among member lines of the facilities and staffing needs considered appropriate aboard cruise vessels."

The guidelines suggest a minimum of one infirmary bed per 1000 passengers and crew, one intensive care unit bed per ship, and it recommends a variety of equipment, but the actual equipment on board may vary depending upon the itinerary, size of the ship, and anticipated demographic makeup of passengers. Included on the list are two heart defibrillators (to provide backup in case one of them fails) and an X-ray machine on new ships delivered after January 1, 1997, and on which there are more than 1000 passengers. Some smaller ships will surely have an X-ray machine, but one can never be too sure. The *Radisson Diamond*, for example, used to have an X-ray machine. The machine broke, so the room labelled "Caution: X-ray" is now used as an all-purpose closet. The placard on the door has not been removed.

Infirmaries on most ships are simply set up to deal with minor injuries, including workplace injuries of crew. They are also equipped for dealing with heart attacks and to stabilize these and other patients with acute conditions. Realistically speaking, the ship's infirmary is more like a neighbourhood clinic than it is a hospital emergency room. It is set up to most effectively deal with routine problems such as scrapes and cuts, sunburn and indigestion. It also is equipped to serve as the "family doctor" for all the ship's crew, treating anything from the common cold and flu to high blood sugar and hypertension.

However, the infirmary also deals with emergency situations. 90 % of the sixty deaths reported by cruise ships sailing out of Miami from 1996 to September 1999 reported a heart attack or heart-related problems as the cause of death. With a fleet of seven ships at the time, Holland America Line indicated in 1996 that it had between three hundred and twenty-five and three hundred and seventy-five emergency evacuations (forty by air ambulance) per year. These numbers, applied industry wide, suggests that there were as many as four thousand evacuations in 1996; potentially as many as six thousand in the current year.

The medical staff on a ship needs to be able to deal with both these routine and emergency situations. However, the staffing of infirmaries varies widely. For example, Disney Cruise's *Disney Magic*, with a capacity of 1750 passengers, has two doctors (one with a background in pediatrics) and four nurses; Holland America Line's ships which carry approximately 1250 passengers have one physician, three nurses, and often a dentist; and Cunard's *QE II* with a passenger capacity of 1715 carries one doctor and two nurses.

## What Are the Qualifications of the Medical Staff?

Not only is there a wide difference in staffing patterns, but there is also a considerable range in qualifications of medical staff on cruise ships. There have been reports of ship physicians who are not licensed, and/or who would not be qualified to practice in the U.S. There have also been reports of physicians who have received their degrees from a diploma mill, and of some who cannot speak good English. In response to the problem, and to criticism from the American Medical Association, the International Council of Cruise Lines issued recommendations in 1996 that cruise ship infirmaries should be staffed with medical personnel who, either individually or collectively, meet the following criteria:

>•*Competent skill level in advanced life support and cardiac care;*
>•*Current valid medical license (international or domestic);*
>•*Medical staff conversant in English;*
>•*General practice experience plus emergency or critical care experience; or Board Certification or similar international certification or equivalent experience, in any of the following areas: emergency medicine, family practice, or internal medicine;*
>•*Three years of clinical experience including minor suturing;*

Within these guidelines fit companies such as Princess Cruises, which uses exclusively U.K. trained and licensed nurses and physicians, and Holland America Line and Norwegian Cruise Line which both use U.S. and Canadian trained and licensed physicians and nurses. The guidelines also include Celebrity Cruises, which uses a large number of Colombian trained physicians, and Carnival Cruise Lines, which uses physicians from a number of different developing and developed countries.

Perhaps more troubling is that the guidelines require competence in advanced life support and cardiac care, but they do not require that the person be ACLS (Advanced Cardiac Life Support) certified. ACLS certification is a standard requirement for any physician working in emergency medicine in North America. Similarly, some may be concerned that while the regulations require that a member of the medical staff hold a medical license, there is no regard given to where the license is issued or where the person is trained. This is not to suggest that physicians in third world countries are less competent than their colleagues in industrialized countries, but their training may not be as advanced in the use of technology and in new innovations and treatments.

Despite the ICCL guidelines, a 1999 *New York Times* article reports that only 56 % of the doctors on Carnival Cruise Line's ships had board certification or equivalent certifications; 85% of the physicians on Royal Caribbean Cruise Lines were board certified. Neither cruise line has violated the International Council of Cruise Line's voluntary regulations. However, the medical care received is potentially qualitatively different than that on a cruise line that maintains higher minimum standards for its medical staff.

## I Don't Plan to Get Sick, so What Difference Does it Make?

No one plans to get sick. But when they do, they tend to take for granted that comprehensive and qualified medical care will be available. In most cases on cruise ships the needed intervention is provided. However, there are cases where passengers have not been as fortunate.

A 1999 *New York Times* article discusses several cases where medical care has fallen short. For example, it describes a case where the doctor on the *Carnival Ecstasy* failed to diagnose a fourteen-year-old girl whose appendix had ruptured and that she had a massive infection. Only on the third visit, when the parents specifically asked whether the problem could be appendicitis, did the physician conduct a physical exam. He responded that he was sure the problem was not the girl's appendix. On the advice of their doctor at home, the family returned home midway through the cruise and the daughter underwent emergency surgery. As a result of the infection from the ruptured appendix, the young woman has lifelong medical problems. The physician who treated her on the ship had finished medical school in his native Italy in 1981 and had held nine medical jobs in Italy, Africa, and England in the fifteen years before joining Carnival Cruise Line. A woman on her honeymoon also had a bad experience on a Carnival Cruise Line ship—in this case the *Sensation*. The woman and her husband returned to the ship from a walk ashore and went to the infirmary because the woman, a diabetic, felt flushed. There, the nurse and doctor checked her blood sugar and because it was very high the woman was administered fast-acting insulin to bring the blood sugar down. According to the husband:

> *Instead of getting better, she got worse and worse...She was totally unconscious and went into a diabetic coma and was wringing wet. I called for the nurse and she said she'd come around. I waited and she started jerking real bad.* [16]

He rushed back to their cabin to get his wife's glucose meter and returned to the infirmary to measure his wife's blood sugar himself. He found that her blood sugar was not too high, but it was too low. The nurse administered glucose, and the woman regained consciousness after about fifteen minutes. The couple claims that the incident caused brain damage, which has left the woman disoriented and unable to return to her job.

The nurse involved in this case, was also involved in a case where a fifty-nine year-old man died of a ruptured abdominal aortic aneurysm, though it was the physician who made the diagnosis and provided the care. The man's family claims that the medical care provided was inadequate. Lawyers for the company suggest that the rupture that killed the man was extremely difficult to diagnose and that it required immediate surgery at a major trauma centre. The condition is usually fatal.

A forty-seven-year old woman on Celebrity Cruises' *Zenith* also died following treatment by the ship's physicians. She went to the infirmary complaining of difficulty breathing and chest pain. The physician took a chest X-ray and diagnosed an upper-respiratory tract infection and acute bronchitis. Over the next three days, as her condition failed to improve, the woman made additional visits to the doctor. The day after she returned to New York, following the cruise, she was hospitalized and she died in intensive care. The woman's family claims that failure of the ship's physician to properly treat the first heart attack had led to an increased risk of her second, fatal heart attack. There were two physicians who provided care to this woman. Both were trained in Colombia, neither was licensed to practice in the United States, and neither had advanced training in cardiac care.

There is also a case—one of the few cases where a passenger has died from outbreak of a gastrointestinal disease—of a fifty-two-year-old man who died while aboard Carnival Cruise Line's *Jubilee* in June 1996. The ship had been struck by a gastrointestinal virus, not unlike the Norwalk virus, and more than 50 passengers (and 16 crew) were afflicted. One of these passengers was Russell Lum, an aircraft mechanic from Berkeley, California. He had complained that he wasn't feeling well the second night, and following a bout of nausea he spent the following day in his cabin.

> *At 1:30 A.M. on the third day, Mrs. Lum said in an interview, she woke when her husband collapsed outside the cabin's bathroom. She said she called the ship's infirmary but the nurse tried to discourage her from bringing him there because it was so late. Mrs. Lum said she insisted, and her husband was put on an intravenous solution to avoid dehydration.*

> *After a time, the nurse took Lum's blood pressure and said he was improving and could return to his cabin. Tired but relieved, Mrs. Lum hurried to the cabin to get towels and a change of clothes, because her husband had soiled his pants.*

> *"My daughter and niece were awake, and I told them he was fine and would be coming back," Mrs. Lum said. "I was gone about five minutes, and when I got back to the infirmary the doctor and nurse asked me to wait in the waiting room." [After several minutes]... "they came back and told me that he had taken a turn for the worse and he had died," she said. "I asked them how that was possible, and they said there was nothing they could do."* [17]

Lum died as a result of extensive blood loss from a tear in his esophagus caused by vomiting and his family is suing Carnival Cruise Line for his wrongful death. Carnival's lawyer, Curtis J. Mase, contends that the company was not responsible because the death was an act of God and that Lum had failed to seek timely or appropriate medical care. "Russell Lum's own negligence contributed to his death and injuries," Mase said.

## Isn't the Cruise Line Responsible for the Actions of its Medical Staff?

When something does go wrong on a cruise ship, passengers are often surprised to find that the cruise line itself assumes no responsibility for the action (or inaction) of its medical staff. In almost all cases, the onboard physician is considered an independent contractor. As far as the cruise line is concerned, passengers pay the physician for treatment—not the cruise line.

The cruise lines' position is based in maritime law. The law of the sea specifies that a ship owner has no duty to provide medical care, and as stipulated in the small print on the cruise contract, is not liable for the ship's doctors and other independent contractors. This precedent is rooted in the 19th century, when ships sailing across the Atlantic would give doctors free passage in exchange for looking after passenger's medical needs.

Maritime law also governs the nature of claims that can be made. The Death on the High Seas Act limits damage to only real monetary losses. It does not allow claims for punitive damages, or payments for pain and suffering. In 1996, the cruise industry tried unsuccessfully to cap the amount passengers could collect for medical malpractice when an ill or injured passenger was referred to a doctor or hospital in port. The measure failed to receive Congressional approval.

In cases involving a claim against a cruise line for the actions of its medical staff, some lawyers have unsuccessfully argued that cruise lines are engaging in false advertising. Because the company's brochures advertise medical facilities, the cruise contract says they provide medical care, and the doctors wear the same uniforms as other officers, the argument is made that the care provided is ultimately under the responsibility of the cruise line. However, courts have not accepted this line of argument. More common in these cases is that cruise lines will settle claims out of court. Like cases of sexual assault, they wish to avoid the undue publicity, and they also want to avoid setting a precedent where a United States court has made a monetary judgment against a foreign-based cruise line. As a foreign-registered corporation, cruise lines want to preserve their rights in relation to the U.S. judicial system. This will be discussed in greater detail later when we address "flags of convenience."

## How Can I be Prepared for a Medical Emergency?

Part of being prepared for an emergency is to recognize that medical care on cruise ships is at the best of times limited in what it can provide—transfusions and even minor surgery are not likely to be practical. It is also helpful to keep in mind that there is a wide range in the qualifications of medical care providers. These differences reflect different standards that companies have for minimum qualifications for their physicians and nurses. They also reflect different amounts of money each cruise line is willing to pay for its health care professionals. The physician with Carnival Cruise Lines discussed above earned a salary of $1057 a month; the physicians with Celebrity Cruises were paid a salary of $2300 a month. These are relatively low when compared with Princess Cruises, Holland America Line, and Norwegian Cruise Line which each pay a monthly salary equal to $100,000 - $120,000 a year. These salaries are in addition to a percentage given to the physician (between 10% and 20%) of all charges made by the infirmary, including the sale of drugs. Though all cruise lines may not be willing to give the information out, this is something about which a concerned passenger should certainly feel comfortable asking.

A cruise passenger can also be prepared by being able in an emergency to give a medical history, and to identify any prescription dugs currently being taken and any known drug allergies. The fact that a ship's physician doesn't know the patient prior to an emergency situation means that the more information that can be given quickly, the easier it will be to make a proper diagnosis and provided needed intervention. I have seen many passengers who have a history of medical problems travel with a copy of documents that may be relevant in the case of an emergency.

This need to be prepared to give a medical history was made vividly clear on a recent cruise. A passenger had been using patches behind the ear to control sea-sickness. Because he didn't think they were working, he used a different patch each day; by day four he wasn't feeling well. He went to the infirmary, complained of abdominal discomfort, and was advised by the nurse to take a laxative and sent on his way. The next day, passengers at his dinner table told another passenger, who happened to be a physician, about the man's condition. Immediately, the physician pointed out that he likely had an overdose from the scopolamine patch he was using. The symptoms were compounded by the fact that he was also taking Ditropan, a bladder control medication. That night at dinner his table companions passed on to him what they had been told. He went to the infirmary immediately after dinner and was catheterized. Because he hadn't volunteered information about the medications he was taking, and because the nurse didn't ask, the man risked serious medical complications.

While this man was fortunate, the simple reality is that people do die on cruise ships. Take for example the winner of Thrifty Car Rental's sixth annual Honeymoon Disaster contest. The couple that won reported five onboard deaths in less than ten days, including a man who collapsed and died in front of them as they were on their way to dinner the first night. Even the comedians on the ship began cracking jokes about the rising body count.

As already pointed out, the vast majority of deaths on ships are from heart attacks, and they often occur such that medical intervention isn't necessary. For example, there were three heart attacks on a transatlantic cruise I took several years ago. Two of the passengers died in their sleep so all the physician could do is to confirm what was already known. In one of these cases, it was quipped that it was a case of death by chocolate—the passenger had a large dinner and then overindulged at the midnight chocoholic buffet and died in his sleep shortly after going to bed. In the case of the third heart attack, the passenger was watching the show. A "Code Alpha" was called, the doctor arrived in a matter of minutes, the man was stabilized, and he was then hospitalized at the first port.

The basic fact is that many more passengers survive a heart attack at sea than the number that succumb. There are also cases that can be cited where the actions of crew have saved the life of a passenger. For example, a Holland America Line ship had a case in the mid-1990's where a sixty-one-year old woman was bleeding internally and was estimated by the doctor to have four hours to live, unless they could get her to a trauma centre. The ship was forty-five miles off the coast of Portugal. The closest town was Leixoes, a relatively small port on the west coast. In the limited time available, the Captain was able to make contact with the pilot station (through his port agent in Lisbon) and to arrange for the ship to be met by the pilot. However, as they got closer to shore, they were told the port had been closed because of dense fog. Given the situation, the pilot station sent a pilot boat to the ship, and then provided guidance to one of the ship's tenders (which could accommodate a stretcher) to the shore where an ambulance was waiting. It had taken three and a half hours to get the woman from the ship to the ambulance. When the ship got to Lisbon the next day, the Captain was told by the ship's agent that:

> *I was on the phone with the doctor just a half-hour ago and she made it. Had you been fifteen minutes later, he said, it would have been too late. She will be out of the hospital in a few days and fly home to the U.S.* [18]

A week later the captain was told that the woman and her husband had filed a lawsuit against the cruise line. Their suit complained that the cruise line had put them through a harrowing experience. They had been placed in a small boat and dropped in a foreign country without help. They stated in their claim that they could have died there, not appreciating that the woman would have died had she not been taken ashore.

This story provides another side of the picture of medical care on cruise ships. It also points to the potential costs associated with illness at sea. In an emergency, there may be costs to the cruise line, and to those who work on the ship. Several years ago, there was a medical emergency involving a woman's eye on Cunard's *Crown Dynasty*. In order to increase the chance of saving the woman's eyesight, the captain gave the order for the ship to turn all screws—the ship is normally powered by two dynamic diesel engines, with another two on emergency standby. With all four engines running, the ship docked in Acapulco ten hours ahead of schedule and the woman was airlifted to Los Angeles for emergency treatment. Her sight was saved. However, the captain sacrificed his operating budget for the cause. Each cruise is a cost-accountable profit-and-loss function, controlled by a budget for every onboard expense.

> Cost savings translate into percentage perks for all from maintenance to master. Despite accolades for his action, the captain lost his percentage benefit by expediting [the trip to port]...because four screws burn twice as much fuel as two. [19]

There are also potential costs to a passenger when there is a medical emergency. Aside from the costs for medical care on the ships—X-rays, electrocardiograms, and prescriptions are comparably priced to what would be paid shore side—one needs to also be prepared for an early disembarkation or an air evacuation. The simple reality is that evacuation from a ship can cost between $20,000 and $50,000, which is the sole responsibility of the passenger. This certainly provides an incentive to having health insurance coverage during a cruise.

In recent years there have also been some technological advances that have improved medical care on ships, but which also have a hefty price tag. Princess Cruises introduced in 1998 a system they call SeaMed (later renamed MedServe). The system provides a satellite link between the ship's physician directly to physicians at Cedars Sinai Medical Centre in Los Angeles. The communication is similar to a live television broadcast and allows for X-rays and electrocardiograms to be displayed on the video screen. The ship's doctor and the passenger are able to receive the advice of a specialist in the treatment of the emergency situation. In a single year, Princess' fleet of ships carries out over three hundred telemedicine consultations. A similar telemedicine system was adopted by Renaissance Cruises in 1999, and is supported by a satellite video link to Johns Hopkins Medical Centre in Baltimore.

The cost to the passenger for using the SeaMed/MedServe system is $500, charged directly to their onboard account. The system as a whole is a much larger investment. It costs approximately $45,000 to install the system on a ship, but diverting a ship to port for medical care can cost the line $500,000 or more, depending on the ship's location.

## So, Is It Safe to Take a Cruise?

Despite all of the potential for problems or even disaster, a cruise is a relatively safe vacation. One can avoid some of the difficulties simply by being aware of the potential for problems and by being prepared. While we can certainly never fully anticipate an accident or an illness, we can be prepared for them when they happen. When it comes to medical care on a cruise ship, we need to take the initiative to be sure to provide to medical personnel all relevant medical information. We need to also be informed users of the medical care system. If the service provided doesn't help, be assertive. Call your regular family physician from the ship—a $20 phone call is a small price to pay for peace of mind—and seek advice. It may be that one's vacation is cut short by an illness or an emergency, but that is the main reason why one should have health insurance when traveling on a cruise ship, or for that matter anywhere outside the country.

[1] Miami Herald, February 5, 1990, page 1BR
[2] Frantz, Douglas. "On Cruise Ships, Silence Shrouds Crimes," New York Times, November 16, 1998.
[3] "Are Ships Safer Than the Streets?", CNN Interactive, July 14, 1999
[4] Korten, Tristram. "Carnival? Try Criminal: What happens when a female passenger is assaulted on a cruise ship? Not much." Miami New Times, February 3-9, 2000.
[5] Korten, Tristram. "Carnival? Try Criminal: What happens when a female passenger is assaulted on a cruise ship? Not much." Miami New Times, February 3-9, 2000.
[6] Kalosh, Anne. "Shipboard Confidential: Love Sex, Death and the Baron's Missing Trousers," Los Angeles Times, September 12, 1993, page L - 1.
[7] Frantz, Douglas. "On Cruise Ships, Silence Shrouds Crimes," New York Times, November 16, 1998.
[8] Chapman, Paul. Trouble on Board: The Plight of International Seafarers, Ithaca, NY: ILR Press, 1992, page 67.
[9] "Former Employee Claims Luxury Liner Allowed Sexually Charged Working Environment," SF Gate News, December 7, 1998.
[10] Frantz, Douglas. "On Cruise Ships, Silence Shrouds Crimes," New York Times, November 16, 1998.
[11] Frantz, Douglas. "On Cruise Ships, Silence Shrouds Crimes," New York Times, November 16, 1998.
[12] Korten, Tristram. "Carnival? Try Criminal: What happens when a female passenger is assaulted on a cruise ship? Not much." Miami New Times, February 3-9, 2000.
[13] Fitten, Ronald K. "Seattle-based Cruise Line Accused in Downing," Seattle Times, August 9, 1999.
[14] Bleecker, Arline. "Cruise Lines Bear the Brunt of Guests' Sticky Fingers," Houston Chronicle, October 20, 1996, page 2.
[15] Frantz, Douglas. "Getting Sick on the High Seas: A Question of Accountability," New York Times, October 31, 1999.
[16] Frantz, Douglas. "Getting Sick on a Cruise May Mean Medical Care with Few Standards," New York Times, October 31, 1999.
[17] Frantz, Douglas. "Getting Sick on a Cruise May Mean Medical Care with Few Standards," New York Times, October 31, 1999.
[18] Mateboer, Hans. "Captain's Log: The Evacuation," Cruise Industry News Quarterly, Summer 1999, page 145.
[19] Courtice, Paul. "Sickness Isn't all That's Out There..." Medical Post, October 19, 1999, page 27.

ross a. klein

# 6 How Green is Green?

My interest in the environmental practices and requirements of cruise lines was piqued on a 1993 cruise of the Mediterranean on the *Song of Norway*. Early on, I noticed that all crew members wore a lapel pin reading "Save the Waves". To that point in time, I hadn't given much thought to what ships were and were not allowed to throw into the sea. On that cruise, largely sensitized by the "Save the Waves" program, I began to wonder, "what is being thrown into the seas?" I read the material provided passengers in their cabins, but also watched several times as what appeared to be food waste was being thrown overboard—apparently contradicting the information in print. At the time, I accepted the insistence of the bar waiter that they would never dump food waste at sea. I am not sure that today I would be as ready to believe.

Cruise lines have generally projected an image of environmental sensitivity and responsibility. Royal Caribbean Cruise Line has had its "Save the Waves" campaign since the early 1990's. Similarly, Princess Cruises has its Planet Princess, and Holland America Line has its program of Seagoing Environmental Awareness (SEA).

More recently, cruise lines have become participants in ocean-monitoring projects. Royal Caribbean International announced in September 2000 a joint project with the University of Miami to collect data from the air and ocean as the *Explorer of the Seas* plies its regular route from Miami to Caribbean stops in Haiti, Puerto Rico, the U.S. Virgin Islands, and the Bahamas. Holland America Line announced one month later that it is participating in an ongoing project of the International Seakeepers Society to monitor the quality of the world's oceans from its newest ship, the *MS Amsterdam*.

Each of these projects and campaigns present a positive image for the company, and projects an impression that the company has a corresponding attitude of responsibility to the environment. It is particularly glaring when a company behaves in ways that contradict the image they project.

These contradictions may be slight, as when a "deck boy" on Holland America Line's *Rotterdam* emptied the contents of each of three containers into a single receptacle at the end of the day. The containers were painted with an emblem and the words "Seagoing Environmental Awareness" on the side. Though each specified a particular type of garbage—paper, plastic, bottles and cans—the contents of each were emptied into the same bin. These contradictions may also be extreme, as in the case of a number of Royal Caribbean Cruise Line's ships dumping oil and hazardous waste in or near a number of U.S. ports.

## The International Convention for the Prevention of Pollution from Ships—MARPOL

There are international regulations that regulate what cruise ships (and other ships) can legally dispose at sea. Established within the framework of the International Maritime Organization, MARPOL is an international convention that sets standards for protection against marine pollution, including specifications for disposal of waste and garbage. MARPOL strictly prohibits the disposal anywhere at sea of plastics, oil, and hazardous waste. It sets limits within which disposal of kitchen garbage and human waste is permitted, and specifies where it is not permitted. As with SOLAS, it is the responsibility of a ship's country of registry to enforce MARPOL's regulations. Infractions observed by any country are referred to this country for its consideration and action.

## What is allowed under MARPOL?

The MARPOL Convention initially came into effect in the mid-1970s and it has been amended many times. The two sections that apply most directly to cruise ships are Annex IV, which regulates disposal of sewage, and Annex V, which regulates disposal of garbage.

The disposal of some things is not controlled under MARPOL. For example, there are no clear limitations for the discharge of gray water—the stuff that goes down the drain in showers and sinks. Cruise ships are not restricted by MARPOL as to where gray water may be disposed, though local laws, such as the Clean Water Act in the United States, may limit how close to shore it may be disposed into the sea.

In contrast, the disposal of sewage is strictly regulated. Known as black water, it must be treated if it is discharged within four nautical miles of land; sewage may be released untreated if the ship is more than twelve miles from shore. MARPOL also requires that any "...sewage that has been stored in holding tanks shall not be discharged instantaneously but at a moderate rate when the ship is en route and proceeding at not less than four knots...." The amount of gray water and black water is considerable given that the average cruise ship passenger (and crew member) generates one hundred gallons of wastewater a day. 10 % of this is sewage.

MARPOL also regulates the disposal of garbage. The regulations distinguish between what are called special areas and all other areas. Special areas include the Mediterranean Sea, Baltic Sea, Black Sea, Red Sea, The Gulfs, the North Sea, the Antarctic area, and the Caribbean region. The only garbage that may be disposed in these areas is food waste, and it may not be disposed any closer than twelve miles from the nearest land.

Though technically a special area, the Caribbean is treated a bit differently. In the Caribbean, ships may dispose food wastes within three miles of the nearest land, as long as the wastes have been ground and can pass through a one-inch screen. Otherwise, the twelve-mile limit applies. Though the Caribbean's status as a "special area" took effect in April 1993, enforcement has been delayed. MARPOL requires that Caribbean ports provide adequate on-land reception facilities for ship's waste. Until they are able to do so, the "special area" provisions do not bind ships. For now, the Caribbean is not treated as a special area.

Outside special areas, ships are allowed to dispose to within twenty-five miles from land dunnage, lining, and packing materials. To within twelve miles of land, they are allowed to dispose "all other garbage [except plastics], including paper products, rags, glass, metal, bottles, crockery and similar refuse." These can be disposed to within three miles of the coast if the refuse is ground and can pass through a one-inch screen. As long as enforcement of the Caribbean's special status is delayed, these same regulations apply to that region.

Though these regulations do limit what can be put into the sea, and where this can be done, they appear somewhat permissive with regard what is allowed and not allowed. Admittedly, some cruise lines have initiated policies that are more stringent than those required by MARPOL. Others have not.

## Are MARPOL Regulations Enough?

Despite the MARPOL Convention, pollution from cruise ships has been a problem. In 1989, in response to the problem of garbage washing ashore, the Governor of Florida proposed that the state fine ships for dumping trash or garbage overboard. Shortly after his call, two passengers on Norwegian Cruise Line's *Sunward II* reported observing trash being dumped overboard on a cruise of the Caribbean. Nothing happened in relation to these events, and the problem continued. The media called occasional attention to the trash floating ashore along the Florida coast, and to the hundreds of tons of trash and debris picked up from Florida beaches each year. It also reported several cleanup campaigns in which a significant amount of the trash had the insignia of cruise lines.

Concern for the protection of the environment from the cruise industry was most strongly expressed by some commonly visited ports. Following an $8500 fine levelled by Bermuda against Royal Caribbean Cruise Line's for a four hundred and fifty meter long oil spill in St. Georges harbour left by the *Nordic Prince*, Caribbean countries began expressing greater concern about dumping in and near their ports. In March 1992, the Cayman Islands announced that it was clamping down on the discharge of unauthorized waste in its ports and coastal waters. Soon thereafter it fined Norwegian Cruise Line's *Seaward* $3750 for discharging "a large quantity of debris" into the sea, believed to include raw sewage. Roughly one year later, Royal Caribbean Cruise Line's *Majesty of the Sea* was fined $2500 by the Cayman Islands for dumping waste containing an "unacceptably high" level of bacteria harmful to marine life.

Given the problem, and the Government's concerns, the Cayman Islands implemented as a preventative measure a new maximum fine for dumping of garbage or other waste within twelve miles of the coast. Previously, fines could not exceed $6250. The new regulations allowed fines up to $625,000. The increase presented a disincentive for ships dumping waste in waters off the Cayman Islands.

Other countries were not as strong willed as the Cayman Islands. According to Dr. David Smith, Executive Director of Jamaica's Conservation and Development Trust, some countries are put under pressure by the cruise lines. If they enforce regulations, the cruise line may withdraw their vessels and use another port. This is something most islands cannot easily afford to lose. As a result, many ports balance the environmental needs with the need for the income generated from cruise ships visits.

Despite individual islands waffling in their position, discontent with the cruise industry was expressed collectively in 1992. The Caribbean Tourism Organization, the regional tourist authorities' lobby group, called on the annual meeting of Caribbean heads of government to speak directly to cruise ship owners and to spell out the region's unhappiness over the conduct of many cruise lines and to make clear to them that they must be more sensitive to Caribbean concerns. The concerns include the feeling that cruise lines are not making a satisfactory contribution to regional economic development, the perception that cruise lines are not adequately participating in international marketing of the region, and the indifferent attitude displayed by many lines toward the preservation of the Caribbean environment.

The level of resentment toward the cruise lines is reflected in a proposal made by St. Lucia's tourism director. He proposed that Caribbean governments should issue licenses to cruise lines and impose stiff fines on ships that dump unauthorized waste in Caribbean waters. If three environmental offences were committed, licenses would be withdrawn. The scheme was not approved.

The U.S. government shared the frustration experienced by Caribbean governments. The Coast Guard had been monitoring violations in U.S. waters, but found that reporting an incident to the flag state had no effect. In October 1992, the U.S.

Government complained at a meeting of the Marine Environment Protection Committee —the Committee charged with responsibility for MARPOL—that it had reported MARPOL violations to the appropriate flag states one hundred and eleven times, but received responses in only 10% of the cases; action was taken in only two.

> *More frustrating was that among the responses, most said either that the crew for the voyage in question had dispersed and could not be located or that a flag-state investigation failed to uncover any evidence to support the U.S. allegation of unlawful dumping.* [1]

Because the U.S. was prohibited by its own law from taking action against foreign flag violators beyond its three mile limit, other than to file a report with the flag state and hope for action that rarely came, the government extended its port-state control of coastal waters to the outer limit of the U.S. two-hundred-mile Exclusive Economic Zone. The U.S. also elevated sanctions for violation of the MARPOL dumping bans from civil administrative breaches handled by the Coast Guard to Class D felonies that must be dealt with in U.S. courts. At the time, there was some discussion of placing undercover FBI agents on cruise ships to document violations, and to implement a whistle blower scheme that would protect the identity of seafarers reporting infractions to U.S. authorities. It isn't clear whether either plan was eventually implemented.

The U.S. began its stricter enforcement in 1993. In April, Princess Cruises was fined $500,000 for dumping more than twenty plastic bags full of garbage off the Florida Keys. The dumping of the bags was witnessed and videotaped by a couple on the cruise. The videotape was used to indict Princess Cruises for unlawful dumping of plastics at sea and was the basis for a plea bargain. Because it is allowed by statute, and as an incentive aimed at encouraging cruise ship passengers to report illegal waste dumping, the court awarded the couple that shot the videotape half of the fine. They received $250,000 for reporting what they saw.

A year later, Palm Beach Cruises was fined $1 million for the *Viking Princess'* intentional dumping of waste oil, leaving a 2.5 mile slick 3.5 miles from the port of Palm Beach. This instance was also videotaped, but in this case Coast Guard surveillance aircraft made the tape. The company was fined for dumping, and for failing to report the incident. Several months later, Regency Cruises agreed to pay a fine of $250,000 after admitting that two of its ships dumped garbage-filled plastic bags in Florida waters.

There have continued to be cases of dumping by cruise lines. The U.S. government reports eighty-seven illegal discharges from passenger ships between 1993 and 1998 (see Appendix B). These numbers include a $500,000 fine paid by Ulysses Cruises for two incidents of plastic-wrapped garbage being thrown from the

*Seabreeze* off Miami (one case was observed by a musician, the other case by a passenger), and two cases of dumping oily bilge water, both of which were detected by Coast Guard surveillance.

These statistics also include a 1995 incident in which Holland America Line's *Rotterdam* dumped oily bilge water overboard in Alaska's Inside passage. In 1998, Holland America Line paid a $2 million fine for the infraction—to date the second largest fine ever paid by a cruise line. The incident had been reported by the assistant engineer, who told the U.S. Coast Guard that he had been ordered to pump overboard bilge oily waste, which he refused to do.

After a three-year investigation, Holland America Line entered a plea agreement, which included a $1 million fine and $1 million in restitution. The assistant engineer was given a $500,000 reward for reporting the incident. Following agreement to pay the fine, the Chairman and Chief Executive Officer of Holland America Line, Kirk Lanterman, said, "We believe that companies should be responsible for their actions. That's why we've accepted this settlement. Today, every one of our ships is equipped with recorder and monitoring devices that enable us to know instantly if water discharge or smoke emission criteria are exceeded."

More recently, Holland America Line was fined $50,000 for an accidental oil spill in Long Beach Harbour. They voluntarily disclosed the accident. In 2000, the cruise line paid a $250 fine for the leak of five gallons of diesel fuel into Juneau Harbour from a tender on the *Noordam*. Again, the company admitted the accident and did not contest the fine.

In 2000, several investigations of environmental violations by cruise ships were undertaken. In July 2000, an investigation of environmental violations aboard several ships operated by Norwegian Cruise Line was announced. This became public when Star Cruises, the new owner of Norwegian Cruise Line, reported to the U.S. Department of Justice that it had uncovered numerous violations. It agreed to cooperate with the investigation, which is ongoing.

In August 2000, Carnival Corporation was served with a grand jury subpoena asking it to produce documents relating to environmental matters. The subpoena covered all the Corporation's six cruise lines: Carnival, Holland America, Windstar, Costa, Cunard, and Seabourn. Though the U.S. government would not comment on the issue, it was suggested by Lloyd's List that the investigation was likely a part of the investigation into cruise lines' environmental record by the U.S. Justice Department's Environmental Protection Agency and Environmental Crimes Section.

At the same time, the Environmental Protection Agency was also investigating a number of cruise lines, including Carnival, for violating funnel emission standards in Alaska in 1999. In September 2000, the Alaska Department of Environmental Conservation cited six cruise lines for air quality violations over the summer of 2000.

These cases pale in comparison to those involving Royal Caribbean Cruise Line— cases that were resolved in 1999 and 2000. The public exposure, and negative image, provided by these events has motivated cruise lines to project a more "green" image. This image includes donations to environmental causes, participation in environmental monitoring programs, advanced garbage and sewage treatment plants on new ships, and new propulsion systems which are cleaner and less costly to operate.

At the same time that they work on their public image, there remain questions about their private behaviour. This was made vividly clear to me on a cruise with Seabourn Cruise Line's *Seabourn Goddess I*. While crossing the Atlantic Ocean, passengers watched as a florescent green stream of liquid was twice released from the back of the ship. Many took pictures, and the matter was a topic of much discussion. A number of passengers asked the chief engineer about the emission. He explained that it was a chemical used to detect leaks and that it was legal to be released while at sea. However, his comments contradicted the MARPOL log on the bridge that listed the emission as food waste, and was inconsistent with an explanation given by an officer who said the chemicals should have been put into a holding tank until they reached shore. There is no way to know which account was correct, and given that the matter would have to be referred to the country under whose flag the ship sailed, there was no point in reporting the matter to U.S. or other government authorities. I did mention the matter in a conversation with a representative of the company's chief executive officer. He showed no real interest or concern.

## Royal Caribbean Cruise Line and the Environment

It is likely you are already somewhat familiar with the case against Royal Caribbean Cruise Line for it's dumping from five of its ships of waste oil and of hazardous waste in several areas of the United States. Given its complexity and its many parts, it is worth briefly summarizing what the case was about and how it concluded.

## When Did the Case Begin?

The case began October 25, 1994 when the crew of a Coast Guard tracking plane reported they observed oil slicks in an area where the only ship was the *Sovereign of the Seas*. Coast Guard officials in San Juan were radioed. They dispatched one team to gather samples of the oil slick that had been observed. A second team was sent to meet and board the ship when it pulled into port. They met with the captain and the chief engineer, both who insisted that the ship was not the source of the slick. The Coast Guard team also took samples of oily water in discharge bins in the engine room.

Later that afternoon, another team of investigators—one with greater experience with larger ships—was sent to the *Sovereign of the Seas*. They inspected the ship's "Oil Record Book" (which must record any discharges) and found that none had been recorded. However, their inspection of the engine room indicated a number of things that weren't right, including that the oil-water separator—a critical anti-pollution device—was not functional, yet it appeared that there had been a recent disposal. The team videotaped what they saw.

The ship arrived in Miami four days later and was again inspected by the Coast Guard. They again videotaped what they observed in the engine room. When this tape was compared with that made when the ship was in San Juan, experts observed that a set of pipes present in the earlier picture were gone in the later picture. It was determined that the pipes had been used to bypass the oil-water separator so that waste could be discharged directly into the sea.

The Coast Guard continued its investigation and within several months discovered similar bypass systems on other Royal Caribbean Cruise Line ships. As their investigation developed, they increasingly questioned the reliability of the ship's oil record book.

> Confronted by evidence, witnesses changed their stories. They testified that Royal Caribbean ships regularly bypassed pollution devices and dumped oily waste overboard, usually at night to avoid detection. An engineer from one ship, the *Song of America*, testified that the oil-water separator was operated so infrequently that it did not work when he did try to use it. They also admitted that the oil record books were falsified so routinely that they were known among many engineers as "eventyrbook," which means fairy tale book in Norwegian. [2]

The obvious question is why the engineer would avoid using the oil-water separator.

> Oil-water separators are notoriously troublesome to operate. But company engineers testified that the bypass systems, which had been in operation on some ships since 1990, were partly the result of the company's bonus incentives. Membranes for the separator cost as much as $80,000 a year per ship and disposing of waste oil in port can cost $300,000 a year. By saving this money, a ship's officers could receive bigger year-end bonuses for staying under budget. [3]

In December 1996, a Grand Jury in San Juan indicted Royal Caribbean Cruise Line for alleged conspiracy to dump waste oil in U.S. waters from five of its eleven vessels. The Grand Jury also charged the Miami-based company—the only cruise line awarded a Det Norske Veritas Safety and Environmental Protection Certificate—and two high level employees with obstruction of justice for allegedly tampering with witnesses and destroying evidence that *Sovereign of the Seas* was bypassing pollution control procedures.

## How Did They Respond?

The first defence advanced by Royal Caribbean Cruise Line was that the discharge of oil near San Juan was an isolated oversight. However, the Justice Department argued to the contrary. According to Coast Guard files, on February 1, 1993, a Coast Guard surveillance plane spotted an oil slick behind the *Nordic Empress* off the Bahamas en route to Miami. Videotape taken from the plane showed a slick that appeared to be a perfect match for the videotaped discharge from the *Sovereign of the Seas*. When questioned by the Coast Guard, the officers of the *Nordic Empress* also denied discharging anything into the sea.

Royal Caribbean Cruise Line's second effort was to avoid indictment. In the fall of 1996, the company offered to plead guilty to some charges and to pay a substantial fine. Officials at the Justice Department rejected the offer and told the company to expect a thirty-five-count indictment. The Justice Department also resisted Royal Caribbean's lobbying the State Department and the Defence Department to persuade the Department of Justice not to file charges. The argument advanced by Royal Caribbean Cruise Line was that the United States lacked the authority to bring charges against the cruise line. They did not refute the accusations of dumping. They argued that the U.S. government asserting jurisdiction was inconsistent with the international Law of the Sea and that it could serve as the basis for other countries interfering with U.S. vessels. Some in the administration saw the strength of that argument.

Legal manoeuvring and lobbying intensified after Royal Caribbean Cruise Line was indicted. They filed briefs with the Court arguing that it lacked jurisdiction in the matter. They also sought the assistance of the Norwegian government, because the *Sovereign of the Seas* flies a Norwegian flag. On March 12, 1997, a delegation from the Norwegian embassy in Washington delivered a diplomatic note to the State Department seeking jurisdiction in the case. Given that the Norwegian government had already looked into the case and decided that no action was necessary, its call for jurisdiction had no effect.

The argument that the U.S. lacked jurisdiction was ultimately rejected by the Federal court in San Juan and the case of the *Sovereign of the Seas* was scheduled to go to trial June 1998. Several months before, in February 1998, Royal Caribbean Cruise Line was indicted in Miami, not for dumping but on a single count of making a false statement to the Coast Guard with regard to the discharge off Bermuda by the *Nordic Empress*. The cruise line again claimed the U.S. lacked authority, and the Liberian Embassy intervened and asked that the case be dismissed.

After a hearing in April, the federal court rejected Royal Caribbean Cruise Line's call that the case be dismissed. While the judge may have conceded that the U.S. did not have the authority to prosecute for the discharge of oil—that would have to be done by the flag state—he ruled that the United States had authority to press charges because of the false statements the company made to the Coast Guard.

On June 3, 1998, Royal Caribbean Cruise Line pleaded guilty in the cases in Miami and San Juan and agreed to pay $9 million in fines. The government called the violations so pervasive and longstanding that the criminal conduct amounted to a routine business practice. Though this settled some cases, investigations in other jurisdictions continued. Eventually, Grand Juries would be struck in Alaska, New York, California, and the Virgin Islands. In sum, there were eight ships that followed an almost identical pattern: they would discharge unclean waste, would lie about it to Coast Guard investigators, and would make false entries in their oil record book. It was:

> *...also discovered that it wasn't just oil involved. Dry cleaning fluids, photographic chemicals and solvents from the print shop operations were being dumped in the water. The dumping continued even though the company knew it was being investigated. Among the accusations:*

> *On one sailing in 1994, the* Song of America *discharged 5000 gallons of oily bilge between New York and Bermuda...In Miami, Royal Caribbean's home port, [and in New York City] it regularly dumped pollutants into the Port of Miami, including silver used in photo labs and....perchloroethylene [which is] used in dry cleaning....In Alaska in 1994 and 1995, its* Nordic Empress *routinely discharged oil-contaminated waste, and in fact didn't use the oil/water separator at all...In St. Croix in the Virgin Islands, the* Song of America, Song of Norway, *and* Sovereign of the Seas *dumped dirty water into the sea on a weekly basis....In California, the* Nordic Prince *dumped its bilge water into the surrounding sea.[4]*

## What Were The Other Charges?

Less than a month after Royal Caribbean Cruise Line agreed to pay the $9 million fine to settle the case in San Juan involving the *Sovereign of the Seas* and in Miami involving the *Nordic Empress*, the company reported a new dumping episode to the U.S. Coast Guard. The offence was reported to the company by crew members and led to the firing of the two engineers. "Engineers aboard the *Nordic Empress* were caught tampering with the sensors that monitor oil dumping and creating false record books to hide their actions even as the U.S. Coast Guard was continuing to scrutinize the cruise line."[5]

Based on this episode, and others investigated in other jurisdictions in the United States, Royal Caribbean Cruise Line pleaded guilty in July 1999 to twenty-one counts of dumping oil and hazardous chemicals and lying to the U.S. Coast Guard. They agreed to pay an $18 million fine. The plea agreements, and the amount in respective fines, were filed in U.S. District Courts in Miami ($3 million), New York City ($3 million), Los Angeles ($3 million), Anchorage ($6.5 million), Puerto Rico ($1 million), and the U.S. Virgin Islands ($1.5 million). In announcing the plea agreements, Attorney General Janet Reno said: "Royal Caribbean used our nation's waters as its dumping ground, even as it promoted itself as an environmentally 'green' company." She warned: "This case will sound like a foghorn throughout the maritime industry."

This essentially settled all charges Royal Caribbean faced in U.S. jurisdictions, but the company was still vulnerable to charges by state and local jurisdictions. Alaska filed suit against Royal Caribbean Cruise Line in August 1999 alleging seven counts of violating laws governing oil and hazardous waste disposal. In January of the following year, the company paid a fine of $3.5 million for dumping toxic chemicals and oil-contaminated water into the state's waters, and it agreed not to discharge wastewater within three miles of Alaska's coastline. Alaska is likely the only state involved with the federal case that was able to pursue civil charges against the company because the violations occurred in Alaska's waters in 1994 and 1995.

In the face of the suit by the state of Alaska, and an increasingly hostile attitude toward the cruise industry among many Alaskans in port cities, the president of Royal Caribbean Cruise Line visited by cruise ship the ports used. He apologized for the company's past actions, and made promises for the future. In most places the reception was cool to hostile.

His visit was also unsuccessful in swaying voters in Juneau against a proposed $5-a-passenger tax on cruise ship visitors. Approved with 70% voter support, the measure had failed three years before, but was successful this time in large part because of negative feelings about Royal Caribbean.

"Blue engine smoke rising over Juneau's harbour, throngs packing Juneau's pavements and streets and incessant noise from sightseeing flights ferrying cruise passengers to glaciers were among residents' complaints about cruise ships," said Joe Geldhof, an attorney for a labour union that organized the campaign. "[The thing with Royal Caribbean]...just put people over the edge." [6]

This tax was the first time any intermediate port in a U.S. state had imposed such a fee. While other ports discussed adopting similar fees, the North West Cruise Ship Association—an association of cruise lines serving the Alaskan market—questioned its legality because it might violate constitutional provisions governing interstate commerce as well as laws covering international commerce. In addition, the association claimed, the fee discriminated against cruise passengers (as compared to those arriving by plane or ferry). The association wanted the $3 million raised by the fee to be used to benefit the ships and their passengers directly. But the city didn't bend. Later that month, Haines took a similar step and approved a new tax on local tours taken by cruise passengers.

At about the same time, Royal Caribbean Cruise Line got a break from the federal court judge. When it went to pay its $6.5 million fine, the judge suspended $3 million of the fine in return for prompt payment of the remaining $3.5 million. So, while the company paid $2 million to the National Parks Foundation, $1 million to the National Fish and Wildlife Foundation, and $500,000 to the U.S. treasury, it got to keep in its own coffers $3 million— an amount equal to that given for purposes of the environment. A parallel situation would be you or me agreeing to pay $250 in cash for a $500 speeding ticket today and being forgiven the other $250. Judges in my town don't offer this option, but perhaps in Alaska's courts it is different.

## What Is the Aftermath of the Royal Caribbean Case?

Federal authorities continue to pursue the individuals in the Royal Caribbean Cruise Line cases who were responsible for the dumping, and who falsified the oil record books. Authorities are also continuing to pursue the question of how far up the organizational structure knowledge of the practice went. To date, several chief engineers have been implicated. One, the chief engineer on the *Nordic Prince* when it was dumping oil and other wastes in the Pacific, was arrested in November 1999 when he returned to the U.S. in his position on the newest mega-ship, the *Voyager of the Seas*. FBI and immigration agents took him into custody when the ship arrived in Miami on its maiden voyage and he was charged with three counts of conspiracy to violate federal oil pollution laws. He potentially faces a 15-year prison term and $750,000 in fines.

There has also been a degree of fallout from Royal Caribbean Cruise Line's behaviour. With increased interest and attention to the issue of shipboard wastes, cruise lines bowed to public pressure in Alaska in December 1999 by assuring government regulators that they would no longer dump untreated sewage or ground up garbage in areas of Alaska's Inside Passage where it is otherwise allowed. In early 2000, the industry narrowly escaped an attempt by the state government to impose a $50 head tax for each cruise ship passenger to Alaska—a move strongly motivated by the cruise industry's disregard for the environment of the Inside Passage. It is not unlikely that these efforts will be renewed.

Also in early 2000, attention began to shift to include air pollution. In February 2000, the Environmental Protection Agency cited six cruise ship companies (involving thirteen ships) for air pollution violations in the 1999 season. The investigation, which was undertaken following a flood of citizen complaints, cited violations in the waters of Juneau, Glacier Bay, and Seward. The companies cited include Holland America Line, Princess Cruises, Celebrity Cruises, Norwegian Cruise Line, Carnival Cruise Line, and World Explorer Cruise Line.

In August 2000, state investigators charged seven companies (the six listed already and Crystal Cruises) for eleven violations of state smoke-opacity standards when their ships were docked in Juneau between mid-July and mid-August. The citations were the result of a new five-year program to monitor emissions. Funded by $250,000 of the $3.5 million fine Royal Caribbean Cruise Line paid to the state to settle state water pollution charges, the program was set to expand to ports other than just Juneau. As a result of the charges, and in a bid to repair its image, Princess Cruises announced in late September 2000, that its ships would plug into Juneau's power supply while in port instead of running their smoke-belching engines in port to generate electricity. Their announcement was a response in part to a call earlier in the month by Alaska's governor that cruise lines use shore side power.

The program monitoring cruise ship emissions also analyzed the wastewater from cruise ships. Under a voluntary agreement, cruise lines agreed to allow the testing, but specific names of ships and companies would not be released unless violations were prosecuted and thereby became part of the public record. Interim results announced in August 2000 indicated more than a subtle violation of federal standards on fecal coliform. Readings as much as one hundred thousand times in excess of regulations were found. As well, all samples taken indicated that "conventional pollutants" were also part of the wastewater. According to the Juneau port commander for the Coast Guard, "The results are so extreme…that all possibilities must be considered, including design flaws and capacity issues with the Coast Guard-approved treatment systems."[7]

A meeting was held November 13, 2000, between the governor of Alaska, the International Council of Cruise Lines, and representatives of eight cruise lines to address environmental issues and to establish rules for discharges in Alaska's waters. The governor described the two and a half hour closed-door meeting as "a good start toward addressing the serious problem of maintaining Alaska's pristine inland waters and protecting our oceans." He said that

> *"the industry agreed on a shared goal of preserving Alaska's clean water through monitoring and regulating of their vessels' discharges, support for legislation now pending in Congress and an industry-funded state monitoring effort."* [8]

Through their support for federal legislation, the cruise lines agreed to refrain from dumping untreated waste in Alaska's waters, including beyond three miles from the coast, and they agreed to refrain from discharging treated sewage and gray water within one mile of shore or while the ship is at rest.

## Environmental Politics

There is little debate that Royal Caribbean Cruise Line's actions produced a public relations nightmare for the cruise industry. Shortly after media exposure of the issue, the International Council of Cruise Lines issued a policy statement and expressed its support for the environment. Individual companies have adopted their own campaigns to project an appropriately "green" image. For Royal Caribbean Cruise Line this includes being particularly generous in its donations to maritime-environmental causes. It has provided millions of dollars of support through its Ocean Fund, including in 1998 a $50,000 donation to Audubon Society's Living Oceans Program. Not only did the company provide financial support, but also in line with the Audubon Society's opposition to the consumption of swordfish both Royal Caribbean Cruises and Celebrity Cruises removed swordfish from their menus. They had been consuming 20 tons of swordfish per year.

We could likely find similar types of decisions by other cruise lines. However, of interest here are the environmental politics that are at play with regard to ports. For example, imposition of the head tax in Juneau, the shore excursion tax in Haines, and near-success in imposing a $50 state fee for cruise passengers, each reflect a political reaction to an environmental issue.

The issue is further politicized by retaliatory measures taken by cruise lines, such as that taken by Holland America Line following passage of the head tax in

Juneau. The company announced it would withdraw much of its support to Juneau charities. "If the community doesn't really want us there, if that's really truly what they're telling us, then we need to reassess what we're doing," Al Parrish, a Holland America Line Vice President was quoted as saying. At the same time that the company was proudly announcing new, environmentally responsible designs for its fleet, it appeared less than sensitive to the scars and hostility that had been produced by environmental irresponsibility.

Though it insists that the decision has nothing to do with the imposition of a new 4 % sales tax on shore excursions, Royal Caribbean International announced in December 2000 that it was cancelling all cruise ship service to Haines, Alaska—a loss of 120,000 tourists during each twenty-week season. The city itself has a population of 1200 residents.

The cruise line's decision to cancel stops at Haines followed the town's passage of the 4 % tax on shore excursions, and a nonbinding resolution to limit the growth of cruise ship visits after the incidents in which oily bilge water and other pollutants were dumped in area waters by Royal Caribbean International's ships. According to the local newspaper:

> The costs of the sudden RCCL pullout to Haines will be about $450,000 in lost moorage fees and sales tax revenues and $5 million in sales to local businesses. [9]

Royal Caribbean International resisted the city's attempts to have the decision reversed. Company officials said that the Haines stop had become a money-loser as fuel costs increased. Cruise ships can save large amounts of money bypassing Haines on their run from Juneau to Skagway.

## The Cruise Lines' Friends in Washington

It is not likely to be surprising that the cruise industry has its friends in Washington. Like any other interest group or industry, cruise lines lobby the U.S. Congress, and they support through campaign contributions the candidacy of certain members of Congress.

Representative Don Young (R-Alaska) is one candidate they have supported. In 1995, he introduced as an amendment to a bill on the House floor, which passed a measure that would restrict the ability of sexual-assault victims to collect damages in court, and to prohibit crew members from suing in courts. The measure never passed into law because opposition quickly erupted, as it became known that it had passed in the House. However, as seen earlier with regard to its relationship with Congress in relation to labour issues, the cruise industry does have its friends in Congress.

A year earlier in 1994, Representative Young and Senator Frank Murkowski (R-Alaska) were successful in forcing the Department of the Interior to increase by 72% the number of cruise ships allowed per year in Glacier Bay National Park, from one hundred and seven to one hundred and eighty-four. Each man was assuming the chairmanship for the committee that had jurisdiction over most agencies and programs of the Department of the Interior. From that position, they were able to instruct the Secretary of the Interior, Bruce Babbitt, to direct the park service to change the vessel management part of its plan so that it endorses one hundred and eighty-four visits per year— a number that corresponds to an average of two visits a day during the 92-day season. Though the media pointed to the fact that Bruce Babbitt and his chief of staff had both previously served as partners in a firm that had Holland America Line as a client, it is not clear that this had any influence on their actions.

The increase in the number of permits for Glacier Bay National Park was opposed by environmentalists and by the park service's own experts. Their concern was for the abundant wildlife in the park, including several species of whales, Stellar sea lions, seals, and otters. The mouth of the bay is a major feeding area. There had been a 20 % reduction in permits for Glacier Bay in 1978, following a sharp decline in the number of humpback whales in the bay, and strict speed limits were imposed on cruise ships. This reduction was slowly rolled back between 1982 and 1991.

Most visitors are interested in observing the far end of Glacier Bay, the head of the sixty-five-mile long bay where they can watch the huge Grand Pacific and Margerie Glaciers calves. Cruise ships normally travel to this area so passengers can observe the magnificent sight of huge chunks of glacial ice breaking off and with thundering sound falling into the sea. As a cruise ship holds its place in the area for an hour or two so passengers can observe this phenomenon, it also discharges into the air black smoke from its smoke stack. In certain weather conditions, these emissions produce a cloud of smog over the bay. In 1992, three cruise lines were fined a total of $50,000 for repeated violations of air-pollution laws. Regardless, additional permits were authorized two years later as environmental concerns gave way to political realities.

## Cruise Lines and Caribbean Ports

Environmental concerns continue to be an issue in the Caribbean. As in the case of Alaska, these have been reflected in efforts to raise the head tax charged for each passenger. But in the Caribbean the situation is a bit different.

There had been several efforts by Caribbean ports to increase their port charges in the early 1990s. For example, the seven-member Organization of Eastern

Caribbean States raised its port fees to a uniform $9.25 per visitor. However, pressure from the cruise industry forced them to roll the fees back to their original level. They raised them to $10 per visitor in 1995, but again were forced to roll them back. The Bahamas successfully resisted pressure from cruise lines to lower its new $15 head tax in 1994, but Jamaica in the same year gave into pressure, reduced its tax, and agreed to phase in an increase over four years. Cruise lines used the credible threat to move their ships to another port as their means of persuasion.

Disputes over port fees resumed in 1997 after six Caribbean islands (Antigua, Dominica, Grenada, St. Kitts, St. Lucia, and St. Vincent)—all members of the Organization of Eastern Caribbean States, announced that effective December 1, they would begin charging an extra $1.50 to cruise passengers. The extra cash was earmarked to defray the cost of improving waste management systems at the islands. Per regulations under MARPOL, the money was being used to increase the islands' ability to handle ship-generated waste.

The islands involved were participating in a region-wide program of waste disposal based in Port of Spain and sponsored by the International Maritime Organization. The entire program across the region was expected to cost $54 million, and it was financed by the World Bank. After almost a year, the cruise lines finally withdrew their opposition to the new tax in April 1998, following intervention by the World Bank. The bank explained that the island governments really had no choice in the matter—they had signed on with the project and collecting the tax from each visitor was part of the agreement. The agreement provided that the World Bank's funding would finance new landfills for each nation, provided they use the new tax revenues to run the landfill.

Though Carnival Cruise Line was one of the cruise lines that opposed the tax, it announced in March 1998 that "it looks like we will accept the $1.50 in the case of Granada, to help the country deal with its garbage problem."

> But... Carnival's vice president for public relations added that the cruise line still views the new tax as unfair and a dangerous precedent for a company that disposes of most of its solid waste on board its modern fleet. He said that Carnival has yet to decide whether to pay the tax in the other five nations that agreed earlier this month to impose it starting May 1. "We do not mind paying for something if it's a service being provided for us," he said. "But we do not want to pay for facilities we don't use."

> Gallagher conceded that $1.50 a head—on top of the current $3 arrival tax, the lowest in the region—seems paltry. But he stressed, "The reason that Carnival Corp. makes the kind of money we do is

*because we pay great, great attention to controlling our costs. Sure it's just $1.50. But it's $1.50 here, then $1.50 there, then $1.50 over there. When you allow people to unfairly charge for things, then you open a Pandora's box." [10]*

Disputes over port charges have continued, but they have been given limited attention in the media. Barbados was considering in 1999 an increase in its $6 a person fee, and was fully aware that any increase would be resisted by the cruise industry. In addition, in November 1999, Carnival Cruise Lines renewed the dispute over the $1.50 fee charged by members of the Organization of Eastern Caribbean States. Claiming that taxes on cruise ships are too high, Carnival Cruise Lines again announced a decision to boycott Grenada as a port. The confrontation appears to be a stalemate.

## The Problem of People Pollution

An item that is given limited attention when considering environmental issues is people pollution—the simple concentration of too many people in a single place. This is seen most vividly in ports such as St. Thomas. I recall being in port in December 1998 when thirteen cruise ships were in port. They disembarked for the day more than 25,000 cruise ship passengers; all crammed into the downtown area and Havensight Mall. That day is an extreme example of people pollution. It is more people than can be comfortably accommodated in the area.

The problem of people pollution varies with the size of a port and with the size of the ship—the larger the port the more passengers that can be comfortably accommodated. With increasingly larger ships, some small ports are becoming inaccessible. However, for other ports the effect of larger ships is compounded by the increase in the number of ships. For example, over the past decade the southeast Alaska market has tripled from 200,000 to 600,000 passengers a year. The towns receiving these passengers have scarcely changed in this same period of time.

Despite increased size of ships, many ports remain physically accessible. However, the mere increase in the number of passengers that go ashore alters the nature of the port experience. For example, it is not uncommon for Skagway, Alaska to receive ten times more visitors in one day than it has residents. This certainly influences the experience cruise passengers have of local folks—by the end of the season most people in cruise ports can't wait to be able to reclaim their town and to walk down the main street unhindered. Local residents simply become tired of the continuous onslaught of tourists. Their patience wanes as the season goes on.

The experience a cruise passenger has of a port is also coloured by the simple fact that other cruise passengers surround one. This presents a different experience than being in a community on one's own. Occasionally, a cruise ship passenger is fortunate. I visited Skagway one year at the beginning of the season, on a ship that had a thousand passengers, and on a day when there was no other ship in port. In addition, ours was the first cruise ship visit of the year. That experience of Skagway was considerably different than that had on a typical day at the height of the cruise ship season.

These comments are not meant to make too much of the problem of people pollution. They are meant to raise awareness of the problem, and that our experience of the problem may be directly influenced by the choice of cruise ship and of cruise itinerary.

[1] "U.S. Cracks Down on Marine Pollution," Lloyd's List, April 17, 1993, page 3

[2] Frantz, Douglas. "Gaps in Sea Laws Shield Pollution by Cruise Lines," New York Times, January 3, 1999.

[3] Frantz, Douglas. "Gaps in Sea Laws Shield Pollution by Cruise Lines," New York Times, January 3, 1999.

[4] Fields, Gregg. "Slick Justice," Miami Herald, September 26, 1999.

[5] Brown, Carolyn Spencer. "Cruise News," Washington Post, October 25, 1998, page E03.

[6] "Lines May Fight Legality of Juneau Passenger Levy," Lloyd's List, October 8, 1999, page 5.

[7] McAllister, Bill. "A Big Violation on Wastewater," Juneau Empire, August 27, 2000.

[8] Sidron, Jorge. "Cruise Lines Agree to Back New Discharge Rules," Travel Weekly Daily Bulletin, November 16, 2000.

[9] Nanney, Dave. "Salvaging the Economic Wreck," Eagle Eye, December 17, 2000.

[10] "Tax on Passengers is a Lot of Garbage, Cruise Lines Say," Los Angeles Times, March 20, 1998, page A-5.

# 7 You Can Squeeze Blood From a Turnip

It should not come as a surprise that cruise lines are in business to make money. However, if one looks at cruise fares, it is easy to wonder how that money is made. A cruise today costs less than it did in the early 1980s. *The Washington Post* reported in 1983 that the average cost for a cruise was between $160 and $200 a day. If we adjust for inflation, the amount today would range from $272 to $340 a day.

Many cruise lines today have average per diems that are significantly lower than this. In 1998/99, a number of major cruise lines had average per diems less than $300: Premier Cruises ranged from $93 to $150, Carnival Cruise Line from $190 to $227, Royal Caribbean International from $168 to $285, and Norwegian Cruise Line from $175 to $240. Cruise lines such as Holland America Line, Princess Cruises, and Celebrity Cruise generally cost today what an average cruise cost in 1983.

There are a number of ways that cruise lines are able to earn incomes other than through pricing. Some of these depend on generating onboard revenue— Princess Cruises' *Sun Princess*, a ship carrying 1200 passengers, was reported in 1997 to generate $6 million in weekly onboard revenue—an amount that is twice the industry norm in 1999 of between $220 and $232 per passenger per day.

Being a foreign-registered corporation that is operating foreign flagged ships also shapes the financial bottom line for a cruise line. Carnival Cruise Lines, which earned approximately $1 billion in profits in both 1999 and 2000, paid less than 1% in income taxes; these taxes were for holdings of Gray Line Westours in the states of Washington and Alaska. If Carnival were an American corporation paying taxes at the 35 % rate, it would have paid taxes of more than $350 million. Royal Caribbean International, which is also a foreign-registered corporation, does not even include a line for income taxes on its financial statements.

Another way in which cruise lines make money is through economies of scale. Like the hotel industry, which has consolidated over the decade to a handful of major players, the cruise industry has undergone considerable consolidation over the past five to ten years. This consolidation has allowed the larger companies to get larger and to increase their overall efficiencies.

While the large companies increasingly benefit from the economic power associated with their size, smaller cruise lines are increasingly disadvantaged. Carnival Corporation, the parent company of Carnival Cruise Line, has been on a buying spree since 1989. In the same decade that Carnival Corporation has been buying new ships and several cruise lines, many other cruise lines have come and gone.

Before she became affiliated with Carnival Corporation, and before her current position as Chief Operating Officer of Cunard Line, Pam Conover predicted in 1992, as vice president of cruise shipping for Citibank NA, that the mass market "...will increasingly become a game in which only players who enjoy economies of scale can play and win." She predicted that three companies would dominate the North American cruise industry by the year 2000 with 90% of the market. She was not too far off the mark.

## Consolidation and the Concentration of Capital

The cruise industry has had several phases of growth. Many of the companies we know today—Princess Cruises (1965), Norwegian Cruise Line (1966), Royal Caribbean Cruise Line (1970), and Carnival Cruise Line (1972) (which was a breakaway of sorts from NCL)—had their start in the late 1960's and early 1970's.

There was another wave of growth in the industry in the early and mid-1980s as cruising for leisure became more popular and as large investors became interested in the earning potential of the cruise industry. Premier Cruises was begun in 1982 by Dial Corporation (the parent company of Greyhound Bus Lines and Armour foods), and in 1984 both Regency Cruises and Sea Goddess Cruises began operations. Windstar Cruises followed in 1986, and Seabourn Cruise Line started in 1989. Premier and Regency were focused on the mass market; the others each provided an up market product with corresponding up market prices.

The growth in number of luxury cruise lines continued in the early 1990's with Crystal Cruises and Renaissance Cruises in 1990, Radisson Cruise Line in 1992, and in 1993 both Silversea Cruises and Orient Lines. There were also a number of new lines directed toward the broader market. These included: Celebrity Cruises in 1990; Crown Cruise Line, Majesty Cruise Line, Seawind Cruise Line, and Star Clippers Cruises in 1991; and in 1993, Star Cruises and two companies that ceased operations within a year: American Family Cruises, which was started by Costa Cruises, and Fiesta Marina Cruises, which was a Spanish-speaking line begun by Carnival Cruise Line.

Not only was there a growth in the number of cruise lines, but the companies operating were increasingly expanding their capacity. Many cruise lines undertook plans for building new fleets in the mid and late 1980s; this building program has continued for almost two decades.

For Carnival Cruise Line, which by the mid 1980's had proven quite success-ful and profitable, there was a need to build new ships. The company anticipated an increasing number of passengers that would fill new cabins, but unlike its competi-tors it also had the assets from its operations that allowed it to pay for the new ships it was building. New ships served the dual purpose of providing for an expanding market, and as an investment for substantial profits from operations.

Carnival's buying was not limited to new ships. Through its parent company, Carnival Corporation, it made a near successful bid for Royal Caribbean Cruise Line (and its sister line, Admiral Cruises) in 1988. It bought Holland America Line instead. Holland America Line, which had purchased Westours in 1975, had recently acquired 50% of Windstar Cruises, and with Carnival's ownership it acquired the remaining 50% in 1989. Two years later, in 1991, Carnival Corporation called off an agreement to purchase Premier Cruises. Later that year it purchased 50% of the upscale Seabourn Cruises. In 1986, Carnival was one of twenty-six cruise companies in North America and it had less than 15% of market share. In 1991, it had more than 26% of the mar-ket (followed by Royal Caribbean (15%), Norwegian (14%) and Princess (12%).

Carnival Corporation was not the only company investing in cruise lines. Premier Cruises took over Home Line in 1987 and Princess Cruises purchased Sitmar Cruises in 1988. Kloster Cruises, the parent of Norwegian Cruise Line, had bought Royal Viking Line in 1984 and added Royal Cruise Line in 1989.

A commercial shipping firm, Overseas Shipholding Group, also tried to enter the cruise industry. It made an unsuccessful play for Royal Cruise Line in 1989. In 1991, it negotiated a purchase of Kloster Cruises (parent company of Norwegian Cruise Line), but pulled out of the deal at the last minute. Later that year it purchased a 50% share of Celebrity Cruises.

As the cruise industry boomed again in the late 1990s, consolidation resumed. While Norwegian Cruise Line was saved from bankruptcy by selling $101 million in bonds to Carnival Corporation in 1995, and narrowly avoided being taken over, it survived the financial crisis and went on to acquire Majesty Cruise Line in 1997, it started Norwegian Capricorn Line (for the Australian market) in that same year, and in 1998 it purchased Orient Lines. In 2000, Norwegian Cruise Line was itself bought by Malaysia-based Star Cruises.

In roughly the same period of time, Royal Caribbean International pur-chased Celebrity Cruises (1997). Its continuing investment is reflected in the com-mitment of both companies to building new ships. As well, Royal Caribbean International expanded its access to the European market through its purchase of a 20% share of British-based First Choice in 2000.

The greatest consolidation in the industry however has been by Carnival Corporation. It gained a minority interest in Greek-based Epirotiki Line in the early 1990s, in part by selling the line its old ships, though divested of its 49% stake in 1995. Following its failed bid for Norwegian Cruise Line in 1995, Carnival Corporation purchased a 28.6% stake in British Airtours (operator of Sun Cruises) in 1996, and later that year (with Airtours as its partner) it purchased Costa Cruises. In 1998, Carnival Corporation bought a majority interest in Cunard Line. It took full control of that company in 1999, and combined it with Seabourn Cruise Line in 2000.

Carnival Corporation again attempted to buy Norwegian Cruise Line in 1999, but after resistance from the NCL parent company's Board of Directors it entered a partnership with Star Cruises (which had also made a bid for the company) in order to make the purchase in early-2000. Carnival ended the sixty / forty partnership with Star Cruises several months after it had been formed and gave Star Cruises full control of NCL. In September 2000, Carnival Corporation bought from Airtours the 50% of Costa Cruises it did not already own.

Four key players today dominate the cruise industry. Carnival Corporation, which in 1999 began marketing its six brands (Carnival, Holland America Line, Windstar Cruises, Seabourn Cruises, Cunard Cruise Line, and Costa Cruises) under the label "The World's Leading Cruise Lines," is the largest force in the industry. Other dominant players are Royal Caribbean International (including Royal Caribbean Cruise Ltd. and Celebrity Cruises), P&O Princess Cruises (which operates P&O Cruises, Princess Cruises, Aida Cruises, Swan Hellenic Cruises, and Seetours International in Germany), and Star Cruises (which also has ownership of Norwegian Cruise Line and Orient Line). There are many smaller cruise lines, but they tend to fill a particular niche. It can be expected that a number of these smaller cruise lines will either disappear or be bought up by the larger conglomerates.

The industry has also consolidated through elimination of companies. Some cruise lines (such as Pearl Cruises in the mid-1990s) have simply decided to cease operations. Others have disappeared through mergers. For example, in the late 1990s, Epirotiki Line, Sun Line, and Royal Olympic Cruises combined under the Royal Olympic name. Several years later, in 1999, Cyprus-based Louis Cruise Lines bought controlling interest in the combined company, but maintains Royal Olympic as an independent brand name. A group of investors similarly bought Seawind Cruise Line, Dolphin Cruises and Premier Cruises and combined them under the Premier name in 1997.

Some cruise lines have gone bankrupt, while a number of cruise lines have barely been saved from bankruptcy. Sea Goddess Cruises leased their ships to Cunard Line when they faced bankruptcy in 1987. Similarly, Renaissance Cruises was sold in 1991 when its parent company was forced to claim bankruptcy. Regency Cruises had no last minute saviour. The company went bankrupt in 1995, leaving many passengers stranded and with little recourse for refunds. Passengers booked on a fifty-nine-day circumnavigation of South America found themselves returning to an unplanned port several days into the cruise. Passengers on the company's other itineraries also had their cruise end abruptly. The World Cruise Company went bankrupt in 2000, similarly leaving many passengers stranded in Tahiti midway through a world cruise.

In the fall of 2000, Premier Cruises, the fifth largest cruise line, suddenly went bankrupt. It cut short the vacation of 2800 passengers and withdrew from the marketplace more than five thousand berths per week. Several months later Commodore Cruise Line also claimed bankruptcy. Unlike passengers with Regency Cruises, those with Premier Cruises received refunds of fares paid. Only some passengers received refunds when Commodore Cruise Line ceased operations.

The U.S. government, through the Federal Maritime Commission, requires cruise lines embarking passengers at U.S. ports to post a $15 million bond. The bond is underwritten by an insurance company, which reimburses to the extent possible passengers who have already purchased fares for voyages that are being cancelled. In the case of Regency Cruises, the bond covered passengers with reservations on a ship operating from a U.S. port, however those taking cruises on ships that were home ported in Jamaica or another foreign port, had no recourse.

In the case of Premier Cruises, the staff weren't as fortunate. Some were "trapped" on ships in port while waiting for several months for back pay and savings held by the company. They lived on provisions aboard the ship and little more. In the case of the *Seawind Crown*, anchored in Barcelona, police were needed to maintain calm on the ship after the initial six weeks or so in the ordeal. Staff on Commodore Cruise Line's *Enchanted Capri* were repatriated to their home country through the efforts and financial support of the International Transport Workers Federation.

## Why Isn't There a U.S. Cruise Industry?

Though many of the largest cruise lines have their headquarters in the United States—both Carnival Corporation and Royal Caribbean Cruises Ltd. have their stocks traded on the New York Stock Exchange—none are actually U.S. corporations. Carnival Corporation in 1999 had revenues of $3.5 billion with over $1 billion in net income, but it paid no corporate income tax. As stated in the company's annual report:

> *Management believes that substantially all of the company's income (with the exception of its United States ("U.S.") source income from the transportation, hotel and tour businesses of Holland America*

*Westours) is exempt from U.S. federal income taxes. If the company was found not to meet certain tests of the Internal Revenue code, as amended, (the "code") or if the code were to be changed in a manner adverse to the company, a portion of the company's income would become subject to taxation by the U.S. at higher than normal corporate tax rates.*

Royal Caribbean International, which in the same year had profits of $383 million on revenues of $2.5 billion, has a similar statement in its annual report. This exemption from tax is based on a section of the Internal Revenue code that exempts foreign corporations' income from ships and aircraft from taxation, if the country in which the corporation is organized offers the equivalent exemption to U.S. corporations. The rules were set up to promote international shipping and air trade. Cruise lines have been able to take unique advantage of the provision by registering in countries that do not impose a corporate income tax. These countries offer what are known as "flags of convenience."

## Why Fly a flag of Convenience?

Most cruise ships are registered in one of three countries: Bahamas, Panama, and Liberia. By registering their ships in these countries, companies are able to seek protection from burdensome income taxes, from U.S. labour laws (including wage scales and the right to collective bargaining), and from U.S. regulation generally. The regulations that the ship must follow are those of the country where the ship is registered. Even enforcement of international regulations is the responsibility of the state where the ship is registered. For example, if you were to observe a cruise ship dumping illegal waste in international waters, it is the flag state that would handle any complaint about the action.

Flags of convenience provide a low cost option for ship registry, and also allow a company to operate a ship with fewer regulations or controls than would be the case if U.S.-registered. Worker salaries and hours are not regulated and workers have limited if any recourse in U.S. or other courts if there is a dispute over wages or a workplace injury. With foreign registries, inspection of safety equipment is often left to the U.S. Coast Guard (or similar authority in some European countries) to inspect and certify as meeting international standards.

The flag of convenience is clearly an economic benefit to the cruise line. Flags of convenience are also easy to purchase. Liberia offers its registry through International Registries Inc. in Reston, Virginia. Panama's fleet-safety operation is based in Manhattan, not Panama City.

Ship registry has become big business. In 1995, Panama earned $47.5 million in ship registration fees and annual taxes—5 % of its federal budget—and another $50 million for maritime lawyers, agents, and inspectors. The government operates fifty-six maritime consulates around the world from which a registration can be purchased. The consul can offer discounts of up to 50% for transfer of multiple ships to Panamanian registry, and a complete waiver of fees for a year in some cases. The consul also receives a bonus based on the amount of business brought in.

There have been regular calls in the U.S. Congress and from the U.S. Coast Guard and the National Transportation Safety Board that cruise lines operating from U.S. ports, carrying U.S. passengers, should be held to U.S. standards, regardless of where the ship is built, under what flag of convenience they are registered, and where their ownership is headquartered. However, these calls have been generally unsuccessful. Yet the government of Panama called on the U.S. Coast Guard to investigate the sinking of Premier Cruises' *Seabreeze* in December 2000. Though some incremental changes have been made, the industry continues to operate largely free from U.S. government regulation.

## Are there Any U.S.-Registered Cruise Ships?

There are several small cruise lines that operate ships registered in the United States. The largest is American Classic Voyages (ACV), which operates the Delta Queen Steamboat Company, Delta Queen Coastal Voyages, America Hawaii Cruises, and the newly established United States Line. The United States Line was formed when ACV bought the *Nieuw Amsterdam* from Holland America Line and renamed it the *MS Patriot*. Two new 1900-passenger ships are also under construction for the line at Litton Industries' Ingalls Shipbuilding in Mississippi. Clipper Cruise Line, Cruise West, and Glacier Bay Tours and Cruises and America West Steamboat Company are several other companies that operate U.S.-registered ships.

To be registered in the U.S., a ship normally must be constructed in the U.S., and it must be crewed by U.S. officers and staff. U.S. labour law, including provision of a minimum wage, and all other federal laws and regulations apply to U.S.-registered ships. The main advantage of being U.S.-registered is that the ship can transport passengers between two ports in the United States and not violate the Passenger Vessel Services Act of 1886. This Act requires that a ship be U.S.-registered if its itinerary is based in only U.S. ports, as is the case of cruises of the Hawaiian Islands.

## What is the Passenger Vessel Services Act?

Have you ever wondered why that cruise to Alaska leaves from Vancouver rather than Seattle? The answer is the Passenger Vessel Services Act of 1886 (PVSA). Originally passed to protect U.S. companies from competition by Canadian ferries that shuttled among resorts on the Great Lakes, the Act states:

> *"No foreign vessel shall transport passengers between ports or places in the United States, either directly or by way of a foreign port, under penalty of $2 for each passenger so transported and landed."*

The fine was increased to $200 in 1889. In 1984, the Puerto Rican Passenger Services act exempted that island from the restrictions of the PVSA.

Stated simply, the Act prohibits a foreign registered cruise ship from taking passengers from one U.S. port to another U.S. port. Consequently, a cruise from San Diego to Hawaii will embark passengers at Ensenada, Mexico in order to avoid taking passengers from one U.S. port to another. Ensenada also serves as an intermediate port for passengers on a round trip Hawaiian cruise that leaves from and returns to San Diego.

The penalty for violating the Passenger Vessel Services Act is payment of a fine for each passenger landed from one U.S. port to another. In January 1999, the Norwegian Cruise Line's *Norwegian Dynasty* made a stop for engine repairs in San Diego while en route from Hawaii to Puerto Vallarta. Passengers were given the option to go ashore for the day, but they were told they would have to themselves pay the $200 penalty under the PVSA. In December 1999, Holland America Line's *Statendam* sailed directly from Hawaii to San Diego, choosing to cancel the planned stop at Ensenada. The ship had left Hawaii eleven hours late and had a choice between paying the fine for the 50 or so passengers who boarded in Hawaii versus stopping in Ensenada and the start of the following cruise (which was a fully-booked Millennium cruise) placing it behind schedule, before it began.

## Is the Jones Act the Same as the PVSA?

There are two laws that control the activity of passenger ships in U.S. waters. One of these is the Passenger Vessel Services Act (PVSA). The other, the Jones Act, is often confused with PVSA. These two laws have distinctly different purposes.

As we have seen, the PVSA sought to protect U.S. passenger vessels from competition in their transport of passengers from one U.S. port to the other. The Jones Act, which is also known as the Merchant Marine Act of 1920, was passed shortly after the World War I and sought to promote the growth of a well-equipped and modern merchant marine that would be available for use in the nation's defence and that would grow foreign and domestic commerce. It also reinforced the intent of the Passenger Vessel Services Act. The Jones Act states:

> *It is necessary for the national defence and for the proper growth of its foreign and domestic commerce that the United States shall have a merchant marine of the best equipped and most suitable types of vessels sufficient to carry the greater portion of its commerce and serve as a naval or military auxiliary in time of war or national emergency, ultimately to be owned and operated privately by citizens of the United States; and it is declared to be the policy of the United States to do whatever may be necessary to develop and encourage the maintenance of such a merchant marine, and, insofar as may not be inconsistent with the express provisions of this act, the Secretary of Transportation shall, in the disposition of vessels and shipping property hereinafter provided, in the making of rules and regulations, and in the administration of the shipping laws keep always in view this purpose and object as the primary end to be maintained.*

These two acts together have posed a barrier to foreign-registered cruise lines operating freely between ports in the U.S. The cruise industry has lobbied for many years for repeal or change in these acts, but to date with no success. The most recent efforts were in 1997, when the Senate considered the United States Cruise Tourism Act, and 1999, when the Senate considered the United States Cruise Ship Tourism Development Act. Hearings were held for both acts, but they did not produce any clear consensus for change.

Opposition to the changes associated with these acts was already well-organized. In late 1995, a broad-based coalition called the Maritime Cabotage Task Force was formed of more than four hundred American organizations and companies to support the Jones Act. The task force has as its members U.S.-flag ship operators, shipbuilding and ship repair yards, labour organizations; rail, trucking and airline groups; marine vendors and equipment manufacturers; and pro-defence coalitions. In 1997, the U.S. House of Representatives passed a resolution of support for the Jones Act, and both Republican and Democratic Senate leaders declared their strong support for the act. It does not appear that the cruise industry has impacted the resolve of groups supporting key provisions of the Jones Act.

In addition to lobbying for changes in these two acts, the cruise industry has actively lobbied against efforts by the U.S. Government to increase its control over the industry. There were several such efforts in 1991, a year in which the cruise industry received more attention from Congress than any year before because of safety concerns brought forward by the Coast Guard and the National Transportation Safety Board, and because for the first time the industry's avoidance of U.S. taxes was raised as an issue. The attention included the Gibbons Bill, which was designed to convince the world to stop subsidizing shipbuilding and repair—the U.S. ended its practice of shipbuilding subsidies in 1981; the Murphy Bill which would bring seafarers on foreign ships regularly using U.S. ports under the U.S. labour laws; and the Taylor Bill which would strip foreign flag vessels of the right to operate casinos unless they sailed on voyages of more than thirty-six hours or made a port call. None of these bills was successful, but they did define the points of difference between the cruise industry and the U.S. government. The battle lines drawn have scarcely changed over the past decade.

## Elimination of Shipbuilding Subsidies?

One of the key elements of the Jones Act is concern for the development of a U.S.-flag merchant marine. An obvious question is why U.S.-flag passenger vessels are not more common than they are. Hearings held on the most recent effort to change the protections in the Passenger Vessel Services Act and Jones Act provide some interesting insight. Speaking in support of current regulations, the president of the Shipbuilders Council of America points out that:

> *U.S.-flag cruise ship operations have been disadvantaged for too long by foreign-flag cruise ship companies operating with considerable competitive advantages. Foreign flag cruise ships today operate virtually tax exempt, while U.S.-flag operators pay U.S. corporate income taxes; foreign flag operators employ third world crews at a fraction of the cost of U.S. flag vessel crew costs; they operate outside U.S. environmental laws, and last but not least, they have long had and continue to have the ability to purchase heavily subsidized vessels in foreign shipyards—some as much as 33 % in direct subsidies plus incalculable indirect subsidies.*

The issue of subsidies was discussed in greater detail several years earlier in testimony by the Shipbuilders Council of America to the House of Representatives in hearings April 13, 1994 before the Committee on Merchant Marine and Fisheries in its consideration of the United States Passenger Development Act of 1994. The Shipbuilders Council pointed to:

*Three ships (Statendam, Maasdam, and Ryndam) constructed by Fancantieri Shipyards in Italy for Holland America Line which received a 28% government grant toward ship construction (worth between $210 million and $224 million), plus a subsidy from the Italian Government for financing the construction;*

*Two ships (Crown Princess and Regal Princess) constructed by Fancantieri Shipyards in Italy for Princess Cruises which received a 28% government grant toward ship construction (worth an estimated $154 million) plus a 30% subsidy for the ships being registered under the Italian flag (worth an additional $165 million)—the two ships, which together cost $550 million received $319 million in subsidies and grants, plus further subsidies in government financing of the construction;*

*Two ships (Costa Classica and Costa Romatica) constructed by Fancantieri Shipyards in Italy for Costa Cruises which received a 28% government grant toward ship construction (worth an estimated $151 million) plus a 30% subsidy for the ships being registered under the Italian flag (worth an additional $162 million and roughly equal to the depreciation in value in the first five years of the ships operation)—the two ships, which together cost $540 million received $313 million in subsidies and grants, plus further subsidies in government financing of the construction;*

*Two ships (Dreamward and Windward) constructed by Chantiers de l'Atlantique in France for Norwegian Cruise Line, which received a grant of 20% on one ship and 40% on the other, meant the two ships costing $220 million each had total subsidies of more than $264 million—sort of a buy one, get one free kind of arrangement;*

*Three ships (Nordic Empress, Monarch of the Seas, and Majesty of the Seas) constructed by Chantiers de l'Atlantique in France for Royal Caribbean Cruise Line with subsidies of between 28% and 36.5%, in addition to government-subsidized financing for construction—the three ships had a total cost of $750 million, and they received total subsidies of between $160 million and $183.7 million; and,*

> *Two ships* (Legend of the Seas *and* Splendor of the Seas*)*
> *constructed by Chantiers de l'Atlantique in France for Royal*
> *Caribbean Cruise Line with a subsidy of 9% ($28.3 million) for the*
> *first ship and 20% ($62.8 million) for the second—the two ships*
> *together cost $628 million; they had subsidies amounting to more than*
> *$91 million.*

The use of subsidies by shipbuilders was an important element in develop-ment of the shipbuilding industry. In the late 1980s, the Italian government made a deliberate attempt to use subsidies to capture cruise ship construction contracts for state-owned Fancantieri. Until Fancantieri secured a cruise ship contract with Princess Cruises in 1988, the shipbuilder had not built a cruise ship since 1966. In just five years, subsidies enabled Fancantieri to make up for more than twenty years with-out cruise ship contracts and become the world's premier ship builder. Its status has only increased since 1994, with the yard accounting for much of the new construction undertaken by Carnival Corporation and by Princess Cruises.

It does not appear that the U.S. is likely to reintroduce subsidies for cruise ship construction. It is equally as unlikely that the government will change its posi-tion on the Jones Act and the Passenger Vessel Services Act. While the cruise industry would like to continue to benefit from the subsidies in foreign ship construction, it is unlikely that they will become unencumbered by laws that encourage and support development of a U.S.-based merchant marine. They will undoubtedly continue to try to effect change.

## But Doesn't the Cruise Industry Have Friends in Congress?

Though the cruise industry does have its friends in Congress, it is unlikely that major changes will be made that would open travel between U.S. ports by for-eign-registered cruise ships. The industry has been successful in winning small bat-tles. For example, it was successful in having a senator insert a single word in the Federal budget bill in 1998 which exempted the seventeen cruise lines operating in the U.S. from a $6 per passenger immigration fee to cover inspection costs for people arriving in U.S. ports. The change saved the cruise lines $20 million a year. The indus-try was also successful in having an amendment made to another bill that protected the foreign-registered cruise lines' monopoly on coveted permits to sail into Glacier Bay National Park in Alaska. However it failed in its 1996-effort to have an amend-ment added to the Coast Guard funding bill that would have barred foreign seafarers from suing employers in U.S. courts. The amendment was dropped after a bitter bat-tle for votes between cruise line lobbyists and seafarers' advocates.

The cruise industry has generally been successful in resisting restrictions considered by Congress. The industry has used a variety of strategies to influence Congress. Until the early 1990s, the industry provided to a number of legislators "fact-finding" cruises in order to provide them first hand knowledge of its product and of the industry. These ended in 1992 after Congressman Taylor raised the issue in the House of Representatives and it was added to the things that were considered "politically incorrect" to accept. The industry has also maintained an active lobbying presence in Washington, at an annual cost of more than $600,000. The International Council of Cruise Lines coordinates these efforts.

The most visible effort to influence Congress began in the early 1990s when the industry first came under scrutiny by Congress. Criticism surfaced about the tax status of cruise lines, and concern began to mount about the cost to the U.S. government of a foreign-registered cruise industry operating out of its ports. The industry responded to congressional and public concerns through a campaign designed to demonstrate how much the U.S. benefited from the industry.

In 1992, the International Council of Cruise Lines commissioned Price Waterhouse to undertake a study and prepare a report that would document the contribution of the foreign-flag cruise industry to the United States economy. The hope was that the report would combat what the industry perceived as a misunderstanding of, and threat to, the industry by the U.S. Congress. The report said the cruise industry directly accounted for 134,780 jobs (with ripple effect, the number was estimated to be as high as 450,166), it paid more than $14.5 billion in wages to United States employees, and had a total impact of $6.3 billion in federal, state, and local taxes. The report appeared to have its desired effect in that criticism seemed to subside.

Since 1992, the study has twice been revised, once in 1997 and again in 1999. In both of these years, Congress had under consideration legislation that would affect the Jones Act and the Passenger Vessel Services Act. The 1997 study indicated that the industry generated 176,433 U.S. jobs. Unlike the 1992 study however, its focus was on the direct economic impact of the industry on the U.S. economy. In 1997, the industry spent $6.6 billion on goods and services produced in the United States. Its total economic impact was estimated at $11.6 billion. It was estimated that this impact would increase to $18.3 billion in 2002. The 1999 study provided a breakdown of the industry's impact by each state in the U.S. It told each state the total economic benefit derived from the cruise industry in that state.

These reports have been used by friends in Congress to project a positive image for the industry. These efforts have been mildly successful. At the very least they have contributed to maintenance of divisions that inhibit legislation that would benefit or hinder the industry.

## Ship Designs That Increase Revenue

Innovations in ship design provide another means for cruise lines to affect the economic bottom line. Though cruise ship design has advanced steadily over the years, the arrival of a new revolutionary ship component has been a relatively rarity. However, one of these innovations appeared in 1997. It has had a major impact on the design and construction of ships since. In that year, Carnival Cruise Line's *Elation* was the first cruise ship to incorporate an Azipod propulsion system.

The Azipod (short for azimuthing podded, which is also known as a right angle drive) propulsion system was actually a logical step in the evolution of cruise ships. It was already common for new cruise ships to depend on diesel-electric propulsion. Electric power being generated by the main engines was transferred via cables to electric motors that run the propellers. With podded drives, these electric motors and propellers are mounted on the underside of the ship's hull (rather than inside the hull). Because the pod can be turned up to three hundred and sixty degrees, it eliminates need for long shaft lines (from the engines to the propellers), rudders, and stern thrusters common to all conventional cruise ships.

An Azipod propulsion system has a number of benefits for a cruise line. They provide excellent manoeuvrability generally, but are also quite effective at slow speeds and during berthing operations. They eliminate a number of main components, which reduces breakdowns and maintenances costs. Long shaft lines, reduction gears, rudders, rudder machinery and transversal stern thrusters can all be eliminated. This means less need for extensive maintenance and fewer mechanical breakdowns. In addition, the Azipod system provides fuel savings because it has greater hydrody-namic efficiency and it reduces the capital cost of ship construction.

There is another key benefit of the Azipod system. Because it frees space that has traditionally been filled with machinery, cruise lines can choose to increase the number of revenue-generating cabins—the CEO of Royal Caribbean Cruise Ltd., Richard Fain, suggests that the space saving provided by the Azipod system, com-bined with the use of gas turbine engines on the Millennium-class ships, provides enough space for up to fifty additional cabins. The space can be used in other ways. Carnival Cruise Line's *Elation* and *Paradise* use the extra space for an additional incinerator and an additional sewage treatment unit.

The Azipod propulsion system is becoming common for new ships. It has been installed on Royal Caribbean Cruise Line's Project Eagle cruise ships (*Voyager of the Seas* and *Explorer of the Seas*), on Celebrity Cruise's Millennium (and is planned for the next three Millennium-class ships), and on other ships constructed at the Chantiers de l'Antique shipyard in France for Radisson Seven Seas and Festival Cruise Line. The system will also be installed on the two new ships being built for the

United States Line of American Classic Voyages, and on a group of new ships being built by Fancantieri for Holland America Line.

## The Design of Space on a Cruise Ship

Ship design is also used in other ways to generate either cost savings or increases in revenues. The most visible design features are those that are used to attract passengers to a particular ship. Unless a cruise ship attracts passengers it cannot earn money.

There are a wide variety of ways that are used to attract passengers. The personality of a ship is one feature of design. Joseph Farcus, ship designer for Carnival Cruise Lines, has produced a unique theme and personality for each of the Carnival ships for which he has had responsibility. What he has done has appeared to work well. Other ships' designers also have their own style and produce personalities for the ships they design. The newer Holland America line ships reflect the work of F.C.J. Dingemans of the Netherlands VFD designs; Robert Tillberg of Sweden has designed the ships for Star Cruises' Libra-and Leo-class ships (as well as the *Norwegian Sky*, Royal Caribbean International's *Voyager of the Seas*, and the *Disney Magic*); and Greece's AMK Architects and Designers have had responsibility for the Millennium-class ships of Celebrity Cruises, and also new buildings for Festival Cruises and Royal Olympic Cruises. The list of designers can go on, but the point here is that each ship reflects a personality desired by the company and its designer.

Different ship design is also reflected in such things as alternative dining options, a two-story water slide, an ice skating rink and rock-climbing wall, elaborate atriums, extensive shopping areas, and glass elevators that look into the atrium or that provide a view of the sea. These and other innovations have all been effective. Many cruise enthusiasts look forward to each new ship and to the options and opportunities that are provided. The innovations keep them coming back, but they also attract new passengers.

When a new innovation is successful, it is often copied by the competition. The success of the rock-climbing wall on the *Voyager of the Seas* was duplicated in the design of a new ship being built for Festival Cruise Line within months of its first appearance. There has also been a proliferation of alternative venues for dining, each of which is promoted as the best or the most innovative afloat.

The copying of innovations from one company to the next fuels a drive to newer and more elaborate features that differentiate one ship from the competition. Historically, this pattern is most visible in the way that cabins with verandas have become increasingly common. Verandas were relatively uncommon in the 1980s, but within a decade they became a norm. In 2000, ships are being built on which every cabin has a veranda. A similar pattern is seen more recently with the increasing number of upscale cabins being offered on new ships. With each new generation, new amenities and new options are offered.

Decisions about what to include and not include on a ship influences onboard revenue. Traditional ocean-going ships always had a library. Newer ships are increasingly built without a library (or a very small reading room), using the space instead for a shop, a bar, or a café.

The presence of casinos is another example. Ships built in the 1950s, 1960s, and 1970s did not have a casino. Casinos only began to be common on ships in the 1980s as the gaming industry generally grew and passengers demonstrated a desire for them. Older ships tended to have small casinos, located in odd places, because the casino was added after the ship was designed and built. Royal Caribbean Cruise Line operated for ten years before a real casino was installed on one of its ships in 1980. Ships built after 1980 were designed to include a casino.

Increasingly, cruise lines are devoting larger amounts of space to casinos and they are introducing schemes that make the casino attractive to its passengers. The motivation for these changes is simple: casinos can easily capture as much as one-third of the cruise passenger's discretionary spending. The casino and the bars together can easily generate the majority of onboard revenue.

## The Art of the Money Grab

Cruise lines can improve their economic bottom line in two ways: that which can be eliminated for cost savings is as important as what can be added to generate revenue. For example, Royal Caribbean Cruise Line stopped placing chocolates on pillows in 1993, reportedly to save $50,000 a year. Later in the decade they eliminated scratch pads, stationery, envelopes, and the two decks of playing cards for each cabin, all without any significant customer response. But when they attempted to cut out their repeaters' parties, passengers did complain and the parties were resumed.

It would appear that Carnival Cruise Line's policy around providing in-cabin amenities is another example of earning money by not spending it. For the longest while, Carnival Cruise Line stood out from among the competition because it was one of the only lines that provided only soap as an amenity. Even in its top-end suites, soap was the only amenity found in the bathroom. The absence of amenities avoided an expense, but it may have also increased the sale of sundries at the ship's shops.

In 2000, Carnival changed its policy and it introduced new in-room amenity baskets that contained a number of name brand products (e.g., Thermasilk shampoo and conditioner, Phisoderm daily skin cleanser, Soft Soap body wash, Breathsavers and Starburst candy, Lady Speed Stick deodorant, etc). Given the "sampler" nature of the products in these amenity baskets, it isn't clear whether they constitute a cost or a benefit to the line. It is as likely that companies are paying (or providing the products free of charge) to have their products advertised by being placed in passenger cabins as it is that the cruise line is paying for them. To some, this viewpoint may appear cynical. After all, isn't the key element of a cruise that it is all-inclusive? That has certainly been the traditional selling point of cruises.

As competition and costs increased, cruise lines sought ways to increase their revenues without raising fares. Carnival Cruise Lines was the first to realize the potential of onboard revenue in making a profit. The goal was to get passengers on board with low fares and then to generate income by spending once passengers are on the ship. J. Norman Howard, previously Business Director for Cunard Line, expresses the orientation as follows:

> *"Attract passengers with good pricing and merchandising. Entertain them at all costs. Fill them up. Strip them clean. Send them home happy."* [1]

There are a wide variety of ways that cruise lines have devised to grab money. Many of these have been introduced in the past twenty-five years. They began about the time that cruise lines created a corporate position of Manager of Onboard Revenue. The sources of onboard revenue are many and varied.

## Bars and Lounges

Given that a cruise is a vacation, it is not surprising that drinking is part of the routine. Most ships begin pushing drinks when the ship leaves port by having waiters with pre-mixed, special bon voyage drinks circulating around open decks and offering drinks (for a price) to passengers. One ship actually begins pushing drinks as passengers embark the ship through the atrium. They are offered a drink, and only after they take one from the tray do they realize that there was a charge. And so it goes.

Passengers become accustomed to having waiters on open decks pushing drinks and waiters in the dining room offering wine or beverages from the bar. They find bars in convenient locations, and increasingly the bars have special themes: the *Carnival Destiny* includes a wine bar among its bar choices, Costa Cruises added a martini bar on its Caribbean sailings in 1998, and many cruise lines have introduced bars that specialize in cigars and cognac. Each of these provides another source for generating sales.

It is so convenient to indulge that some passengers find themselves spending much more than they intended. Several newspapers published stories in 1997 about a man who was not allowed to leave Norwegian Cruise Line's *Dreamward* until he paid off the nearly $500 in booze and other extras he had rung up during a seven day cruise. He expressed surprise that he had spent that much and was feverishly working to find some way to pay the bill so he could disembark.

Revenues from drinks have increased phenomenally over the past couple of decades. In the early 1970s, a mixed drink on most cruise ships cost between 35 cents and 50 cents. In the early 1980s, cruise ships were charging between $1 and $1.40. Today, mixed drinks cost $4 or so, unless one goes for one of those fruity drinks in the souvenir glass—then the drink is likely to cost as much as $7.50. The cruise lines continue to purchase alcoholic beverages duty free, but their prices have come to match those normally found at land-based resorts. According to Bob Dickinson, President of Carnival Cruise Lines, land-based prices are their reality-check to be sure that they aren't overpricing what they sell. "On our three and four day product we compare prices with Disney and Universal Studios," he says.

In addition to price increases, cruise lines have devised other ways to increase bar revenues. One cruise line operating three and four day cruises in the Caribbean decided in the mid-1990s to capitalize on the popularity of line dancing.

> *It replaced the traditional midnight tropical fruit buffet with a country and western theme buffet. The activity proved successful as passengers who had previously come to the buffet to look briefly or sample some foods, began staying longer and either participating in, or observing, the line dancing. The result was an increase in bar revenue of $1.10 per passenger. On a 2000 passenger ship sailing fifty weeks a year, that is an annual increase to the bottom line of 4 million dollars.* [2]

Not only did the cruise ship increase revenue, but also it saved $50,000 because of a lower food cost for the western theme buffet.

Cruise lines have also worked to eliminate competition with their bars. Beginning in the mid-1990s, many cruise lines began prohibiting passengers from bringing onboard their own beer, wine, or liquor. While passengers may be able to sneak a bottle or two aboard when they embark, even though all carry-on luggage is subject to inspection, they are unlikely to be able to sneak anything onboard when returning from a port. This policy is designed to ensure that passengers who want to drink will be purchasing their desired beverage from the ship. It is roughly the equivalent of going to a hotel and being told that if you want to drink in your room you must use the minibar or room service.

The explanations given by cruise lines for this policy are somewhat interesting. A spokesperson for Norwegian Cruise Lines, probably the most restrictive of those serving the mass market, suggests:

> *"A big part of this is really to have control of minors getting a hold of alcohol...In years past there have been some situations where we have had underage drinking going on, and those passengers were disruptive."* [3]

A spokesperson for Carnival Cruise Line, which has a strictly enforced ban on passengers taking any alcohol onboard, any time, indicates:

> *...if a passenger brings back a bottle in a shopping bag with other items, that infraction may go unnoticed, and 'if you drink in your cabin, so be it—that's your business...But you're not going to get away with bringing in a large volume of drinks at a port of call. We're going to take it from you and give it back to you at the end of the cruise.*

The reason for this: 'There are some guests who would interpret that as meaning it is OK to bring large quantities of liquor on board, and then that leads to issues of disruptive behaviour. If you're buying it on board at typical prices, it's likely that you're not going to consume as much as if you had 10 cases of beer in your cabin.' In addition...glass bottles inexpertly packed into luggage could pose 'a minor safety issue.'

Perhaps passengers should be thankful that the cruise lines look so carefully after their interest. It is a small price to pay for that case of beer at $84 (twenty-four bottles at $3.50 each) so that one doesn't over-indulge. At these prices, it is no wonder that the bars on ships are first, or second only to the casino, in generating onboard revenue.

## Casino Gambling

As already mentioned, casinos were not a common feature on cruise ships until the 1980s. By the 1990s, there was considerable competition between cruise lines for having the biggest or the best casino afloat. When it first appeared in 1998, Princess Cruises' *Grand Princess* claimed to be the largest and most expensive casino afloat. The 13,500-square-foot gaming area, designed to be comparable to any top-of-the-line Las Vegas-style casino, features a number of games and innovations never before offered at sea. The casino was recognized in 1999 by CasinoGuru.com as one of the Top 10 Casinos in the world. *Grand Princess*, the only cruise ship to make the list, was placed in the same category as Caesar's Palace, the Bellagio and Mandalay Bay in Las Vegas, and the Monte Carlo Casino in Monaco.

There are other methods used to attract passengers to ships because of the casino. Crystal Cruises advertises its Ceasar's Palace at Sea, and like other lines presents inviting pictures in its brochures. Carnival Corporation, like casinos in Las Vegas and Atlantic City, has its Ocean Players Club: a complimentary cruise is available to players who agree to a minimum level of gambling. Norwegian Cruise Line began advertising complimentary cruises for "qualified players" in its 2001-2002 brochures. Some cruise lines have been reported to also provide complimentary drinks to "high rollers."

Cruise lines have several ways to attract passengers to the casino once they are on board. It is not uncommon for a casino to offer free lessons, to offer a limited number of "free play" chips to get a passenger started, or to offer free champagne or cocktails the first or second night of the cruise to get people into the casino and to familiarize them with what is available to play. In addition, most casinos on cruise ships have tournaments that attract a fair number of people.

The bottom line is that the ship's casino is a major source of entertainment for many passengers and also a large generator of revenue for the cruise line. The author of a 1997 article in the *Los Angeles Times* shares his observation of one red-faced man who lost $400 in twenty minutes as he learned the ins and outs of black-jack. I met one man on a circumnavigation of South America who fully expected to lose $15,000 on the cruise.

## Shore Excursions and Port Lecturers

Another source of income for the cruise line is shore excursions. Depending on the port, cruise lines can expect between 50 and 80 % of their passengers to avail of one of the shore excursions offered. Most passengers are willing to pay the price for the convenience. The port lecturer sells them on the benefits of the shore excursion, which further encourages them.

Most passengers do not realize the port lecturer is usually not an employee of the cruise line. S/he is an employee of a company contracted to provide the lectures and port shopping program. The same company often also supplies the ship's shore excursion program. The port lecturer's income may be tied to the revenues generated.

There are three main companies in the United States that operate shore excursion and port lecturer programs. These include International Voyager Media of Miami, On-Board Media of Miami, and the PPI Group (which through its Panoff Publishing produces *Porthole Magazine*). These companies provide the cruise line with trained port lecturers who provide information on each port of call, including recommended shopping, and who also work closely with the shore excursion manager in marketing the ship's shore excursions so that shopping and tour revenues are maximized.

So how do these folks earn money? The shore excursion a passenger purchases on a ship has been marked up several times. Tour operators in a particular port bid for the contract to provide the shore excursion to a ship's passengers. The tour operator offering the lowest price often gets the contract, but in any case there is great pressure to keep tour prices down.

The shore excursion concessionaire contracts with the tour operator and normally marks up the cost of the shore excursion as much as 100% before offering their program to the cruise line. The cruise line, in turn, will also add an additional mark-up in order to provide additional profit. A shore excursion that is offered for $15 or $20 by a tour operator may be priced as high as $60 when it is finally offered to the passenger. These mark-ups in price can create resentment among passengers who expect more than what they receive for what they pay. The passenger blames the tour operator for the inflated prices, rather than realize that only a percentage of the price paid makes its way to the tour operator.

A passenger has options. The going rate for half-day coach tour of an island in the Caribbean costs about $30 per person, or $60 for two. An alternative for people who don't want to travel with a group, or who want to see different sights, is to negotiate a half-day island tour with a private taxi at the pier.

Depending on the port, one can often find a taxi that will offer what they want for $50 or $60. A couple will gain the freedom afforded by a private guide, and yet pay no more than they would for the group tour for 50 people. If they join with another couple, the private shore excursion will cost half as much per person as that offered by the ship.

It is not just shore excursions that provide income to the companies providing port lecturers. As anyone knows who has been on a cruise, most cruise lines include in their port lectures a map that includes a list of "approved" stores. Passengers are told these stores have been chosen because of their quality and reputation. However, passengers are not always told that stores on the list pay a fee to be included.

These fees have replaced a situation that was common in the 1970s and 1980s. What used to happen is that the cruise director or tour director would visit all the shops frequented by a ship's passengers, either at the end of the day or on the ship's next visit, and would collect his or her "royalties" for sending passengers to the store. The cruise director or tour director on a major cruise line was able to earn as much as $250,000 per year in royalties.

When cruise lines realized that this income could be theirs, they formalized the arrangements through contracts with shore excursion/port lecturer concession-aires and they took their share of the kickbacks. Today, some merchants pay a promo-tional fee based on the number of ships that call at the port. Others may pay a fee based on the dollar value of transactions a merchant conducts. These fees vary widely.

In 1994, fees ran as high as $500 to $700 for a large, upscale retail operation in St. Thomas serving passengers from large, upscale ships. This may sound a bit high, but consider that in that year the average spending among the 1.24 million pas-sengers who visited St. Thomas was $394 per person—an 80% increase over two years before. In that same year, the average spending per passenger per Caribbean port was $154.

In 1996, the average spending per Caribbean port fell to $124. According to a 1996 survey by Price Waterhouse, the average passenger on a seven-day cruise with an average of 31/2 ports of call spends $434 at ports. St. Thomas is the leader at $255, followed by San Juan ($158), and Ochos Rios ($101). Ports with the lowest spending are Key West ($41), St. Kitts ($47), and Montego Bay ($57).

Passengers are told that one of the main advantages of using the cruise line's approved stores is that they will guarantee the quality and value of the merchandise purchased, and that they will facilitate refunds if the product purchased is not as it was advertised and sold. They are clear that refunds cannot be had in a case of buyer regret.

The most common dispute over port purchases is in relation to the value of jewellery. Passengers are often told that it is guaranteed that the item purchased is priced better than it would be at home. While most accept this guarantee without question, there are cases where buyers have found that the claim was unfounded. Consider the following:

The *Conde Nast Traveler Ombudsman* reported in December 1996 a case where a passenger on Carnival Cruise Line's Sensation, during a shore excursion in Ochos Rios, purchased a diamond engagement ring at Colours for $2350. An apprais-al certificate accompanied the ring for $4450. When the passenger returned home, he took the ring for an independent appraisal and was told that it was worth $600 less that he had paid: $1750 instead of $2350. The passenger followed the instructions that were given on the ship for a refund, but to no success. The store refused to accept the credentials of the passenger's independent jeweller, and Carnival stood behind the store's position. However, when the passenger secured the Ombudsman's assistance a refund was finally given.

The "Consumer Beat" in the *Boston Globe* reported December 19, 1999 on a similar case. The passenger had purchased a tanzanite and diamond ring at Rachat & Romero in Cozumel while traveling with Celebrity Cruises. He had paid $2400 for a ring that the Mexican jeweller appraised at $6530. When the passenger returned home, he sought an independent appraisal and was told the value was $1900. When the matter was raised to the Rachat & Romero, they said the appraised price was more like a suggested retail price, even though it was identified on a document entitled "certified appraisal." Though the *Boston Globe* was able to secure a refund for the passenger, the passenger rejected the offer saying that to agree "...to a refund would be letting the cruise line and jeweller off too easily. 'They're basically saying you caught us at fraud so what we'll do is give you your money back. I think that stinks. How many other people are they ripping off?' he asked."

The *Boston Globe* article provides some useful insights. It cites a gem and jewellery specialist who suggests that:"...jewellery fraud is rampant abroad," and she described cruise ship passengers as lambs being herded to slaughter. "These stores are taking advantage of the fact that people are looking for bargains. Everyone wants a memento of their trip and, for women, jewellery is one of the favourite mementos."As for the cruise line's guarantee, she said it was the first she had ever heard of it. "But it's an easy promise to make since most people, quite frankly, don't bother to check out anything when they get home."

The point of raising these cases is not to frighten readers from making purchases when on a cruise, nor to warn people off a cruise line's approved stores. These cases reinforce the need to be an intelligent consumer and to realize that the store, the concessionaire providing the port lecturer, and the cruise line are all in business to make money. With that fact in mind, one needs to be as cautious in their purchases abroad as they are when at home.

## Onboard Shopping

There was a time when shipboard shops sold only sundries such as toothpaste and candy bars, a few items with the company's logo such as t-shirts and sun hats and a small selection of duty-free perfume, jewellery, and gift items. As cruise lines began to realize the amount of shopping being done at ports, they also realized that shipboard shopping had the potential to be big business. Not only could they compete on price with shops in many ports, but they also had the advantage that passengers would be tempted by items in the shop windows because they would pass by the displays many times in the course of their cruise.

One of the first ships to introduce the concept of a collection of shops was Norwegian Cruise Line's *Norway*. On its enclosed promenade deck it had "streets" called Champs Elysees and Fifth Avenue lined with shops and boutiques offering everything from mink coats and diamonds to costume jewellery and casual sportswear. The *Norway's* success only encouraged similar development on other ships. Perhaps the most lavish was the collection of shops on Cunard Line's *QE II*. They offered a seagoing branch of Harrods department store, and included other boutique names such as Gucci, Dunhill, Christian Dior, Louis Vuitton, and H. Stern. Passengers could buy anything, from a can of caviar to a logo t-shirt; from flatware service for twelve to a sweater knitted with Scottish Shetland wool.

The shops on cruise ships, like port lecturers and shore excursion programs, are provided by a concessionaire—a company that pays to use the space on the cruise ship and that often shares a portion of its profits. There are two companies that dominate the industry. The largest of these is Miami Cruiseline Services, which in 2000 was bought by LVMH Moet Hennessy Louis Vuitton. The company has shops on one hundred ships spanning twenty-six different cruise lines. These shops sell many products, including many brand names owned by LVMH. The company's wines and spirits include Moet & Chandon, Dom Perignon, Veuve Clicquot Ponsardin, Krug, Pommery, Chateau d' Yquem, Chandon, Hennessy and Hine; its fashion and leather goods include Louis Vuitton, Celine, Loewe, Kenzo, Givenchy, Christian Lacroix, Fendi, and Pucci; its fragrances and cosmetics include Parfums Christian Dior, Guerlain, Givenchy, Kenzo, Bliss, Hard Carndy, BeneFit Cosmetics, Urban Decay, Make Up For Ever, and Fresh; and its watches and jewellery include TAG Heuer, Ebel, Chaumet, Zenith, Fred, and Omas.

The other company that provides shops on cruise ships is Greyhound Leisure Services' International Cruise Ships Division. It serves a total of seventy-seven ships. Greyhound Leisure Services began operations as a duty free retailer in 1958 and it entered the cruise ship market in 1963 with shipboard operations on P&O Line and Yarmouth Line.

Onboard shops have proven to be a significant source of income. The items offered on a particular ship are usually chosen based on the clientele that the ship serves. But most ships have several items in common. Gold by the inch, precious gemstones, and designer watches at duty-free prices are some of the most popular items. They make up a significant proportion of sales, but are also effective in getting passengers into the shops so they can see (and be tempted) by other items. Cruise lines further motivate purchases through fashion shows, often using passengers as their models, where the clothing available in the shops are shown. The shows attract a fair number of passengers, including those interested in the clothing and those who just want something to do.

The sale of sundries by the shops on a ship is influenced by the amenities provided by cruise lines in passenger cabins. One analyst has suggested that Carnival Cruise Line's longstanding practice of providing only soap in cabin bathrooms was a way to increase the sale in the ship's stores of such items as shampoo, toothpaste, sewing kits, and shoe shine mitts—all items that most travelers come to expect will be provided at a hotel.

To be fair, shipboard shops can be a service and a value to passengers. I have bought overstocked items at prices that were hard to believe —including cartons of cigarettes (in 1999) for as little as $5—and have also used the shops to know what price I would need to beat if I were to buy an item ashore. While the shops are there to make money, the smart shopper can do quite well as compared to prices at home and prices in many ports.

## Shipboard Photographers

The photographers on most ships is another outlet sold to a concessionaire. Notable exceptions are Carnival Cruise Line and Princess Cruises, both of which moved the operation of their photo services in-house a number of years ago. They realized they could run the operation themselves and earn greater profits.

As much as people are prone to purchase photos in which they appear, there is a limit to how many photos one person is likely to buy. The number of photo sales on a seven-day cruise is not proportionately as high (per day) as on shorter cruises. Daily sales on longer cruises are even lower. Thus the greatest profit is on shorter, three-or four-day cruises.

With this in mind, a number of schemes have been tried to increase sales. Most shipboard photographers offer passengers an opportunity for portraits to be taken on formal nights and often on theme nights. In addition, photos are taken as passengers leave the ship for shore excursions, as they return to ship from shore excursions, and when they are just hanging out on deck. They are also taken at dinner. On some cruise lines these are only taken on formal nights. On others, they are taken on formal nights and on other nights when there are different costumed characters that come to dinner tables and pose for pictures with the passenger. It may be a person dressed as a pirate who makes a vicious face as he puts a plastic knife up to a person's neck, a Las Vegas-style dressed showgirl who offers to pose with the men, or a Mexican bandito who makes a threatening face for a photo with a passenger. The fact that so many pictures are taken suggests that people must be buying them.

Another way that has been used to sell photographs is to offer increased value for increased spending. For example:

One operator recently developed a photo promotion where passengers were offered a discount and a souvenir photo album for pre-purchasing six photos. When passengers selected photos early in the cruise, they were offered a package deal that included five photos (value $7 each), an 8 x 10 portrait (value $12) and a souvenir album (value $20). A $67 value for $40. Through this method, the operator increased net photo revenue by $1.39 per passenger, per day. For a ship carrying 2000 passengers 50 weeks a year, that is an increase of just under a million dollars from this one idea.

Some photo concessionaires have also increased income by offering photo-finishing services. Like the local photo shop, they have a drop off slot where one leaves their film and the pictures can be picked up the next day. On several upscale lines, photo concessionaires even offer a selection of cameras at quite competitive, duty-free prices. While each of these is a service to the passenger, it is also a source income for the concessionaire and for the cruise line.

## Spa Services

Spa services such as massages, hair styling, and manicures and pedicures have also become big business aboard cruise ships. These services, provided by a company that pays the cruise line for the concession on its ships, have generally been provided by a single company. Until recently, Steiner Leisure Limited has had almost exclusive control over spa services provided to the cruise industry. The company has the concession for twenty-nine cruise lines, including more than 100 ships. The company's success is perhaps best reflected by the fact that in 1999 it earned almost $22 million in profit on sales of almost $130 million.

The services provided by Steiner Leisure are equivalent to that received in any urban area, and is generally at prices common in New York City or Los Angeles. A massage that in 1980 cost $20 to $24 for an hour is now priced between $79 and $99. Interestingly, pricing varies from line to line and from ship to ship within the same line. A one-hour massage on Royal Caribbean International's *Voyager of the Seas* is priced at $99. On all other Royal Caribbean ships, the cost is $79. At the same point in time, a one-hour massage on the *Seabourn Goddess I* cost $102. The difference in price is unlikely to dissuade a passenger who wants a massage from availing of the opportunity. However, these differences in price provide an insight into the lucrative nature of spa services as a source of revenue.

A major break in Steiner's dominance in providing spa services on cruise ships came in November 2000 when Norwegian Cruise Line announced it would not renew its contract with Steiner's. Instead, they contracted with Mandara Spa, headquartered in Hawaii, to provide spa services on their ships. This is their first contract with a cruise line, though Mandara Spa already operates some 35-resort spas in Bali, Thailand, Malaysia, The Maldives, Micronesia, Tahiti, Hawaii, Aruba, and the new spa at the 3,000 room Paris - Las Vegas Casino Resort. Time will tell whether they (or others) will present a challenge to Steiner Leisure's dominance.

## Private Islands

Private islands, too, were first introduced for their economic benefits. The concept was the brainchild of Bruce Nierenberg, when he was with Norwegian Cruise Line. The private island was meant to address several problems. The introduction of the *S.S. Norway* brought to light that too many passengers were often arriving in port on the same day and some ports didn't have adequate mooring facilities and infrastructure to accommodate a large number of passengers in a single day. As well, ships were often in ports like Nassau on Sundays, when the shops were closed. With increases in the number of ships and the capacity of ships, NCL found it needed to find additional ports. A private island filled this need.

The first generation of private islands consisted of very basic facilities such as bathrooms, a barbecue, and some covered eating areas. After twenty years of development, private islands now include options for water sports and nature hikes, and they generally offer craft and souvenir shops, bars, and barbecues. The main attraction of most private islands is its pristine beach lined with chairs and stocked with towels.

There are several ways that a private island produces revenue. The principal source of revenue is sales generated to a captive market: beverage sales and concessions, such as tours, water activities, souvenirs, and convenience shops. The cruise line has no competition, so all money spent on the island provides revenue and profit. In addition, the private island has a lower per person port charge than is common at many ports. Between lower cost and the fact that passengers tend to enjoy the experience, a private island provides a positive impression of the cruise line. It is an indirect source of increased revenue in the form of future passenger referrals.

One other way that private islands have contributed to the economic bottom line is that cruise lines are able to save fuel by cruising at a slower speed to an intermediate port of call. For example, rather than sailing non-stop from St. Thomas to Miami, a ship may reduce speed with a scheduled stop at the private island between the two ports. The ship can save money by burning less fuel and yet increase passenger satisfaction.

Today, most major cruise lines operating in North America include a stop at a private island as part of some of their Caribbean itineraries. A notable exception is Carnival Cruise Line, however it retains the option of using Half Moon Cay (the name given to Little San Juan Island), the private island constructed and used by sister Holland America Line.

## Communicating with the Outside World

Like the private island that draws income from a captive consumer, cruise lines also offer communication with the outside world, but at prices that can be quite extreme. The cost of a telephone call can range from $3.95 to $15 a minute. The concessionaire that provides communication services to the ship provides these services, and the cruise line sells the service to passengers.

The most common concessionaires are COMSAT Mobile Communication and Maritime Telecommunications Network. In some cases, the concessionaire provides the hardware for voice, fax, and data communication, and also certified radio crew for each ship. The cost of investment and maintenance of equipment is the responsibility of the concessionaire, and its revenues from sales to passengers are shared with the cruise line.

Passengers have a choice to wait until they reach port to use the phone, but many don't realize until they receive the bill the cost of making a telephone call to home. To be fair, cruise lines are clearly open about the phone charges, placing placards near the phone that inform the passenger of the cost. But many passengers simply ignore the cards, thinking, "How bad can it be?"

There can be wide differences in the price of a telephone call. I often found it interesting that while Norwegian Cruise Line in the mid-1990s consistently offered discounted prices for its telephone calls (between $3.95 and $4.95), its competition (using the same concessionaire for its phone and radio links) offered the same service for twice or three times the cost.

With the popularity of the Internet, cruise lines have introduced cyber cafés. Crystal Cruises was among the first when it debuted in 1997 its Computer University @ Sea. They installed 22 computers in a computer room, and offered laptop computers for rental to those who wanted to work on a computer elsewhere on the ship. Their computers are available for passengers to surf the net and to check their own e-mail accounts (at a cost of $1.25 per minute with a ten minute minimum). A passenger also may use a personal shipboard e-mail address for sending and receiving e-mail. The cost is $3 per message. In either case, there is a $5 fee to set up a computer account.

Several cruise lines introduced cyber cafés in the summer and fall of 1999. Royal Caribbean International introduced "royal caribbean online." It is a joint effort of two companies: Xcelerate and CAIS Software Solutions. They were contracted to manage the development, design, and deployment of all of Royal Caribbean's online services.

The largest concessionaire providing Internet connections for cruise ships is Digital Seas International. Working with ICG Satellite Services, Digital Seas International installed its first cyber café on Norwegian Cruise Lines' *Norwegian Sky* in July 1999. It has since expanded to other NCL ships, Holland America Line's ships, and others.

The arrangement the company has with the *Norwegian Sky* stipulates that Digital Seas International and ICG Satellite Services absorb the cost to set up the eight to twelve computer stations in the cyber café (approximately $300,000), and that they also provide the staff for supervision and maintenance. They charge 75 cents a minute (with a minimum charge of five minutes), and share revenue with the cruise line. Current fees on other cruise lines range from 75 cents to $1.50 a minute, with minimum charges of as much as fifteen minutes.

There is little doubt that cyber cafés will quickly become a common feature on most if not all cruise ships. The next wave, already begun, is for Internet access in passenger cabins. This provides an opportunity to generate income during typical down times, such as when passengers are relaxing in their cabins.

## Generating In-Cabin Revenue

Also in the mid-to-late 1990s, cruise lines introduced interactive multimedia to passenger cabins. Carnival Cruise Line has its "Fun Vision"; others have SeaVision, CruiseView, and similar names.

Interactive multimedia brings to cabins the ability for passengers to preview shore excursion options and to reserve their choices, to order wine for dinner from the ship's wine list, and to review the charges made to their room. In addition, passengers can order movies on demand (including, on some cruise lines, movies that are x-rated), they can play video poker and similar games, and in some cases they can even shop. Like computer access in cabins, the interactive television makes the traditional shipboard revenue downtime—when passengers are in their cabins relaxing or dressing—into revenue generating times.

Many of the interactive television systems initially were run much like the current system used for Internet access. The cruise line would contract with a company such as Allin Interactive or The Network Connection to install and maintain the hardware, at the expense of the concessionaire, and the revenues generated would be shared between the cruise line and the concessionaire. Recently, cruise lines have begun to purchase the systems from these companies and run the system themselves. The initial capital cost for installation is now borne by the cruise line, but the income generated is no longer shared.

Another recent revenue generating introduction to cabins is minibar systems, similar to those found in hotel rooms. However, those designed for a ship have two challenges: space for the minibar is more limited in a ship's cabin than in the typical hotel room, and the cruise line doesn't always have the available staff to maintain and restock the bars. Several systems have been successfully used which means there is now increased presence in cabins of both snack foods and beverages.

Disney Cruise Lines is among the first to introduce in-cabin minibars. Interestingly, in Disney's case the minibars are built with a clear glass front. As the manufacturer states, this allows passengers to see all the snack items and this precipitates the impulse sale. Given that the clientele on Disney's ships is largely families with children, this marketing technique may be effective in increasing revenue, but it is unclear whether parents appreciate it. Time will tell whether there is sufficient passenger dissatisfaction with this system to warrant a change to the more common opaque door used on most minibars.

The most recent innovation in minibars addresses the problem of available staff for checking and refilling supplies. Recently introduced on Royal Caribbean Cruise International's *Voyager of the Seas* is an on-line, totally integrated system that uses infrared technology to bill the customer as soon as an item is taken from the minibar. When first introduced, there were a number of false charges because passengers found they were billed just for picking up and looking at an item. Billing was not reversed by the infrared system when an item was returned to its original place.

This system is attractive to cruise lines because of the convenience it provides. It eliminates the need for someone to daily inspect a minibar to see what has been consumed. A printout is provided of items used and only the cabins needing to be refilled need to be visited. In addition, from an inventory standpoint, ship managers know at any point in time the products that have been sold, and they can identify those items that are the fastest moving by both quantity and margin. All the information that would otherwise take days to manually compile are at the fingertips of any manager who simply checks his or her computer.

## Bingo and Video Games

Bingo games have been common on cruises for at least the past three or four decades. It was first introduced as a form of entertainment and was directed under the supervision of the cruise director. In the "early days," the income generated was either kept by the cruise director or shared among the cruise staff. It wasn't until the 1980s and 1990s that cruise lines began to realize the amount of money that was being foregone with this arrangement. Increasingly, they have brought the bingo games under their control and have directed the income from the Cruise Director to the cruise line.

Bingo has proven to be a very popular activity. Participation is encouraged by larger jackpots. Norwegian Cruise Line even offered passengers a chance to win a free cruise as a way of attracting participation. With the larger prizes have also come increases in the price of game cards. I recall in the early 1990s paying $5 for a package of game cards for a session of bingo games. Today, the cost of playing bingo has increased significantly. Though it varies from cruise line to cruise line, charges of $25 or more for a package of cards is not unusual. This isn't a deterrent for most people who want to play.

In the mid-1990s, cruise lines introduced video games as another activity that would provide entertainment and generate income. In some cases, the games are clearly directed toward children; in others, they are of as much interest to young adults as children. These game rooms can be found on most new ships. The size of the space devoted to the games varies with the nature of the clientele attracted by the cruise line. Carnival Cruise Line, Royal Caribbean International, and Princess Cruises devote more space to video games than upscale lines. They are certainly a convenience to the parent who is traveling with children, but they are an added expense to the "all-inclusive" holiday.

## Art Auctions

The auction of art is another activity introduced in the 1990s. Norwegian Cruise Lines was the first to introduce the concept, and other lines quickly followed suit. These auctions are one more activity that is provided by a concessionaire, and one more activity designed to generate revenue.

The same companies that offer shore excursions and port lecturers also offer art auction programs. For example, Onboard Media provides art auctions through its sister company, Cruise Management International, which has a partnership with Park West Gallery. It serves Celebrity Cruises, Costa Cruises, Carnival Cruise Line, Crystal Cruises, Holland America Line, Princess Cruises, and Royal Caribbean International.

The PPI Group provides art auctions to several other major cruise lines. As PPI states at their website:

> *Fine Art Auctions are an enjoyable and entertaining onboard activity. The auction program initially became popular as they enhanced the cruise experience for the guests. However, it was soon realized that the auctions were an excellent source of onboard revenue, currently generating revenues that can surpass that of the Gift Shops and sometimes the Casino...The use of sophisticated marketing tools and cross promotions, videos, and brochures also ensure that the maximum possible revenue is generated.*

Attendance at the auctions is encouraged by providing free champagne and by employing auctioneers who are often entertaining. I recall one auctioneer who was successful in generating considerable interest in the art auctions by announcing, when introduced to passengers along with other staff at the start of the cruise, that if a passenger ever found him without his gavel, he would buy that passenger a drink. The tactic effectively got passengers interacting with him and generated considerable interest in seeing him at work. Once attending, passengers get drawn into the energy of the auction, and may find themselves bidding on items that they hadn't originally intended to buy.

The art auctions gain some interest because they include among the pieces available serigraphs and lithographs from well-known artists, including Picasso, Dali, Erte, and Chagall. The auctioneer provides background about the art, and emphasizes the excellent price available, suggesting that pieces may be had for as much as 80% off shore side prices. He will also provide a brief education to the two hundred to three hundred works of art being offered in three or four sessions during a seven-day cruise. While the auctioneer will likely explain the importance of the numbering on lithographs and serigraphs, it is not generally made apparent to passengers that the work received by a purchaser is rarely if ever the same number as that which was viewed and purchased onboard the ship. The reason is that the art purchased is normally shipped directly from the company's warehouse to the passenger's home—ostensibly for the passenger's convenience so that s/he doesn't have to travel with a large, bulky package.

For the person who is simply buying art because they like it, that the piece of art shipped to them is not the exact piece (in numerical sequence) they purchased makes little if any difference. However, for the novice collector, which is the way that auctioneers normally project their pitch, this can be a major issue. A serigraph numbered five in a series of three hundred prints has a different value to the serious collector than does serigraph numbered two hundred and ninety-eight of three hundred.

I have never heard an art auctioneer on a cruise ship discuss this small, but quite significant point. If they did, they would be undermining their own sales. Passengers are attracted by the convenience of having the art shipped, free of charge, to their home. They may be dissuaded from buying if they feel they have to take a piece of art home with them in order to receive the exact same piece that they purchased.

## They Even Have Cash Machines

Cruise lines began introducing Automatic Teller Machines (ATMs) to their ships as early as 1995. Some cruise lines initially placed them in the casino because passengers were not allowed to use their shipboard account to charge their casino purchases. More recently however, as lines have become permissive about what can be charged to the onboard account, cash machines are being placed in central areas such as around the shops. In some ways, the machines appear out of place given that there is nowhere on most ships (except in extending gratuities) that passengers can spend cash. Even gratuities are increasingly being placed on shipboard accounts.

ATMs are presently available fleet wide on Carnival Cruise Line, Royal Caribbean International and Celebrity Cruises, and Norwegian Cruise Line. They are likely to appear on other cruise lines in a short time. The machines operate just like those at home, but they levy a $5 charge (on top of the passenger's bank's charge for using a different company's cash machine) for their use. These fees are revenue that is shared by the cruise line and the company that is contracted to install and maintain the machines.

## Revenue Generation Or a Convenience to Passengers

Though I have taken a view that focuses on how each of the items discussed is intended to generate income for the cruise line, this is not a view that would be shared by many of the cruise lines involved. A statement made by Tim Gallagher, Carnival Cruise Line's Vice President of public relations to a reporter for the *Orlando Sentinel* projects a different perspective:

> *"Those optional items available for purchase on board are there as a convenience to our guests, not as a revenue generator"* he said, adding that a la carte items are not being used to fund cruise discounts.* [6]

This view is contradicted by comments made by other corporate executives, particularly those who suggest that onboard revenue adds 20 to 30% to the cruise line's economic bottom line. Whether these added charges are viewed as a convenience or a money grab likely varies from passenger to passenger.

## Squeezing Out the Last Drops From the Turnip

In addition to those things already discussed, cruise lines in recent years have introduced other ways to generate revenue, or to offset cost. In some cases, they have taken away things previously provided. Celebrity Cruises, for example, discontinued its free tender service from Naval Pier to downtown Hamilton (Bermuda) in 1996. It continued the service, but began charging $20. In the mid-90s, Royal Caribbean Cruise Line introduced fees for shuttles from a port to town, even though the distance many times was relatively short.

The idea of a cruise being an all-inclusive vacation was further eroded by the introduction of charges for onboard activities. Though not alone, Royal Caribbean International's *Voyager of the Seas* has been given considerable attention for the venues that have added charges. Use of the ice skating rink costs passengers $6 an hour, the rock climbing wall costs $8 for a ninety-minute session, and the golf simulator costs $20 an hour. Some cruise lines have even begun charging for their lecture programs. Radisson Seven Seas Cruises offered a series of culinary workshops on the *Seven Seas Mariner*, charging passengers who want to avail of the opportunity a fee of $295.

Similar charges have also been added for food items. Carnival Cruise lines offers coffee and pastries at its "sidewalk café" at charges ranging from $1.50 to $2.00. Princess Cruises charges $1.90 for a scoop of Haagen Dazs ice cream at its ice cream bar; a sundae costs $3.75. A cup of cappuccino costs $2 on Princess Cruises, $1.50 on Royal Caribbean International, but is free on Holland America Line.

With the offer of alternative venues for dining have also come added charges. Princess Cruises charges a reservation fee of $3.50 per person for those wanting to dine at its alternative restaurants. The company claims the charge is necessary because without it passengers wouldn't take their reservations seriously and they couldn't adequately plan for the number planning to eat in one of the two alternatives offered. Crystal Cruises charges $5 per person for its alternatives; Portofino's on Royal Caribbean International's *Voyager of the Seas* has reportedly charged as much as $15 per person (raised from $8) and Portofino's on the *Radiance of the Seas* has a reported charge of $26 per person; and Costa Cruises *Costa Victoria* charges $18.75 for its alternative restaurant. Royal Caribbean International tried charging shore side prices at the Johnny Rockets concession on its *Voyager of the Seas,* but negative reactions from passengers led them to discontinue charges for food. Charges were retained for milkshakes, sundaes, and other specialty items.

The logic of extra charges for food is sometimes difficult to understand. A passenger on Celebrity Cruises, for example, can order a glass of orange juice from room service and there is no charge. However, if the passenger orders a glass of orange juice at one of the bars it will cost $2. The same glass of orange juice, if ordered in the dining room on a night when it is not "the juice of the night" will cost $1.50.

One other way of generating revenue is to create and market items that would be of interest to passengers. Carnival Cruise Line has done this with a number of items. In 1995, the cruise line introduced Cruise perfume, which quickly became the second largest seller on board ship (after Obsession) and which was also stocked by Burdines department store. The perfume was produced by F.U.N. (Fragrance Unlimited Network), a company in which a principal owner is Mickey Dorsman, the brother-in-law of Carnival Corporation Chief Executive Officer Mickey Arison. The perfume was withdrawn from the market in late 1997 after it was noticed that it was turning brown in the bottle.

Carnival Cruise Line followed Cruise perfume with a Carnival Cruise Line Barbie doll. Produced in 1997 by Mattel, Barbie was properly attired for a cruise. In addition to sunglasses, she wore a sporty nautical-themed ensemble consisting of white shorts, a red and white striped crop top, and a smart, short red, white, and navy blue jacket with gold trim. She carried a carry-on bag and wore a sailor's hat with the Carnival Cruise Line logo. The doll sold on Carnival's ships for $45. It was sold via a toll-free phone number for $50.

In 1998, Carnival Cruise Line introduced two books: a nine chapter, forty page book entitled *Carnival Cocktails* that sold for $3.95, and, an eighty-six page book entitled *The Buffets of Carnival: Entertaining Secrets from Carnival Chefs,* that sold for $12. Both of these books were available on board Carnival's ships, and through a toll-free telephone number.

## Some Economic Unknowns

There are two other items relating to revenue, but it is difficult to know the extent to which these are "money grabs." One of these relates to port charges.

In 1996, a class action law suit was filed in California, Florida, New York, and Washington state alleging that cruise lines inflated port fees as a way of charging passengers more than advertised fare prices. Joseph Lipofsky, an attorney for New York-based Zwerling, Schachter, Zwerling & Koppell, the lead law firm in the suit, said the cruise lines inflated their fees because fierce competition had forced them to cut prices on base rates. He estimated that 50 % of the total amount collected for port charges is used to cover overhead rather than the fees charged by ports of call. The total overcharge was estimated to be as high as $600 million and involved seven companies (Royal Caribbean Cruise Line, Celebrity Cruises, Norwegian Cruise Line, Princess Cruises, Carnival Cruise Line, Holland America Line, and Renaissance Cruises).

The case ultimately involved twelve different cruise lines and was also pursued by the Florida attorney general's office. It was finally resolved in 1997, with the cruise lines agreeing to change the way they computed port charges and to eliminate some of the items that were previously included as port charges.

It came to light during negotiations to settle the lawsuit between the state of Florida and the cruise lines that port charges included not just government fees, but they also incorporated pilot and tugboat services, stevedoring, and garbage hauling. Attempts to get a detailed picture of what cruise lines included as port charges were generally unsuccessful. Princess Cruises refused to specify what was included under the label. General counsel for Holland America Line asserted that cruise lines keep mum on the details because full disclosure would mean spilling the beans on various transactions with contractors, and would put a company at a competitive disadvantage. He suggested that there were a lot of costs incurred when a ship is in port and that these are included as port charges.

Presumably, the situation has been corrected and it continues to be monitored by the Florida attorney general and several private law firms. Passengers can have reasonable confidence that the port fees charged are justified and fair.

Another issue that has potential for a similar scandal is the move by several cruise lines in 2000 to begin to automatically charge tips to passenger ship board accounts. Passengers can change the amounts, if they make the request to the purser's desk, but if they do nothing they will be charged the amount of gratuities recommended by the cruise line.

Norwegian Cruise Line introduced this system first in the summer of 2000 with their introduction of "Freestyle Cruising". With "Freestyle Cruising," passengers no longer have an assigned waiter that serves them each day/night in the dining room. To be sure that the staff receive gratuities, the cruise line initiated a program whereby each passenger is automatically charged $10 per day. The money is then, presumably, distributed fairly and evenly to all staff.

In the fall of 2000, Princess Cruises introduced "Personal Choice Dining." Again, because the new system eliminated the consistency in a passenger having the same dining room staff for the duration of the cruise, a $6.50 per day gratuity is automatically added to each passenger's shipboard account. While we can assume the money is distributed fairly and equitably, we have no way to be sure.

Regardless of whether distribution is fair and equitable, the system seems to be contrary to the notion of what is meant by a gratuity. Strictly speaking, a gratuity is extended as a gesture for the quality of service provided by an individual. With a system of automatic charges, the gratuity is no longer linked to the work of a service provider. Passengers are challenged to deal with the difficulty of having an excellent waiter one night and a mediocre waiter the next, knowing that the gratuity extended will be evenly divided between two people providing a qualitatively different level of service.

[1]  Howard, J. Norman. "Cruising, Better than Ever?," Cruise Industry News Quarterly, Summer 1993, pages 62-63.

[2]  Marjerison, Rob. "Maximizing Onboard Revenue," Cruise Industry News Quarterly, Winter 1995/96, page 82.

[3]  Reynolds, Christopher. "A Toast to Your Cruise! Now Hand Over That Booze," Los Angeles Times, October 19, 1997, page L-2.

[4]  Reynolds, Christopher. "A Toast to Your Cruise! Now Hand Over That Booze," Los Angeles Times, October 19, 1997, page L-2.

[5]  Marjerison, Rob. "Maximizing Onboard Revenue," Cruise Industry News Quarterly, Winter 1995/96, page 82.

[6]  Bleeker, Arline. "Extra Cruise Charges Add Up to Dismay: All-Inclusive Vacation Drifting Toward a la Carte," [7]

[7]  Denver Post, September 20, 1998, page T-10.

# 8 In Closing

I began this book feeling very positive about cruising. Taking a cruise is a type of vacation that I have chosen and that I have enjoyed. I never tire of the mix of being at sea and of seeing ports of call, nor of the blend of sheer laziness and shameless indulgence. I continue to feel positive about cruising, and my reasons remain the same. With experience and knowledge I have been able to tailor my choice for a cruise to what I want and need at that particular time. In this way I can minimize disappointment and maximize the simple enjoyment of my vacation. I enjoy cruising more now than I did then (and I had a great time "then").

My positive attitude may surprise some. They may question how, after what they have just read, I can still look positively upon cruise vacations. My response: it is because of what you have just read that makes it easier to positively view a cruise vacation. It is better to know than it is to not know. Or as the saying goes, "the devil you know is better than the devil you don't know."

It is undisputed that cruises have their problems. Some of these problems are endemic to the sheer size of cruise ships and the scale of their operations—the process of serving more than 3500 passengers their meals, three times a day, is still mind boggling to me. Other problems are endemic to the process of travel, whether it be by air, car, train, or cruise ship—there are the occasional delays, mechanical breakdowns, and even accidents. And other problems are endemic to social groups—greed, the potential for victimization, and social stratification are all present, whether on a cruise ship or at home.

By being aware of the potential for problems, one can be an informed consumer. With information, there is less likelihood for surprise and for disappointment. When something does happen, there is a better foundation from which to handle it. The information in this book should make your next cruise not only better, but given the information you now have it should also be more interesting.

## Choosing That Next Cruise

The move toward ever-larger cruise ships makes it more difficult for some to find a cruise that fits their need. When I began cruising, a large cruise ship carried 700 passengers. Today, a 700-passenger ship is considered small, though "small" also includes those in the 100-to 300-passenger range. Ships with 1500 to 2000 passengers are considered medium-sized; and the label "large" is reserved for ships holding between 2500 and 3800 passengers. The nature of the cruise experience certainly differs when on a ship with 200 passengers than when part of a group of 3300 passengers. There is no debate that each cruise is enjoyable in its own right, but their respective size influences what is possible and impacts the overall cruise experience.

With increased size, cruise lines have introduced different styles of cruising. Many of these new innovations were simply not possible on smaller ships. With increased activities and amenities (many at an additional cost), cruise lines are trying to effectively compete with land-based resorts. They are working to attract the family market by a greater emphasis on being youth focused, and they are increasingly stressing a cruise unstructured by set meal times. These changes reflect the desires and needs of a large block of potential first time cruisers which the cruise lines want to attract.

For those wanting to cruise on a small ship, the choices are limited. There are several budget cruise lines and several niche cruise lines that operate older ships and which carry 700 to 1000 passengers. The other choice is cruise lines catering to the luxury and ultra-luxury market. Clipper Cruise Line, Star Clippers, and Windstar Cruises offer sailing ships which accommodate between 200 and 300 passengers. Silversea Cruises, Seabourn Cruise Line, Radisson Seven Seas Cruises, and Renaissance Cruises operate ships ranging in size from 116 passengers to 800.

## Getting a Good Price

One consideration in deciding to take a cruise is, What is it going to cost? If you look at cruise line brochures, there is an initial shock at what a cruise can potentially cost. Brochure prices are like the prices found in a Turkish bazaar—they are only there to make you feel like you got a great deal with the discounted price with which you ended up. The brochure price is just a figure on which discounts are applied.

If you plan in advance, you can expect to find minimum discounts of 20 to 30 %. Depending on the itinerary and time of year, discounts can run easily as high as 50 % and at times as high as 70 %. In April 1998, I took an early-season

Mediterranean cruise (Rome to Istanbul) with Princess Cruises at 70 % off brochure price—it cost US $133 a day. In December 1999, I took a sixteen-day Hawaii cruise with Holland America Line at a fare that was 61 % off the brochure price. The three transatlantic cruises (totalling thirty-five days) I have taken ranged in cost from US $110 a day with Norwegian Cruise Line, US $133 a day with Radisson Seven Seas Cruises, and US $200 a day (including air fare) with Seabourn Cruise Line. These are not the prices shown in the brochure.

The simple fact is that cruising has become accessibly priced. A careful and intelligent consumer can find the cruise that fits their needs and desires at a price that is lower than they probably expect.

As you consider your choice of cruises, widen your scope of possible ships and cruise lines to include those that you may have excluded because of perceived cost. If you are flexible with your travel dates and your choice of itinerary, it is possible to travel on premium or ultra-luxury cruise ships for the same price per day as you would pay for a mass market cruise ship. There is no trick other than doing research and watching for bargains when they are announced. Look at brochures for comparative pricing and have your travel agent (or do it yourself) compare prices for different dates on the same ship or of different ships on the same date. If you have access to the Internet, you can also make good use of the numerous resources available. Several cruise lines have live booking engines at their web site, and they provide real-time prices.

## Pre-Cruise Anxiety

Once a decision to take a cruise is made, some turn their attention to pre-cruise anxiety. For some, the anxiety is simply a natural part of traveling; it is nothing out of the ordinary. For others the anxiety is specific to the cruise. There is a full range of things that one can possibly be anxious about. Below are a couple that are perhaps more common than most.

One concern expressed in chatrooms and newsgroups is about the luggage one plans to use. The first issue is the appearance of the luggage. Some talk of buying new luggage specifically for their cruise—they say that the old stuff just wouldn't do. Others ask whether those in the group think they should buy new luggage—they too are concerned about what other passengers will think if they see their old beat-up suitcases. Given what some people travel with, I personally wouldn't be the least concerned. Travel with what you've got. Another concern about luggage is, How much is enough? Some passengers can manage with carry-on luggage only for a cruise of one or two weeks. Others bring three or four suitcases each. No matter how much you bring, it will likely be more than enough. The thing that always keeps me under control in terms of the amount of luggage is remembering that somewhere along the way I may have to carry the luggage from point A to point B. I always ask whether that is possible given the amount that I have.

What to bring to wear is another pre-cruise anxiety. Perhaps because of the "Love Boat" television series, and perhaps because of advertising and brochures, many go on cruises expecting that they will be underdressed. There are always some passengers who dress stylishly and who have many changes of outfits, but most people on a cruise simply dress as they would at home. On any ship, no matter what its label (mass market or luxury), dress during the day ranges anywhere from "down home casual" to "traditional cruise wear." No matter what you wear, you will never be (or feel) out of place.

Dressing for the night time is another common pre cruise anxiety. The question is usually some variation of "How formal is formal?" Here again there is a wide variation. On many cruise lines, dress for men on formal nights ranges from a dark jacket and tie or a dark suit to a tuxedo. The proportion wearing a tuxedo varies from ship to ship, but I have never seen it exceed 50 % of the men; on some cruises it may be as few as 10 %. Women also vary widely in their dress. There are always women in gowns, and there are also always women in simple dark dresses or in dark slacks and "smart" tops. Basically anything goes, from a kind of "business casual" to "traditional formal." The key for both men and women is to dress in a way that feels comfortable.

Concern about airline arrangements for getting to and from a cruise is another common source of anxiety. If you make your own arrangements, it is best to arrive a day before the cruise, and to leave the port city mid-to-late afternoon the morning you disembark the ship. The reason: if you have made your own air arrangements and you miss the ship, that is a problem for you to solve with the airline; if the ship is delayed in arriving in port and you miss your flight (on that nonrefundable or frequent flyer points ticket), that is your problem—not theirs.

This brings into focus the main advantage of buying a cruise line's air/sea program. If you miss the cruise and are using their air/sea arrangements, they will take responsibility for getting you to the ship. If the ship is delayed in its arrival in port and air arrangements need to be changed, the cruise line will normally take care of those changes for those on their air/sea.

The disadvantage of using a cruise line's air arrangements is that one loses control over the time of travel and routing. While cruise lines are unlikely to accommodate all requests (at least not without a charge), I have found that my travel agent is often able to learn the routing early enough that she can lobby for changes in routings that are wholly inconvenient. At the same time, one has to be realistic that for what is being paid for airfare and transfers they might expect occasional indirect routings. So what...you're on vacation. At worst, it is just another possibility for the unexpected.

## Living With the Unexpected

As with anything in life, part of taking a cruise includes living with the unexpected. The more we know about what to expect, the less likely we are to be surprised and disappointed—we are less likely to find the unexpected. As a result, we are more likely to be satisfied with our cruise experience.

Satisfaction is strongly influenced by the expectations we bring to a cruise. A Swiss economist I met on a cruise shared with me an equation he used in his classes. It may be useful here:

$$s = p - e$$

The "s" in the equation stands for satisfaction, "p" refers to the performance of the cruise ship, and "e" refers to your expectations.

In this equation, if the cruise ship performs better than you expected, you will leave the ship satisfied; the greater the positive difference between their performance and your expectation, the greater is your satisfaction. In contrast, if your expectations are higher than what you actually experienced on a cruise, then you will leave a cruise ship unsatisfied; the greater the negative difference between performance and expectations, the greater is your dissatisfaction.

One cannot totally avoid the possibility for an unsatisfactory cruise experience. However, this equation emphasizes how we can sometimes be our worst enemy. My wife often says, "no expectations, no disappointments." If we go on a cruise expecting nirvana, we will undoubtedly be dissatisfied. If our expectations for a cruise experience are modest, we are likely to be very satisfied.

Similarly, if we go on a cruise believing the cruise line's brochure or advertising, if we romanticize what we hope to happen on a cruise, and/or if we expect seamless service and flawless entertainment, we are bound to be disappointed. We are bound to be dissatisfied. However, if we let go of unrealistic expectations, and adopt an expectation that the unexpected is likely to happen, we then approach a cruise with a different attitude. We will more likely end the cruise feeling satisfied.

This position is not one that endorses keeping your mouth shut and enduring whatever you are given, particularly if what you are given is unsatisfactory. There are means to appropriately express concerns while onboard a ship. Sometimes this will work. Sometimes it doesn't. When it doesn't, keep notes to yourself and write a letter to the company when you get home. They will normally respond: some by form letter, others by personal correspondence. There is no pattern to suggest whether to expect a response, and what type of response you are likely to receive.

So, how do I approach a cruise in order to maximize the likelihood that I'll come home satisfied? I personally go on the cruise with realistic expectations (always lower than that advertised to be the case) and always expecting that the unexpected will happen. I endure my share of inconveniences, and I try at the time to minimize them as best I can. On the whole I have been more than satisfied by most of the cruises I have taken. Every cruise has not been perfect, but each has been its own adventure and its own respite from the everyday world of work and home.

## The Book Wouldn't be Complete Without...

As one puts together material for a book such as this there are things found that you know must be used but just can't be sure where it will fit. Below is one of the only items that just didn't fit anywhere else. To not include it would be a major omission. The book would be incomplete without it.

Cruise directors and other staff hear a range of questions from passengers. There are many lists that have been offered. Below are some of the more interesting and entertaining questions from some of those lists.

What do you do with the ice carvings after they melt?

Do the elevators go to the front of the ship?

Can we water ski behind the ship?

On which deck do you keep the tour buses?

Do we need to declare to customs all the liquor we drank on board?

Does the ship manufacture its own electricity?

Can we get a discount if we don't eat?

How much above sea level is the ship?

Does the ship's crew sleep on board?

How much do we tip the captain at the captain's dinner?

## APPENDIX A: Events at Sea

### A. Cancellations and Delays

| Year | Ship (Cruise Line) | Event |
|------|--------------------|-------|
| 1983 | Caribe (Commodore) | No air conditioning – 2 cruises cancelled |
|      | Caribe (Commodore) | Broken propeller and mechanical problems – Delayed departure |
| 1988 | Monterrey (Aloha Pacific) | Seized for unpaid bills – Maiden voyage delayed |
| 1994 | QE II (Cunard) | 190 left in Southampton because cabins not ready; sails with renovations still being done. |
| 1996 | Regency Cruises | Ceases Operations -Leaves many passengers stranded |
| 1997 | Disney Magic (Disney) | Delays in delivery – Cancels first 6 voyages |
|      | Rhapsody of the Seas (RCCL) | 2 cruises cancelled while engines fixed |
|      | Rotterdam (Holland America) | Delay in delivery – First three cruises cancelled |
|      | Paul Gauguin (Radisson) | Engine problems on sea trials – Inaugural cruise cancelled |
| 1998 | Rembrandt (Premier) | Arrives two days late in Barcelona for cruise |
|      | Oceanic (Premier) | Prevented from sailing - inadequate safety documentation |
|      | Enchanted Capri (Commodore) | 3 cruises cancelled - USCG safety concerns |
|      | Pacific Princess (Princess) | 25 kg cocaine found onboard – Detained for more than a week in Piraeus |
| 1999 | Grandeur of the Seas (RCCL) | Taken out of service to replace connecting rods in engine |
|      | Stella Solaris (Royal Olympic) | Departure from Galveston delayed for 4+ hours - crew complained of unpaid overtime and poor working conditions |
| 2000 | Sea Breeze (Premier) | Cruise cancelled - engine boiler breakdown |
|      | Destiny (Carnival) | Mechanical difficulties – 1 cruise cancelled, next delayed 1 day and at slower speeds |
|      | Riviera I (World Cruise) | Ship seized in Tahiti for failure to pay fuel bills – Pax left stranded |
|      | Big Red Boat III (Premier) | Maiden voyage cancelled at last minute – not ready for passengers when arrived in NYC |
|      | Millennium (Celebrity) | June: Delay in delivery – Inaugural cruise cancelled. November: Several cruises cancelled for engine repairs |
|      | Sea Breeze (Premier) | Problems with air conditioning, plumbing and propulsion – Several cruises cancelled |
|      | Paradise (Carnival) | Malfunction in Azipod system just outside Miami - 4 cruises cancelled |
|      | Elation (Carnival) | 2 cruises cancelled for preventative maintenance of Azipod system |
|      | Big Red Boat II (Premier) | Passengers stuck on ship when in port - power failure causes malfunctioning elevators and no clean water |
|      | Island Breeze (Premier) | Tugboat struck ship in Houston – damaged propeller; Tug sinks. 2 cruises cancelled |
|      | Seabourn Sun (Seabourn) | Propeller damaged - Cruises cancelled for repairs |
|      | Stella Solaris (Royal Olympic) | Taken out of service for three months - reduced performance of one of the engines |
|      | Premier Cruises | Ceases Operations - Leaves many passengers stranded |
|      | Commodore Cruises | Ceases Operations - Cancels future cruises |

## B. Minor Events – Minimal to Moderate Disruption

| Year | Ship (Company) | Description |
|---|---|---|
| 1991 | Nieuw Amsterdam (Holland America) | Bumped pier while docking - $10,000 damage to pier |
| | Frontier Spirit | Ship turns around – Arctic Ice too thick to continue through NW Passage |
| 1994 | Regent Sea (Regency) | No air conditioning for three weeks |
| | Independence (American Hawaii Cruises) | Plumbing and air conditioning problems on several cruises |
| | Canberra (P&O) | Lost power, almost grounded. Returned to port under own power – out for 2+ weeks |
| | QE II (Cunard) | Detained in NYC for 25 hours – Fire and safety violations need repair |
| 1996 | Maasdam (Holland America) | Dragged anchor over 1000 metres of Soto's Reef, Cayman Islands |
| | Island Breeze (Dolphin) | Company refused to turn on heat from NYC to Florida – Investigated by US Coast Guard |
| | Royal Odyssey (NCL) | Engine problems – missed ports. Out for 2 weeks |
| | Sensation (Carnival) | Power failure; restored a couple of hours later. Arrived in San Juan one day late and missed St. Thomas |
| 1997 | Norwegian Crown (NCL) | Loss of electrical power and propulsion – restored in one hour |
| | Rhapsody of the Seas (RCCL) | Engine problems (50% power) causing it to miss ports on Alaska itinerary |
| | Norwegian Star (NCL) | No a/c, plumbing problems, no drinking water and power outages for several cruises. Passengers sleep out doors. Christmas cruise a disaster; New Year's cruise cancelled |
| 1998 | Norwegian Majesty (NCL) | Mooring line dropped into water, drawn into propeller, snapped back and broke double pane dining room window. 1 passenger hospitalized with minor injuries |
| | Enchantment of the Seas (RCCL) | Engine problem – missed port of Key West. Change in ports and times on later cruises until engines fixed |
| | Black Prince (Fred Olsen) | Freak wave outside Dover smashes 3 windows on bridge and causes electrical equipment to fail – return to Dover for repairs. Next day, left and hit heavy weather off France. Cruise cancelled |
| | Enchantment of the Seas (RCCL) | One of four engines fail; short power outage – Continues at 10% reduced speed. Caribbean port times adjusted for June and July |
| | Jubilee (Carnival) | No air conditioning (San Diego - Miami) and broken toilets |
| | Rotterdam VI (Holland America) | Loss of propulsion for an hour between St. Thomas and Bahamas – Restored |
| 1999 | Norwegian Majesty (NCL) | Fire in pizza oven delays departure from Boston – 1 passenger injured. Problems cause 38 to leave cruise in Bermuda and initiate a class action suit for the "Cruise from Hell" |
| | Sovereign of the Seas (RCCL) | Repairs being made during cruise: carpeting replaced, areas blocked off due to construction, pool being painted and outdoor carpeting being laid, Windjammer Café closed for entire cruise (no buffets) |
| | Norwegian Wind (NCL) | Engine problems – skips two ports in Alaska. |

| | |
|---|---|
| Zenith (Celebrity) | Engine problems - Reduced speed (Acapulco to San Juan and reduced time in ports |
| Crown Princess (Princess) | Propeller damaged while in Alaska – plan to repair in two months |
| Tropicale (Carnival) | Reduced power – Misses Key West |
| Norwegian Crown (NCL) | Power blackout for four hours while in port in Bermuda – No fresh water, no a/c, no toilets |
| Flamenco (Festival) | Engine problems - cruise stopped short |
| Ryndam (Holland America) | Rudder glitch, Sudden 6 degree list in Alaska. 13 injured, 2 hospitalized |
| Tropicale (Carnival) | Toilet problems - 41 passengers leave ship at first port |
| Statendam (Holland America) | Power failure - delayed in port 10 hours. Passengers from Hawaii landed at San Diego – HAL pays fine under PVSA |

2000

| | |
|---|---|
| Holiday (Carnival) | Passengers complain about 6 hr delay (because of wave conditions) leaving LA & delays in boarding tenders. |
| QEII (Cunard) | Passengers complain about cleanliness, sewer and a/c problems, poor maintenance |
| Clipper Adventurer (Clipper Cruise Line) | Trapped in ice jam off Antarctic - freed by Argentine Navy icebreaker. No damage – 24 hour delay |
| Rotterdam (Holland America Line) | Hit by rogue wave leaving Japan - damage to anything not bolted down. Rough seas plague whole crossing |
| Seabreeze - Big Red Boat II (Premier) | Leaves port w/ anchor down. Strikes underwater power lines – causes 17 hour power outage for 6000 people in Newport, RI |
| Aegean Spirit (Golden Sun Cruises) | Fuel leak and vessel listing. Repaired while in port at Crete and continues |
| Rembrandt (Premier) | A/C problems on several cruises |
| Oriana (P & O) | Hit by 40 foot wave - smashed windows in 6 cabins. No injuries, but itinerary is delayed |

## C. Disruptive Events – Engine Failures and Extended Power Failures

| | | |
|---|---|---|
| 1977 | Monarch Star | Loses power – Passengers transferred |
| 1980 | Norway (NCL) | Power failure - adrift for full day when restored |
| 1981 | Norway (NCL) | Power failure – adrift for full day when restored |
| 1986 | Mikhail Lermontov | Sinks off New Zealand |
| | Unnamed Russian ship | Sinks in Black Sea |
| 1991 | Oceanos (Epirotiki) | Loses power and sinks Off South Africa |
| 1994 | Canberra (P&O) | Machinery problems - power failure |
| 1995 | Sagafjord (Cunard) | Engine Problems – Reaches Vancouver 2 days late (LA-VCR) - Cruise cancelled |
| 1996 | Sapphire (Thomson) | Engine failure near Rhodes – Out for 10 weeks |
| | Royal Odyssey (Royal) | Engine failure – Passengers unloaded in Panama (on way from Florida to San Francisco). |
| | Alla Tarasova (Russian) | Flooded engine room – Adrift in North Sea for 10 hours |
| 1997 | C. Columbus (Hapag Lloyd) | Engine failure – Passengers evacuated |
| | Dreamward (NCL) | Electrical explosion – adrift for 20 hours, 30 miles from Nova Scotia. Power restored. |
| 1998 | Sea Breeze (Premier) | Boiler blows – 10 hour power shutdown (no a/c, lights, or toilets). Arrive in NYC one day late |

| | | |
|---|---|---|
| 1999 | Norwegian Dynasty (NCL) | Engine failure - Goes to San Diego for repairs fromHawaii to Puerto Vallarta). Passengers restricted to ship during repairs unless they pay $200 fine under the Jones Act. |
| | Oriana (P&O) | Engine failure – Out for two weeks |
| | Carousel (Sun Cruises) | Technical difficulties (fresh water supply system failed 3 days out on Transatlantic (maiden voyage)- returns to port. |
| 2000 | Paradise (Carnival) | Engine problems – itinerary for millennium cruise changed. Public protest by passengers. |
| | Destiny (Carnival) | Propulsion problems - adrift off Turks and Caicos for 27 hrs. Regains some power |
| | Sundream (Sun Cruises) | Failing generators (no a/c and limited power for 2 days). Similar problems previous week |
| | Ocean Explorer (World Cruise Company) | Engine failure; world cruise ended |
| | Aurora (P & O) | Problem with overheated propeller shaft (18 hours into maiden voyage) – Cruise cancelled. |
| | Oriana (P & O) | Engine failure and power failure - adrift for 30 hours |
| | Seabreeze (Premier) | Engine problems – adrift for 14 hours |
| | Veendam (Holland America) | Electrical generator failure - no electricity for 3 hours |
| | Grandeur of the Seas (RCCL) | Loss of electrical power - towed to port. Delayed 12 hours |
| | Sovereign of the Seas (RCCL) | Partial loss of electrical power - cruise ends at Port Canaveral instead of Port Everglades. Next cruise cancelled |
| | Crown Princess (Princess) | Loss of generator power - reduced speed. 3 hours late for one port; substitution for another port |

## D. Running Aground

| | | |
|---|---|---|
| 1972 | Mardi Gras (Carnival) | Maiden Voyage – runs aground leaving Miami Harbour. Stuck for 24 hours |
| 1978 | Kungsholm | Aground for 5 days at Martinique |
| 1982 | Alaskan Majestic Explorer (Exploration) | Grounded – Evacuated, 1 dead; 2 injured. Captain charged with negligence |
| 1984 | Rhapsody | Grounded off Cayman Islands – Evacuated after 4 days; freed after 12 days |
| | Yankee Clipper (Clipper) | Grounded after tearing from anchorage at St. Martin's |
| 1985 | Bermuda Star (Bahamas) | Grounded off Key West |
| | Amerikanis (Fantasy) | Grounded off Mexico – 5 days to free |
| 1986 | Dolphin (Dolphin) | Grounded in Bahamas |
| 1989 | Frontier Spirit | Grounded in storm off Fiji |
| 1990 | Bermuda Star (Bahamas) | Grounded off Nova Scotia – Evacuated. Freed after 13 hours |
| 1991 | Seaward (NCL) | Runs aground near Miami after plastic bag caught in an air intake and engine shut down |
| 1992 | Tropic Star (Starlite) | Runs aground in Freeport |
| | Mermoz (Pacquet) | Grounded off Scandinavia – 2 cruises cancelled |
| | QE II (Cunard) | Grounded off Cape Cod – 74 foot gash – Cruises cancelled |
| | Nantucket Clipper (Clipper) | Aground off Maine - 4 minor injuries. Refloated 3 hours later – Damage to hull and diesel tank |

| | | |
|---|---|---|
| 1993 | Ocean Princess (Pacquet) | Grounded near Belem – Life boat evacuation Declared a total loss |
| | Yorktown Clipper (Cliper) | Grounded in Glacier Bay -- Spills 28,000 gal of fuel 45 west of Juneau Evacuated. |
| 1994 | Sally Albatross (Effjohn) | Grounded in Gulf of Finland – Half-sunk |
| | Nieuw Amsterdam (Holland America) | Grounded in SE Alaska – 200 ft crease in hull, damaged propeller, puncture in ballast tank, 260 gallon spill. Refloated in 30 minutes – Out for 2 weeks. |
| | Starward (NCL) | Grounded on St. John, VI – oil spill of 100 gallons |
| | Royal Odyssey (Royal) | Grounded leaving Rome – Out for one month. |
| 1995 | Renaissance Six (Renaissance) | Grounded, eastern Aegean – Evacuated. One cruise cancelled |
| | Royal Majesty (Majesty) | Grounded off Nantucket - 17 mi off course |
| | Star Princess (P&O) | Grounded in Alaska – 40' long, 8" wide gash + 100' gash, modest pollution. Evacuated by tender. Out for 6 weeks |
| | America Queen (Delta Steamboat) | Grounded in Ohio River for 1 day – Refloated |
| | Sovereign of the Seas (RCCL) | Grounded in mud bank in San Juan Harbour – Freed after 80 minutes; Towed to port, leaves 24 hours late |
| 1996 | Tropicale (Carnival) | Grounded while leaving Tampa – Freed. Harbour pilot complains that ship failed to respond to 3 different orders to turn |
| | Royal Viking Sun (Cunard) | Collision with reef in Red Sea – Holed. Out for 2 months |
| | Gripsholm (Cunard) | Grounded 2 miles from Swedish port – Out for 2 weeks Officers resign |
| | Hanseatic (Hapag-Lloyd) | Grounded in North passage – Refloated after being evacuated |
| 1997 | Albatros (Phoenix Horizon) | Holed while leaving Isles of Scilly – Out for 2 weeks |
| | Hanseatic (Hapag-Lloyd) | Grounded in Norwegian Arctic - Evacuated, refloated, continues |
| | Noordam (Holland America) | Soft grounding off Mexican coast – Propeller damage. Passengers sent home. Out for 1 week |
| | Leeward (NCL) | Collides with Great Mayan Reef near Cancun – damages 460 sq yard swath of coral |
| 1998 | Monarch of the Seas (RCCL) | Strikes charted reef at St. Maarten – holed. 27,000 sq feet of coral reef damaged. Out for four months. |
| 1999 | Wilderness Explorer (Glacier Bay) | Grounded west of Juneau – Refloated |
| | Spirit of 98 (Sightseeing Tours) | Grounded in mouth of Tracy Arm (SE of Juneau)Holed. Evacuated |
| | Radisson Diamond (Radisson) | Grounded near Stockholm – Refloated |
| | Norwegian Sky (NCL) | Grounded in St. Lawrence – Out for 8 weeks |
| 2000 | Carousel (Sun Cruises) | Ran over rocks causing propeller damage and oil leak (50 ton spill) – Abandon ship at Calica |
| | World Discoverer | Hit rock or reef and holed – Forced to beach. 100 passengers rescued - Solomon Islands |

## E. Fire on Cruise Ships

| | | |
|---|---|---|
| 1979 | Angelina Lauro (Starlauro) | Fire in galley – Burns and sinks while at St. Thomas |
| | Skyward (NCL) | Engine room fire 30 mi from Miami – Evacuated to life boats; transferred to Seaward |
| 1980 | Unnamed British-registered cruise ship | Fire in laundry room while in USVI – Evacuated |
| | Prinsendam (Holland America) | Engine fire 140 m from Alaska – Evacuated to life boats at 1AM. Ship sunk. |

| 1982 | Norway (NCL) | Boiler room fire – 7 cruises cancelled |
|---|---|---|
| 1984 | Scandinavian Sea (SeaEscape) | Fire – Evacuated - 45 hours to put out fire |
| | Scandinavian Sun (SeaEscape) | Electrical fire while in port – Evacuated – 2 dead, 31 hurt |
| 1986 | Oceanic (Epirotiki) | Electrical fire while in port – Evacuated |
| | Emerald Seas (Eastern) | Fire while docked at Bahamas – Evacuated – 18 injured (smoke inhalation) and airlifted to Miami |
| 1987 | Unnamed (NCL) | Engine fire off Key West – Delayed 48 hours |
| 1988 | Scandinavia Star (SeaEscape) | Fire while in Gulf of Mexico – Evacuated |
| | Song of America (RCCL) | Engine fire – Return to port |
| 1990 | Fairstar (Sitmar) | Engine room fire – Not disabled – 1 crew member dies |
| | Scandinavian Star (International Shipping) | Fire while in North Sea – Evacuated 159 die. Possible arson. |
| | Regent Star (Regency) | Fire - put under control. Possible arson. |
| | Regent Star (Regency) | Fire and grounded while approaching Philadelphia – Evacuated |
| | Crystal Harmony (Crystal) | Temporarily disabled from fire in auxiliary engine room Drifted for 16 hours. Evacuated at port |
| 1991 | Sovereign of the Seas (RCCL) | Fire in lounge while in port at San Juan – Evacuated. Cruise resumed. |
| | Eurosun (Europe Cruise Line) | Fire while off Canary Islands |
| | Pegasus (Epirotiki) | Fire while berthed in Venice – Total loss |
| | Unnamed ship | Fire on cruise ship, prepares for evacuation, extinguished |
| 1992 | Starship Majestic | Fire – Evacuated |
| 1994 | Pallas Athena (Epirotiki) | Fire while berthed in Piraeus – Total loss |
| | Regal Empress (International Shipping) | Fire when 30 min from NYC – Evacuated. |
| | Achille Lauro (Starlauro) | Fire and sunk in Indian Ocean (near Seychelles) – 4 die, 8 injured |
| 1995 | Celebration (Carnival) | Engine room fire when 370 miles south of Miami – Adrift for more than 2 days. No a/c or hot food or elevators. Passengers transferred to Ecstasy. |
| | Regent Star (Regency) | Engine room fire while in Prince William Sound, Alaska – Disabled. Passengers transferred to Rotterdam |
| 1996 | Sagafjord (Cunard) | Fire – Stranded off coast of Manila (listing) – Towed to dock. |
| | Discovery I (Discovery) | Fire in engine room – Towed back to Freeport |
| | Golden Princess (Princess) | Fire in engine room – Towed to Victoria |
| | Universe Explorer (Commodore) | Laundry room fire – 5 seamen killed, 67 crew and 6 passengers injured |
| 1997 | Fair Princess (P&O) | Fire in casino - passengers called to muster stations - fire contained. Continues with cruise |
| | Vistafjord (Cunard) | February: Fire while in Straits of Magellan - disabled for two days. Possible arson |
| | | April: Fire in ship's laundry room – 1 crew member dies. Cruise cancelled after reaching Freeport (20 mi away) |
| | QEII (Cunard) | Fire – contained; no casualties |
| | Romantica (New Paradise) | Fire 10 mi off Cypress (total loss) – Evacuated |
| 1998 | Ecstasy (Carnival) | Fire in laundry room while leaving Miami – 54 injured and 4 hospitalized. Out for 2 months |
| | Edinburgh Castle (Direct Cruises) | Fire in main galley – no casualties |
| 1999 | Enchantment of the Seas (RCCL) | Engine fire/failure 60 miles from St. Thomas – 6 next cruises cancelled |

| | Sun Vista (previously Meridien) (Sun) | Fire in engine room – Sinks off Malaysia. Large oil spill |
|---|---|---|
| | Norway (NCL) | Fire in turbocharger room while in Barcelona mid-cruise – This, and next 3, cruises cancelled |
| | SunCruz Casino Ship | Engine room fire before it left port – Evacuated |
| | Tropicale (Carnival) | Engine fire – Disabled. Arrives in port 2 days late – Cancels next 6 cruises |
| 2000 | Celebration (Carnival) | Fire in generator -- Adrift for 6 hrs until power restored. No toilets or air conditioning |
| | Nieuw Amsterdam | Fire in crew quarters while in Glacier Bay – Delayed 12 hrs until given clearance by US Coast Guard. |

## F.  Collisions and Near-misses

| | | |
|---|---|---|
| 1988 | Jupiter (Epirotiki) | Collision at entrance to Piraeus – Sunk |
| 1989 | Crown Del Mar (Crown Cruises) | Collision with barge entering Miami Harbour – No passengers aboard |
| | Celebration (Carnival) | Collision with Cuban cement freighter (25 miles NE of Cuba) – 3 on Cuban vessel dead, 13 injured;  passengers on Celebration shaken. |
| | Viking Princess (Palm Beach) | Steering mechanism fails; rams Navy vessel in port |
| 1990 | Azure Seas | Struck while moored by container ship in LA harbour |
| 1991 | Regent Sea (Regency) | |
| | Island Princess (Princess) | 2 ships collide in strong winds at Skagway – Regent Sea has its steel hull plating on the stern ripped; Island Princess has a 50' gash 30 ft above water line and 11 cabins are exposed. |
| 1992 | Europa (Hapag Lloyd) | Collision with freighter 180 miles off Hong Kong |
| | Royal Pacific | Sinks in a collision with fishing vessel – 2 dead and 30 - 100 missing |
| 1993 | Noordam (Holland America) | Collision with freighter in the Gulf of Mexico |
| 1995 | British-registered passenger ship | Near miss with reefer ship |
| 1996 | Statendam (Holland America) | Near miss with barge carrying 80,000 litres of propane and pallets of dynamite in the Discovery Passage, British Columbia |
| 1997 | Regal Empress (Regal) | Gash in bow from running into pier in St. Andrew's, New Brunswick – Continues after temporary patch |
| | Unnamed | Cruise ship slams into Chelsea Piers sports centre, pier 62 in New York City |
| | Jubilee | Near-miss collision with fishing boats – Evasive action at 2 AM.  Passengers complain of jolt. |
| | Island Princess | Collision with unmarked obstruction at Civitavecchia – 2 cruises cancelled |
| 1998 | Rhapsody of the Seas | Hits pier in Curacao causing a 7 metre hole above water line --Repaired and continues |
| 1999 | Norwegian Dream | Collision with cargo ship in English Channel -- Out for 2 months |
| 2000 | QE II | Collided in a three-ship incident in NY harbour. Damage limited to scrapes and dents |
| | Victory (Carnival) | Hits NYC Pier - Damage to pier; ship proceeds |

## G.  Other Catastrophes

| | | |
|---|---|---|
| 1995 | Club Royale | Gambling cruise ship Sinks while riding out storm – no passengers aboard; no casualties |
| 1996 | Amira Jihan | Nile River cruise capsized during storm and trying to berth near Luxor - 7 die, 14 missing, 16 injured |
| 1997 | Island Princess (Princess) | Explosion during sea trials - 1 killed, 3 injured |
| 1998 | Fantome (Windjammer) | Sunk trying to outrun Hurricane Mitch - more than 30 crew perish |
| 1999 | S.V. Sir Francis Drake (Tall ship Adventures) | Sunk in hurricane while moored |
| 2000 | Seabreeze (Premier) | Sunk in 30 foot seas - no passengers aboard; no casualties |

# APPENDIX B: Illegal Discharge Incidents by Cruise Ships, 1993-1998

## A. Illegal Discharge Incidents in U.S. Waters

| Year | Ship (Cruise Line) | Nature of Incident |
|---|---|---|
| 1993 | Regent Rainbow (Regency) | 30-40 plastic garbage bags found 35 miles offshore traced by their contents |
| | Regent Sea (Regency) | Passengers witness dumping of garbage, including plastics |
| | Viking Princess (Palm Beach) | Discharge of unknown quantity of oil - 3 mile long sheen |
| | Noordam (Holland America) | One quart of oil discharged after oil-water separator failed - in dry dock at the time |
| | Golden Odyssey (Royal) | Plastic bag of garbage discovered in Endicott Arm, AK - traced by its contents |
| | Europa Jet (Europa) | Spill of 20 gallons of oil - linked to ship by chemical analysis |
| | Majesty of the Seas (RCCL) | 300-400 litres of lube oil discharged into Port of Miami |
| | Golden Princess (Birka) | 10 gallons of oil discharged into San Francisco Bay |
| | Star Princess (Princess) | 264 gallons of oil discharged into Taiya Inlet, AK after propeller shaft seal broken by fishing line |
| | Pacific Star (Starlite) | 500-1000 gallons of oil spilled in San Diego Harbour - linked to ship by chemical analysis |
| | Regal Empress (Regal) | Two cases of illegal discharge of garbage, including plastics |
| | Discovery I (Discovery) | 30-40 gallons of oil spilled into Port Everglades - linked to ship be chemical analysis |
| | Regent Rainbow (Regency) | Oil-based paint dripped into Tampa Bay harbour while hull being painted |
| | Pacific Star (Starlite) | 200 gallons of fuel spilled in San Diego harbour - linked to ship by chemical analysis |
| | Dolphin IV (Dolphin) | Observed pumping oil into oil into the water while 5 miles from coast |
| | Santiago de Cuba (Ferry Charter) | 25 gallons of oil spilled into Mobile River, AL - ship in dry dock |
| | Westward (NCL) | 20 gallons of fuel spilled during transfer operations |
| 1994 | Fair Princess (Princess) | Hydraulic connector failed - 1 gallon of oil spilled into Los Angeles Habour |
| | Golden Princess (Birka) | 210 gallons of oil spilled into Los Angeles harbour |
| | Starward (NCL) | Spilled 100 gallons of oil - grounded at St. John, VI |
| | Sea Princess (Sea Princess) | 1 gallon lube oil spilled when tank overfilled |
| | Saint Lucie | 150 gallons of fuel spilled at Port Everglades due to rupture of fuel pipe |
| | Vistafjord (Cunard) | Discharge of 15 gallons of oily bilge water during internal transfer |
| | Regent Sun (Regency) | Fuel spilled into San Juan Harbour, PR, because valve left partially open |
| | Golden Princess (Birka) | Oily waste discharged into Lynn Canal, AK - crew ignored alarms |
| | Universe (Seawise) | Small amount of oil leaked into Gastineau Channel, AK from ship's tender |

| | | |
|---|---|---|
| | Starship Atlantic (Premier) | 5-gallon can of red paint fell into Port Canaveral - broke open when hit water |
| | Fair Princess (Princess) | 42 gallons of oil spilled into San Francisco Bay |
| | Westerdam (Holland America) | Failure of oil-water separator caused discharge into Stephens Passage, AK |
| | Regent Sea (Regency) | Lube oil spilled into Gulf of Alaska when equipment failure - 26 mile sheen |
| | Nieuw Amsterdam (Holland America) | 260 gallons of oil from the propeller leaked when grounded off Gravina Point, AK |
| | Saint Lucie | 150 gallons of oil spilled into Port Everglades - linked to ship by chemical analysis |
| | Rotterdam (Holland America) | Discharged oily waste 13 times in 10 days into Alaskan waters - ship had permanent piping that allowed oily waste to be discharged directly overboard |
| | Starship Majestic (Premier) | 1 gallon oil accumulated on deck and spilled into East Bay, Tampa, FL |
| | Emerald Princess (Fernandina) | Oil-based paint dripped into Amelia River, FL while being painted |
| | Golden Princess (Birka) | 10 gallons of oil discharged into Gastineau Channel, AK - equipment failure |
| | Nordic Prince (RCCL) | Unknown quantity of oil discharged into Gastineau Channel, AK |
| | Sovereign of the Seas (RCCL) | Oil bilge waste discharge 8-12 miles from San Juan Harbour |
| | Starship Majestic (Premier) | 2 gallons of oil-based paint dripped into Tampa Bay Harbour while painting |
| | Fair Princess (Princess) | Oil-based paint dripped into Los Angeles Harbour while painting |
| 1995 | Nieuw Amsterdam (Holland America) | 25 gallons of oil spilled into East Bay, FL because tank overfilled |
| | Star Odyssey (NCL) | 10 barrels of waste oil and sewage spilled into Southwest Pass, LA |
| | Emerald Princess (Fernandina) | 20 gallons of oil leaked into St. John's River, FL |
| | Star Odyssey (NCL) | 126 gallons of heavy fuel oil spilled into Mississippi River because tank overfilled |
| | Seabourn Pride (Seabourn) | Residue from bilge flushed into Port Everglades |
| | Rotterdam (Holland America | One-half gallon of oil leaked from bow thruster |
| | Seabreeze I (Dolphin) | 60 gallons of fuel oil discharged into San Juan Harbour - linked to ship by chemical analysis |
| | Star Princess | 50-75 gallons of oil spilled when ran aground in Lynn Canal, AK |
| | Majesty of the Seas (RCCL) | 1 gallon of oily bilge discharged into Intracoastal Waterway, Florida |
| | Jubilee (Carnival) | Oil-based paint dripped into Port of Los Angeles/Long Beach during painting |
| | Legend of the Seas (RCCL) | 10 gallons of oily bilgewater discharged into Gastineau Channel, AK |
| | Regent Star (Regency) | 10 gallons of lube oil discharged into Whittier Harbour, AK - equipment failure |
| | Regent Star (Regency) | 5 gallons of lube oil discharged into Whittier bay when decks were washed down |
| | Tropicale (Carnival) | 1 gallon of fuel leaked into Tampa Bay through hole in fuel tank on lifeboat |

|      |                             |                                                                                           |
|------|-----------------------------|-------------------------------------------------------------------------------------------|
|      | Scandinavian Dawn (Discovery) | 20 gallons of oil discharged at Port Everglades - leak in seals of propeller hub        |
|      | Discovery Sun (DFDS)        | Oil-based paint dripped into Port of Miami while painting                                  |
|      | Holiday (Carnival)          | 5 gallons of waste oil discharged because valve in wrong position while in dry dock        |
| 1996 | Dolphin IV (Canaveral)      | 50 gallons of fuel oil spilled into Port Canaveral                                         |
|      | Cunard Countess (Cunard)    | Garbage, including plastic, washed ashore on St. Croix, VI - identifying information linked to ship |
|      | Starship Oceanic (Premier)  | 200 gallons of oil spilled in Port Canaveral - linked to ship by chemical analysis         |
|      | Meridian (Celebrity)        | Food waste mixed with garbage illegally discharged into Crown Bay, St. Thomas, VI          |
|      | Queen Odyssey (Seabourn)    | 1 gallon of fuel oil spilled into Caribbean Sea, St. Croix, VI                             |
|      | Tropicana (Tropicana)       | 80 gallons of oil spilled into Port of Miami - linked to ship by chemical analysis         |
|      | Oceanbreeze (Dolphin)       | 150 gallons of oil discharged into Biscayne Bay                                            |
|      | Leeward (NCL)               | 70 gallons of oil spilled into Port of Miami - linked to ship by chemical analysis         |
|      | Leeward (NCL)               | 1 gallon of fuel discharged into Port of Miami during fuel transfer process                |
|      | La Cruise (Louisiana)       | 15 gallons of fuel leaked into St. John's River, FL                                        |
|      | Song of Norway (RCCL)       | Pint of oil-based paint spilled into the Port of Los Angeles/Long Beach                     |
|      | Viking Serenade (RCCL)      | Discharge of 5 gallons of hydraulic fluid into San Pedro Bay, CA - equipment failure       |
|      | Ukrania (Prime Express)     | 40 gallons of waste oil spilled into Port Everglades - waste oil tank overfilled           |
| 1997 | Sundream (RCCL)             | 65 gallons of fuel oil spilled into Patapsco River, MD - tanks had been overfilled         |
|      | Radisson Diamond (Radisson) | 10 gallons of oil discharged into San Juan Harbour - faulty valve                          |
|      | Radisson Diamond (Radisson) | 10 gallons of waste oil spilled into San Juan Harbour because a valve was left open        |
|      | Club Med I (Club Med)       | 76-100 gallons of diesel spilled into San Juan Harbour during transfer of bulk oil         |
|      | Sea Breeze I (Dolphin)      | 80 gallons of black diesel oil discharged into St. Thomas Harbour, VI                      |
|      | Holiday (Carnival)          | Gallon of oil-based paint spilled into Los Angeles Harbour while painting                  |
|      | Regal Voyager (ISP)         | 30 gallons of oil spilled into Port of Miami - linked to ship by chemical analysis         |
|      | Nordic Empress (RCCL)       | 1 gallon of oil spilled into San Juan Harbour during transfer of waste oil                 |
| 1998 | Liberty II (Sea Co.)        | 1 gallon of lube oil spilled into Sheepshead Bay, NY - equipment failure                   |
|      | Acqua Azzurra               | 2 gallons of diesel fuel entered New River, FL from ship's generator exhaust               |
|      | Statendam (Holland America) | 210 gallons of oil spilled into Los Angeles Main Channel when contaminated ballast water released |
|      | Stella Solaris (Royal Olympic) | 5 gallons of diesel fuel discharged into Galveston Ship Channel                         |

| Island Dawn (ISP) | 26-30 gallons of fuel discharged into Port Everglades during fuel transfer |
|---|---|
| Tropicale (Carnival) | Gallon of hydraulic fluid discharged into East Bay, Tampa Bay during test of hydraulic winches |
| Statendam (Holland America) | 1 gallon of oil discharged into Tongas Narrows, AK when hydraulic line ruptured |
| Norwegian Star (NCL) | 30 gallons of lube oil discharged into Barbours Cut Channel, TX when tank overfilled |
| Island Adventure (Meridian) | 200 gallons of fuel oil spilled into Port Everglades during transfer operations |

## B. Alleged Illegal Discharge Incidents Referred to Flag States by the U. S.

| Year | Ship | Incident |
|---|---|---|
| 1993 | Nordic Empress (RCCL) | Coast Guard aircraft observed 7-mile slick trailing ship – midway between Bimini and Florida coast |
| | Statendam (Holland America) | Passenger videotaped garbage (including plastics) being discharged between Panama Canal and Golfo Dulce |
| | Ecstasy (Carnival) | Coast Guard observed several-mile-long slick trailing ship |
| | Seaward (NCL) | Coast Guard observed a three-mile-long slick trailing ship – 11 miles off Key Biscayne, FL |
| | Seabreeze (Premier) | Passenger reported observing discharge of garbage, including plastic, while en route to San Juan, PR |
| | Starship Atlantic (Premier) | Coast Guard observed a mile sheen as ship traveled 4 miles off the Bahamas |
| | Starship Oceanic (Premier) | Coast Guard observed a 6-8 mile sheen trailing ship in New Providence Channel |
| | Britanis (Celebrity) | Passengers reported the discharge of garbage, including plastics, into the Gulf of Mexico |
| | Crown Jewel (Cunard) | Coast Guard observed an 8-mile sheen trailing ship – 35 miles west of Freeport, Bahamas |
| 1994 | Oceanbreeze (Dolphin) | Passengers reported the discharge of garbage, including plastics |
| | Discovery I (Discovery) | Coast Guard observed a 2 mile slick trailing ship as it was en route to the Bahamas |
| | Seabreeze I (Dolphin) | Passengers reported the discharge of garbage, including plastics |
| | Britanis (Celebrity) | Passengers reported the discharge of garbage, including plastics |
| 1995 | Star of Texas (Ulysses) | Coast Guard observed a 1.8-mile (150 feet wide) sheen trailing ship as it traveled near Miami |
| | Royal Majesty (NCL) | Coast Guard observed a 3-mile sheen trailing the ship |
| | Seabreeze I (Dolphin) | Passengers reported discharge of garbage, including plastics, 2-25 miles from US coast. Also discharged oil into the North Atlantic 1 mile from coast |
| | Scandinavian Dawn (SeaEscape) | Coast Guard observed a 3-mile sheen trailing the ship |

Source: United States General Accounting Office, Marine Pollution: Progress Made to Reduce Marine Pollution by Cruise Ships, but Important Issues Remain, Washington, DC:GAO, February 2000. (Document #GAO/RCED-00-48)